HARVEY CUSHI[NG]

SURGEON, AUTHOR, AR[...]

By Elizabeth H. Tho[mson]

Foreword by John F. Fulton

A decade has passed since the death of Harvey Cushing, a great surgeon and a controversial figure in his time. The whole field of brain surgery is built on the foundation he laid so brilliantly.

This biography has caught not only his restless and sometimes rebellious spirit, but the great personal charm which made him beloved by his patients and his friends on three continents. Among these were some of the most illustrious names of his generation—in medicine, in art, in literature, and in public affairs.

In addition to unusual scientific acumen Dr. Cushing possessed the talents of artist and writer, through which in his spare moments he added luster to an already enviable reputation. For his achievement in reducing the mortality in brain operations from nearly one hundred per cent to less than ten per cent, governments, universities, and scientific societies the world over honored him. His biography of the great physician Sir William Osler, won him a Pulitzer Prize in 1926.

A conservative Ohio Republican, he became the friend of Franklin D. Roosevelt, whose son had married his daughter, yet he refused at first to vote for him. Although he sometimes exhibited a Middle Western lack of respect for outmoded Eastern conservatisms, he was something of a Victorian

(Continued on back flap)

HARVEY CUSHING

Surgeon, Author, Artist

HARVEY CUSHING
From a crayon portrait by Deane Keller in 1939
Courtesy of the Yale University Art Gallery

Harvey Cushing

Surgeon, Author, Artist

ELIZABETH H. THOMSON

Foreword by John F. Fulton

1950
Henry Schuman
New York

This book is affectionately dedicated to

My Mother

Julia Bristol Thomson

And the Memory of my Father

Walter Ira Thomson

FOLLOWING THE APPEARANCE OF HARVEY CUSH-
ing's detailed two-volume *Life of Sir William Osler*, there
were requests for a briefer account which would come more
within the purse and compass of the lay reader and the medical student. Mrs. Edith Gittings Reid, an old friend of Baltimore days, responded with her well-known volume that
appeared in 1931 under the title, *The Great Physician*.

After the publication of my biography of Dr. Cushing, a
number of reviewers and many correspondents expressed the
same hope—that a shorter story might sometime be prepared
for the general reader and the young physician and surgeon
who might be put off by the size of my text. Having had misgivings about publishing so extended an account, I welcomed
Mr. Schuman's proposal that Miss Thomson, who had helped
me prepare my biography for press, undertake an account of
Cushing for The Life of Science Library to which she and
I had already contributed a life of Benjamin Silliman.

Inevitably when a new biography is written, fresh source
materials and new anecdotes come to light which give further
insight into the character of the subject. In the case of Dr.
Cushing these new materials have been of particular interest,
and Miss Thomson has utilized them freely. She has also re-
studied the sources that I used and in many instances found
sidelights that I had missed. Such is the wealth of material
that, except for official correspondence, the letters selected
for this volume are for the most part entirely different from

those which I included. The result is a completely new biography, written with the general reader in mind. For this reason, and because the story has been most skillfully woven, I believe Miss Thomson's biography will have a wider appeal than my earlier account.

A welcome feature of the book is that it gives a much clearer picture of the large part that Mrs. Cushing played in influencing Dr. Cushing's career and in directing the energies of their children. During her lifetime I was unable adequately to emphasize Mrs. Cushing's role, and I feel that Miss Thomson has told this aspect of the story with sympathy and keen apperception.

The chapter on Dr. Cushing's relations with his patients casts light, also welcome, on a phase of his life that a number of reviewers felt I had not adequately brought out in my biography.

Following Dr. Cushing's good example of keeping himself out of the Osler biography, I attempted to do likewise in my account of him. However, Miss Thomson has felt that her readers might care to know something of our relationship, so with some diffidence I have placed my files at her disposal and although she has quoted rather more widely from my letters than seems decent, I have not felt inclined to protest because, having written one life of Dr. Cushing, I wanted in no way to influence his next biographer. I can add that this is entirely Miss Thomson's book and that it is written with an insight which a man seldom, if ever, achieves.

John F. Fulton

Yale University
October, 1949

TO WRITE A BIOGRAPHY OF A MAN WHOSE LIFE AND
work were as rich and varied as Harvey Cushing's is both a
privilege and a pleasure. My enjoyment of the task was increased by the challenge created by the wealth of source
material. Many books could be written about the different
periods of his life, or about his different facets—surgeon, author, artist. But for a volume in The Life of Science Library
the primary aim was to convey to the general reader, within
a brief compass, some idea of Dr. Cushing's scientific contributions and his importance to this and succeeding generations.

By devoting his life to neurological surgery and its problems he made operations on the brain of little more hazard
than those involving the abdomen, and this of itself has assured him a place for all time among the great contributors
to the science of medicine. To his achievement in developing
this specialty an ever-increasing number of people will owe
their lives, and the record of his accomplishments will always
be a source of inspiration to students and to those already established in the profession. But Harvey Cushing's life has
meaning for a much deeper reason than this. By example he
taught that a physician is obligated to consider more than a
diseased organ, more even than the whole man—he must view
man in his world. To do this, he must himself have breadth
and vision and courage. In living this philosophy, Cushing
joined the ranks of those humanist-physicians who have stood

out from their fellows because of their broad approach to medicine and to life. Obviously their credo has application far outside medicine—its relevancy is universal. For any man who entreats his fellows to raise their eyes beyond the narrow confines of their own existence, who by "mild persistence urges man's search to vaster issues"—such a man speaks to anyone, anywhere, any time.

I have had a great deal of assistance in writing this book which I am happy to acknowledge. The opportunity came to me in the first instance through Dr. John F. Fulton under whose tutelage I have learned much and who has cajoled, prodded, encouraged, and helped me untiringly throughout the writing. I have leaned heavily on him for assistance with the technical passages; also on his wide knowledge of medical history and education and on his intimate knowledge of Dr. Cushing. My debt to Miss Madeline Stanton, who was for nineteen years Dr. Cushing's secretary, is also not easily acknowledged. She has generously contributed many hours to filling in background behind the printed word, to guiding me among the materials, and to reading and adding constructive suggestions to the manuscript. Dr. W. W. Francis, Librarian of the Osler Library who was a close friend of Dr. Cushing's from the Hopkins days, has read the entire manuscript and given me the great advantage of his close familiarity with the time and the people. And anyone who works with the Cushing memorabilia is grateful to Miss Julia Shepley, who also served as his secretary for many years, for her orderly arrangement of the materials after Dr. Cushing's death.

There are still others to whom I am indebted: Dr. Louise Eisenhardt, the Curator of the Brain Tumor Registry, long associated with Dr. Cushing, and Mr. Frederick G. Kilgour, Librarian of the Yale Medical Library, who have read the manuscript; Mrs. Henrietta T. Perkins, Chief Cataloguer, who has helped with the index and in many other ways; Dr. Lewis H. Weed, Dr. Ernest Sachs, and Dr. Gilbert Horrax who patiently answered many questions; Dr. Walter W. Boyd and Dr. Richard U. Light who have generously supplied photographs from their voluminous files, and Mr. Frederic G. Ludwig of the Yale University Library and Mr. Howard J. Reynolds of the School of Medicine who have assisted in preparing the illustrations for press; and finally to my long-suffering mother, family, and friends, whose interest has been a continuing source of cheer. I was preparing a copy of the manuscript for Mrs. Cushing to read and was deeply disappointed that I was unable to finish the book before she died.

The publisher is always mentioned last, but he belongs well in the forefront—especially Mr. Henry Schuman, for his belief in the importance of the history of medicine and science in helping the world to a better solution of its problems is so strong that he plays a more personal role in the production of his books than does many a publisher. He had a large hand in this one, and for his advice, encouragement, and patience I am very grateful.

Historical Library
Yale University School of Medicine
October 7, 1949

CONTENTS

xiii

ILLUSTRATIONS

PLATES

xvii

HARVEY CUSHING

Surgeon, Author, Artist

"Rarely is it safe to prophesy any durability of recognition, whatsoever the accomplishment. Fame that is contemporary, fame that for a time endures, and fame that actually accumulates, differ in quality as differ the flash of a meteor, the glow of a comet, the permanence of a fixed star. Only when the contemplation of both the man and his achievement truly inspires and ennobles us will they remain indivisible to be praised by the people for time everlasting."

Harvey Cushing, "Emancipators," 1927

THE WESTERN RESERVE...
OF CONNECTICUT

Chapter 1

Harvey cushing, an intern on the south side of the Massachusetts General Hospital in Boston, entered one of the wards on an autumn morning in 1895 to do the routine surgical dressings. Among the patients who watched his progress from bed to bed was Lucy Hogan, who had come all the way from New Brunswick, Canada, for treatment. Sometime before, Lucy had developed a persistent sore on her foot, and having heard that there was a priest some thirty miles from her home who worked miracles, she had saved her money and made the journey to the town. She found that the priest was itinerant, but the kindly wife of the station agent took her in until he should return. The priest must have been a wise man, for he gave her some salve and told her that if the sore did not heal, she should go down to the Massachusetts General Hospital in Boston, and if they thought best to cut off her foot, she must let them do it.

The sore did not heal, and now, two years later, Lucy Hogan was in Boston. It was the first time she had ever been in a big city, the first time she had seen a hospital. She was frightened, and when the doctor and the nurse assisting him came to her bedside and she saw the doctor reach for the scissors, she was terrified lest her foot be cut off then and there. But the gentleness with which he took off her bandage, the warmth in his voice and smile, and the confident and interested manner in which he examined her foot completely reassured her, and from then on she knew she was in sympathetic hands and was no longer afraid.

This meeting was the beginning of a lifelong devotion to the young intern on the part of Lucy Hogan, and she felt a personal pride when he subsequently became famous as a surgeon. Years later, after his death, she wrote a letter to her friend, Miss Ida M. Cannon, Chief of Social Service at the M.G.H. Lucy was nearly blind then with an incurable eye condition and she had returned many times to the hospital because the Raynaud's disease, which had caused the sore on her foot, had grown progressively worse and over the years eight partial amputations had proved necessary. The letter went:

Dearest Miss Cannon, I am enclosing dear Doctor Harvey Cushing's letter which you asked for. he is not dead he lives in the hearts of his Pacients and friends if Doctors knew what they give to their pacients that is not in bottles or pills, I am sure they would find strength and joy to carry them over the very hard places they are called upon to travel. . . . loveingley and greatefully yours, Lucy H. Hogan.

The story of Harvey Cushing did not begin with his birth on April 8, 1869. The forces which shaped his destiny had been at work long before that date—perhaps as far back as a September day in 1835 when Erastus Cushing, the young physician of the town of Lanesboro in the Berkshire Hills of Massachusetts, climbed into his carriage and turned his horses westward. Among those wishing him Godspeed was his mother, Freelove Cushing, who could not be persuaded to leave New England, for it was here that her husband, David, Jr., the first Cushing physician, was buried. But it was the very thought of David and his early death from overwork and prolonged exposure under the cold New England stars that caused Erastus now to say farewell to all that was dear and familiar to him and to make his way farther west where a milder climate and new opportunities beckoned.

The Western Reserve, a portion of the grant made to Connecticut by Charles II in 1662, had been settled largely by mass migrations from Connecticut and Massachusetts. This "largest, strongest, and most characteristic single, compact colony in the West, the last distinct footprint of Puritanism," became part of Ohio when it achieved statehood in 1803.

When Erastus had gone to Cleveland earlier, on an inspection trip, the town had appealed to him strongly and he had chosen it as the place in which to make a new start. As he now set forth with his family, he took with him "the strength of the hills," the cherished memory of his father, and his father's books. These well-used and familiar volumes, so often a source of comfort to David, gave Erastus a feeling of security as he left the green hills and friendly valleys of his home and traveled over the mountains into New York State by the trail which still winds tortuously between mountain and rushing brook. With his young wife, Mary Platt Cushing, and their three children (the oldest eight years, the youngest four months), he eventually reached Troy, the first leg of the difficult journey behind him.

From Troy they had a week's travel across the state by canal boat to Buffalo where they embarked on a sailing vessel for Cleveland. Ordinarily this passage was short, but stormy weather forced them to seek shelter along the Canadian shore for two days, so that it was the 15th of October before they climbed the bluff from the shore of Lake Erie and saw the town of Cleveland stretched out before them. It was a beautiful, clear autumn day; and to a family seeking relief from the long, severe New England winters, it was gratifying to have the pleasant weather continue until after the new year—an auspicious beginning for their new life.

Warmhearted and friendly, Erastus soon made a place for himself, and it was not long before he had a thriving medical practice. He built a house and adjoining office on the lot he had bought opposite the green in the center of town and having established himself as a man of education and integrity, he became a much loved and respected member of the community.

In the meantime, Henry Kirke, his eldest son, grew into a tall, thin lad with a tendency to be shy and nervous. In the autumn of 1845 he entered Union College at Schenectady, New York, in the sophomore class and was graduated in 1848 "with a fair stand in some things only." He then returned home for three years to apprentice himself to his father and to attend lectures at Cleveland Medical College.

During this period he was often a caller at the home of William Williams—where his father, as family physician, was also a familiar figure. Henry Kirke engaged one of the younger Williams boys (at a sum which made him the envy of his brothers) when he wished to make a study of the normal human heart, but he was more interested in the heart of the eldest daughter, Betsey Maria—a pretty, vivacious girl with large dark eyes, and shining black braids wound around her head. As time went on, his intentions became obvious.

Nevertheless, in 1850, Henry Kirke went off to Philadelphia to complete his medical education at the Medical Department of the University of Pennsylvania. Erastus wrote him frequently, encouraging him to make his own decisions and assuring him of support in whatever he thought it wise to undertake.[1] He was pleased that his son was to room with a divinity student instead of a medical student because it would give him a broader outlook and, "if he is an intelligent, gentlemanly man, and reasonably well acquainted with human nature, as every clergyman ought to be, he will be both a pleasant and profitable companion." His only advice was on a familiar subject—"One thing I forgot to mention I deem of great moment for you. It is this—that you give yourself more time to sleep."

In December, 1850, when Henry Kirke, nearing the end of his course, was offered the position of assistant physician in a private retreat for mental patients, his father, after pointing out the good and bad aspects of such an affiliation, wrote him thus: "When you leave there, however, you will not find the world or your patients all in strait jackets & as entirely under your control as in such an institution—but it's to be hoped that you would acquire an ability in managing men that would be of

---

[1] Erastus had had the best medical education then available (a two-year apprenticeship to a local physician, a year at New York Hospital, and a year at the Berkshire Medical School at Pittsfield, the Medical Department of Williams College), and he was eager that Henry Kirke should benefit from the advances in medical education since his time.

use to you in managing the world generally after you leave there." And when Henry Kirke did not get the position, he wrote him sympathetically: "The turn things have taken relative to the expected appointment I would not let trouble you —it is undoubtedly a disappointment, but would not have been if your expectations had not been previously raised, so you have lost nothing. . . . It's only one of the minor mishaps to which we are constantly subject thro life. If you had no abiding place and were entirely afloat in the world, it would be of more moment to you."

The decision as to his future was, however, taken out of his hands, for Erastus became very ill and Henry Kirke went home to fill the breach without having the desired year of internship. Instead, he joined his father in the practice that was becoming too large for Erastus to carry alone. In June, 1852, he married Betsey Maria Williams, and soon the responsibilities of a growing family left him little time for regrets.

Ten children were born to the Cushings, only seven of whom reached maturity.[2] Because of the rapid growth of the city and the encroaching business interests, they were forced to move several times during the early years of their marriage, finally settling at 786 Prospect Street (now No. 3112) near the Erastus Cushing household on Euclid Avenue.

For the next forty years Dr. Kirke, as he was called, was never absent from the demands of his large practice except while on duty in the Civil War and when laid up for a year with an injury to his knee after slipping on an icy step. He became professor of midwifery, diseases of women, and medical jurisprudence at the Cleveland Medical College and later served for over ten years as a trustee of Western Reserve University. He played an active but inconspicuous part in medical affairs in Cleveland. Although greatly respected, he had few close friends, for the innate shyness and diffidence that had kept him from making many friends in college had, in the busy

---

[2] William Erastus (1853-1917); Alice Kirke (1859-1918); Henry Platt (1860-1921); Edward Fitch (1862-1911); George Briggs (1864-1939); Alleyne Maynard (1867-1903); and Harvey Williams (1869-1939).

years of his maturity, taken the form of an austerity and reserve difficult to penetrate.

Many people, and even his own children, would have been surprised had they known that, when he closed his study door on the rare evenings he had at home, the books he read were tales of adventure in strange places—of Lewis and Clark in Oregon, Livingston in Africa, and Gordon in China. He read much about the tribes of Africa and of the Indians in America, of their customs and how they fought; he knew the history of several of the British regiments—their uniforms, their traditions, their battles and campaigns. Had he been able to share these interests with his children, much of the formality that existed between them would have been dissolved, but it was not until they were grown that they really came to know and understand him. He did, however, teach them something of the stars, which he had studied so that they would be company for him on his long night rides, and he encouraged their interest in natural history, especially in trees, of which he had extensive knowledge.

One by one they came to realize that beneath his quiet, forbidding exterior was a lively curiosity that matched theirs. William, his eldest son, later remembered his father's description of his first trip in an automobile. Dr. Kirke had carefully watched the driver until he was convinced that had anything happened to the man, he could have driven the machine home although he had asked no questions about the "modus." On another occasion the matter of whether or not elephants were pacers engaged his interest. Failing to find the answer in any book, he made a point of taking William to the next circus that came to town. When the elephants went by, all pacing, he nodded his head with satisfaction and turned around and went home.

But this was much later. When the children were growing up, it was Betsey Maria who filled most of their needs. It was she who doctored their ills from her own medicine cabinet, treated scraped knees and wounded feelings. It was she who taught them their catechism and helped them with their French, Latin, and Greek—subjects in which she had excelled

at the best classical school in Cleveland. She tried to create
for her children something of the atmosphere in which she
herself had been reared, for she had been one of ten children,
and their home had always been the lively center of a large
family clan. She inherited some of her energy, humor, and
warm friendliness from her father, William Williams—an outgoing man of wholehearted enthusiasms and infinite good
nature. "Olympians in Homespun," [3] Lucien Price has called
these early settlers of the Western Reserve. Like the Cushings,
the Williams family had also come from New England and,
being thrifty and enterprising, had prospered in business. As
many as thirty or forty people of all ages were in the family
group that frequently gathered at William Williams' home on
Euclid Avenue. They created their own diversions—reciting
original poems with gusto, singing (for all the Williamses were
musical), and presenting plays. On one occasion they even succeeded in persuading Dr. Kirke to take the part of Gruff
Tackleton in *The Cricket on the Hearth*.

Because of the early death of her mother and long invalid-
ism of her stepmother, responsibility for her brothers and sisters fell to Betsey Maria while she was still very young. When
her own children arrived, she was already well versed in the
art of motherhood. During the winter evenings when Dr.
Kirke was off on a case, she could be found in a chair before
their open grate fire, holding one of her own babies in her
arms while she continued to help her brothers, first one and
then another, with their lessons. Or she would read with her
book propped up in a rack while she knitted endless socks and
mittens. When the children were old enough, she took them
with her to lectures and musicales.

Through the years, Betsey Maria thus offered her children
rich companionship, so that they did not gravely suffer from
their father's preoccupation with his profession. She rarely
lost her cheerfulness and serenity even when Henry Kirke
would withdraw into days and sometimes weeks of silence be-

---

[3] In 1926 Lucien Price, who is "Uncle Dudley" of the *Boston Globe*,
wrote this warmly appreciative essay, "Olympians in Homespun," about
his native Western Reserve for the *Atlantic Monthly*.

cause of weariness or worry, for she was aware more than anyone that his deep-hidden vein of humor and sentiment underlined and supported her own spontaneity. The most intimate view of their relationship with each other is to be had from an incident recounted by their youngest son. Henry Kirke came home one day and told her solemnly that he had just given all his money for a woman who had lost both her arms and he had brought her home in his carriage. Betsey Maria, as he had anticipated, was immediately full of sympathy and concern and she hurried outside—to find, on the front seat of the carriage, a bronze reproduction of the Venus de Milo!

"AS THE TWIG IS BENT"

Chapter II

Harvey Williams Cushing, the tenth and last child of Betsey Maria and Henry Kirke, was born on the 8th of April, 1869. He had a happy, secure childhood with the companionship (and discipline) of a sister, brothers, and innumerable cousins. Although their large, comfortable house was on a city street, there was room enough in the back yard for a barn where they kept a horse and where the boys housed their pigeons, cats, and dogs—room, too, for their mother's garden, a chicken yard, a croquet set, fruit trees, and a cemetery for departed pets.

Each season had its special pleasures—spring brought the first sapsuckers to the Norway birch in front of the house and the first fragrant violets in the garden. It brought baseball and top spinning and a new family of kittens in the barn. In summer there were family picnics and excursions into the country, swimming in Lake Erie after a dusty walk cross-lots, croquet, and the excitement of poaching in the neighbors' cherry trees. In autumn the Cushing boys flew homemade kites after school, and in winter they skated (on rinks made by flooding someone's back yard), coasted, and had snowball fights. When it rained, they were content for long hours in the attic with their collections of postage stamps, coins, butterflies, and birds' eggs.

Yet the days were by no means entirely lazy and carefree. They helped their mother plant her flowers and their father with the spring chores. They mowed the lawn, swept the walks, shoveled snow, and helped with the semiannual upheaval of house cleaning—a task as distasteful as washing behind the ears. They also had other responsibilities. Punctuality at meals, at school, and at Sunday School was a strict requirement. Departures from grace were punished by spankings from either mother or father, Dr. Kirke using a hairbrush across the open palm when he didn't put the culprit across his knee. The last such punishment that Harvey remembered was administered by his mother when she caught him with a forbidden, and therefore irresistible, ten-penny thriller about a Wild West desperado who, despite his lawless exploits, was always the soul of courtesy to ladies.

Harvey's earliest memories were of the stories that were read to him at bedtime and of the poetry that his mother recited, after he had said his prayers, until he fell asleep.

His particular companions were his brother Alleyne and his cousin Perry Harvey, who was the nearest his age of all his Crehore, Williams, Day, and Harvey cousins. Perry, more often known as "Tot," was the oldest of four boys and always gave Harvey healthy competition in their constant companionship. Except for Alleyne, most of Harvey's own brothers were far ahead of him—when he was eight, Will had already finished at Western Reserve and at Harvard Law School and had begun practice in Cleveland; Harry was about to enter Cornell University;[1] and Ned, at fifteen, was almost ready for Cornell. Harvey was the recipient of their "guidance" and their cast-off clothes, but it was Alleyne, only two years his senior, with whom he shared the joys and trials of brotherhood.

On Sundays, the Cushings attended Sunday School and services at the Old Stone Church, arranged in the family pew from William, next to the straight, unbending figure of Dr. Kirke, down to Harvey, who sat by his mother. The sermons were long and it was hard to sit still. Occasionally Mr. Parsons, a sympathetic neighbor, would slip Harvey candies—thereby, he was later fond of saying, flavoring his Presbyterianism with

---

[1] He later became an eminent geologist, occupying a chair at Western Reserve University for many years.

peppermint. Their two-and-a-half-mile walk home always stirred up a good appetite for Sunday dinner at which they were joined by Grandfather Erastus, now a widower. In the afternoon, someone, often Erastus, read aloud from Oliver Wendell Holmes, the "Autocrat of the Breakfast Table," or another popular author of the day, while Alice, Harvey, their brothers, and perhaps a few cousins, sprawled about on the floor or sat on the bumpy horsehair sofa in the front window watching the Sunday strollers.

At six, Harvey began to attend the private school across the street from his house. After two years there, he entered the Sterling Grammar School, where he acquired a fondness for baseball and the reputation for being the worst speller in the school. His mother would often drive him back after lunch in her carriage rehearsing him in his lesson, but, although seemingly learned, it was soon forgotten, and there were certain words he misspelled all his life. Many years later when he wrote by hand to the president of Yale University in regard to a chair at that institution, he was still writing "privaledge" and "definate." [2]

Harvey was a handsome child, with the quick grace that characterized the movements both of his father and his grandfather Erastus. This litheness made him adept at all kinds of sports, and in the gymnasium they had rigged up in the barn loft he excelled at the parallel and turning bars, at the rings, and at tumbling. His skill at sports and his ready wit made him popular with his classmates when he entered Central High School in February, 1883. But despite the predominance of a gay and mischievous spirit, he had early displayed signs of a quick temper, which at home had earned him the nickname "Pepper Pot." This tendency sometimes led him into difficulty.

On one occasion he quarreled with the Presbyterian minister's son, Robert S. Carroll, during baseball practice with the Sterling Grammar boys. Robert, although two years younger,

---

[2] Other words he misspelled were exhonourate, fortolled, neybour, swoolen, hammard, Sweed, church quire, characature, moskito, Turkish bizarre, sacaraligious, exchecour, malitia, and mediocher. Throughout this book his spellings have been left untouched.

was several pounds heavier than Harvey, and while both had had considerable gym training, what Harvey gained in experience, Robert made up in brawn. Neither knew exactly what incited them to wrath, but Harvey shortly called Robert a "freckle-faced freshy"; Robert retaliated with enthusiasm by calling Harvey a "stuck-up snob." This was more than either could stand, and for forty minutes the two boys wrestled, breathless and perspiring. Finally, they became winded and sitting down on the ground to rest, their faces grotesque with sweat and dust, they grinned at each other sheepishly—and baseball practice continued.

Paralleling Harvey's enthusiasm for sports was a growing interest in natural history. He collected all sorts of bugs, caterpillars, butterflies, and leaves and discovered that his father was a great help in their identification. He did not, however, show his father the present someone made him of a brown and white spaniel puppy, for after their last dog died, Dr. Kirke had flatly refused to let the children have another. Harvey kept Jack well hidden in the barn and patiently taught him tricks when his father was not about. Jack learned to carry articles to people and, being a very talented dog, to p' the piano. Finally the inevitable happened, the dog was discovered, and Harvey waited for the storm to break. But his father remarked only that from his observation the dog might better have been named Jill. Dr. Kirke thereafter ignored the dog until one day he found Jack sitting proudly on the front seat of his carriage which he had left at the front gate. From then on he allowed the dog to accompany him on all his calls.

When Harvey was exercising one day at the Y.M.C.A. during his second year at high school, he slipped from a turning bar and broke his wrist. His father was immediately summoned, and Harvey awaited his coming with considerable anxiety, fearing more than the bonesetting the stern questioning he expected as to what he had been up to. To his surprise, his father said nothing at all but set the bone and fixed the splint with infinite care and gentleness. So fascinated was Harvey by the whole operation that he scarcely felt the pain, and in the days that followed, his interest in the mending process

HENRY KIRKE CUSHING   BETSEY MARIA CUSHING

CUSHING HOUSE AT 786 PROSPECT STREET, CLEVELAND

PLATE I

SONS OF ELI

left to right: Alfred M. Coats, Perry W. Harvey,
Harvey Cushing, G. Beekman Hoppin

BASEBALL TEAM OF THE CLASS OF '91
Harvey Cushing holding bat at lower left

PLATE 2

considerably mitigated a boy's natural impatience with a temporarily useless arm. This was the first time he had seen his father in his role as physician, the first time he had come into close contact with medicine.

It was also in this year that he came under the influence of a remarkable young man, Newton M. Anderson, who taught physics at Central High. Anderson, after graduation from the University of Cincinnati, had installed the first telephone exchange at Liége, Belgium, for the Bell Telephone Company. In addition to being a born teacher, he understood boys and possessed the native talents which they admired. He was a master of all sorts of tools himself, and, convinced that manual dexterity was a valuable asset to any boy, he accordingly set out to establish a manual training course. He rented a barn back of Perry Harvey's house, bought the necessary tools, and gathered in for instruction twelve boys, among them Harvey and several of his cousins. The following year, through the interest of a number of Cleveland citizens, he was able to build and equip a three-story building which became known as the Cleveland Manual Training School, a forerunner of the modern technical high school. Several years later, the courses he gave there were incorporated into the public school system in Cleveland. The boys were taught carpentry, bent-metal work at a forge, mechanical drawing, wood turning, and the use of machinery.

During the summer of 1884, Anderson took Harvey and his cousins, Ed Williams and Perry and Al Harvey, on a fishing trip up the Great Lakes. One of the boys wrote home: "I have rowed so much and got so much muscle that I can turn you city folks inside out. The insides of my hands are all calloused and as hard as bricks." During the following winter, Anderson bought an island in Lake Huron, not far from Sault Ste. Marie, and there Harvey, his cousins, and other Cleveland boys spent several happy summers.

The first year they left Cleveland on a lake steamer on the night of July 3, 1885. A week later they arrived at the island which they named Maskenoza—the Indian word for pike which it somewhat resembled in shape. It was beautifully situated, one end facing the open lake, the other in a deep bay where the water was calm even on the roughest day. Newton Anderson liked nothing better than roughing it in unfamiliar country, and during this and succeeding summers he and the boys felled the spruce with which they built their cabin, explored, surveyed, and mapped the island, shot the game and caught the fish which supplied their larder.

On the 24th of June, 1887, Harvey was graduated from high school, the president of his class. With the help of his mother, he had made a good showing in Latin and especially in mathematics. His grades in Greek and English history were not so high, but he stood eleventh among eighty-three, with an average of 89.34. He took no part in the Commencement activities but he had a leading role in the class play and also gave a tumbling exhibition with one of his classmates.

The summer following his graduation was his last at Maskenoza. During the winter, Anderson had had a 42-foot schooner-yacht built, and eight of the boys sailed the *Susie* to camp. Harvey wrote home that the place seemed prettier every year. He was very much a member of the group during these summers and stood apart from the others only in his knowledge of natural history. He told his father with offhand pride that he was constantly interrupted by the boys yelling: "Oh, Harve, what's this?" The boys cooked their meals in squads of three, and Harvey reported that on one of his squad days their menu consisted of stewed dried beef, corn patties, rice croquettes, baked potatoes, and corn bread, "besides the usual standbyes of hard tack and such things." Frequently, if their luck had been good, they also had duck or woodcock—all this after a breakfast of twelve to fifteen pancakes along with ham and bacon.

Many of the boys were seventeen and eighteen in the summer of 1887 and ready for college in the autumn. Harvey and "Tot" had passed their entrance examinations for Yale, and the happy days on Maskenoza were drawing to a close. Some seven years later, when he was a second-year medical student, Harvey was delighted to discover that one of the house officers from Chicago named Cobb had "sailed the good and great lakes even more thoroughly than the Maskenozeites. . . . He had actually been aboard a small craft by the name of *Susie* which hailed from Cleveland 'run by a lot of boys and a school teacher named Anderson.' The world seems small indeed."

Thus the mention of Maskenoza always stirred vivid memories of their high school days in the minds of the Cleveland boys who had come under the influence of the "school teacher named Anderson." One of his boys wrote of him many years later: "He taught us a lot about being independent and made us so by the duties he inflicted upon us during these summer vacations. We were all undoubtedly better disciplined and better prepared for life from the teachings of this man and from association such as we had with him."

Chapter III

WHEN HARVEY CUSHING AND PERRY
Harvey, who was to be his roommate, arrived in New Haven
on September 18, 1887, they went immediately to 166 York
Street (a lodginghouse still standing), where they had engaged rooms. Harvey's excitement had been mounting steadily
since they had boarded the train in Cleveland. Of the large
group of boys who had come east together, many had already
had a year or more at Yale, for it was a natural choice for the
sons of Ohio families whose forebears had come from the Connecticut Valley.

Mysterious allusions as to what was in store for the freshmen, learned upperclassman talk of the forthcoming football
season, and what sounded like daringly frank comments on
various professors made a deep impression on the Yalensians-
to-be. When separated at the station from their more seasoned
companions, the two boys felt a little lost, and Harvey, who
all his life was to show distrust of new surroundings and an
impatience growing out of being unsure of himself in a strange
place, was definitely disappointed with his first glimpse of
Yale. Their rooms on the third floor, with only two small
windows and a slanting front wall on which nothing could be
hung, had just been calcimined, and the "smell was frightful."
Their landlady, Miss Prescott, was "knee high, old as the hills
(young hills), very fat and wrinkled, and exceedingly fawn-
ing." And the College itself, mixed up as it was with stores and
business blocks along narrow streets, was a sad contrast to

Williams College, which he had visited on his way to Yale. And at Williams the boys seemed to know one another; at Yale, they said, you hardly got to know the members of your own class.

The cost of living also disturbed and alarmed him. In his first letter home he complained that he had had to pay sixty-five cents for a poor meal in a "tony" place and that breakfast had cost him fifteen cents. Later, however, he and Perry made up for these lavish expenditures by eating enough for both lunch and dinner at Professor Ladd's where they had been invited for "tea."

Professor Ladd, a cousin of Mrs. Cushing's, kept a watchful eye on the Cleveland boys, especially Perry and Harvey, during their years at Yale. Harvey found him in his official capacity as Professor of Mental and Moral Philosophy very boring and "a big bag of wind," and when he took his turn in chapel, as did all the professors, Harvey attended with reluctance. He was wholly in sympathy with one of the upperclassmen who on a warm spring day gave an organ-grinder fifty cents to play under Professor Ladd's window while he was lecturing on the self-conscious ego. But as "Cousin George," Harvey found him more tolerable, especially since invitations to his house usually included food.

In 1887 the College was under the presidency of the younger Timothy Dwight, grandson of the Timothy Dwight who had chosen for Yale's first chair of chemistry a young lawyer, the twenty-two-year-old Benjamin Silliman. During the younger Dwight's term of office, the process of changing Yale from a college into a university was well begun. The elective system, the honors system, the general examination, and other innovations in method and curriculum were beginning to take shape.

It was a challenging time to be making a start in the world. The role which science could play in the development of the nation was now well recognized, thanks in large part to Silliman, whose voice had been raised in its interests from his appointment to the faculty in 1802 until his death in 1864, and whose *American Journal of Science* had carried the scientific achievements of the new world to the old and vice versa. Of the 305 students who entered Yale in the autumn of 1887, 100 enrolled in the Sheffield Scientific School which Silliman had been instrumental in founding, and which in the forty short years of its existence had developed from a small group of graduate students and two professors (who served without remuneration) into a thriving organization with a strong faculty. The rapid growth of this school, the first in the country to offer practical instruction in the sciences on a graduate level,[1] was a clear indication of the trend of the time toward utilitarian pursuits and of the need for trained scientists. But when Harvey Cushing began his freshman year, the classical course offered by Yale College was still generally considered the only right road to education for a gentleman.

On his first Sunday in New Haven, Harvey began the custom, faithfully adhered to throughout his student years, of writing every week both to his father and to his mother. Since he often repeated news, he apparently took it for granted that his parents would not share their letters. Occasionally he included sketches which indicated considerable talent for drawing. After his mother had sent him one of those typically Victorian ornaments, a lambrequin, he drew for her their mantel, appropriately draped.

When classes began, Harvey found that he had sixteen recitations a week, one at eight-thirty, immediately following the compulsory chapel at eight-ten; the others at twelve and five every day except Saturday. His program included geometry, Livy, Homer, Cicero, German, algebra, and Greek prose. He liked all of his tutors except Mr. Moore, his geometry teacher, who, he reported to his father with due apology for using the term, was a stinker.

Although he was now walking familiarly in the classics, he was still struggling with his youthful *bête noir*—spelling. But it appeared to cause him more amusement than distress. Once, after he had spelled pneumonia first "pheeunemia" and then

---

[1] It was to Sheffield graduates that Yale was to offer the first Ph.D. degrees to be awarded in this country.

You can see by the clock that it is time for one to stop. I hope this attempt may made up for my short letter. Love to all, from.

Harvey.

Lambrequin-draped mantel of Harvey Cushing's room at 166 York Street, New Haven, in 1887.

had crossed that out and written "phneumonia," his mother wrote him: "I'm sorry your friend is sick. . . . You had quite a struggle with the word pneumonia, which ended in unnecessary generosity on your part in the way of letters of the alphabet. It is well to have a lexicon at hand, if one gets bewildered in spelling as everyone does sometimes. Have you or Perry one?"

A later comment brought this reply from Harvey: "I was very much amused by your lecture on using Yale slang which originated from my attempt to spell succumbed. I admit that I am very poor at spelling but why you imagine that I am swearing or using slang every time I spell a word wrong is more than I can comprehend. Now what manner of slang did you make out of a misspelled succumbed?"

He and Perry survived without a scratch the hazing and rushes which were a vital part of college life in those days, but the high cost of living continued to cause him considerable anxiety. He was appalled at the ease with which money slipped away—for books, furniture, room rent, board, the newspapers and college publications a man was obliged to subscribe to, and such unexpected demands as the support of the crew and the Junior Prom. That he feared his father would suspect him of extravagant living was apparent in every appeal for funds— and these were frequent because he was never given a regular allowance but had to write each time he needed money. In case his father should demand an accounting, he preserved his receipts—*Yale News*, $4.00; *Yale Record*, $1.50; *Yale Literary Magazine*, $3.00; and $10 for the Boat Club. "The News and the 'Lit,' " he wrote, "are very good papers but I can't say much for the Record."

As for the Junior Prom—although he considered it foolishness to buy tickets to an affair the freshmen were not allowed to attend, he reluctantly took two, pointing out to his father that his strength of character had exceeded Perry's, for Perry had been induced to buy five and had furthermore been "stuck" for $25 for the Boat Club. When the night of the Prom came around, he looked in on it at the approximate time for refreshments in an attempt to get some return on his investment. "I succeeded pretty well, too," he wrote his mother.

To offset these unproductive expenditures, he and Tot had bought a second-hand lounge from Miss Prescott's church to make up for their lack of comfortable chairs. This, he felt, was a sound investment, though he wrote his mother somewhat wistfully that he wished he had as much time to sit on it as some of the other boys did.

The matter of rugs for their rooms was his next problem. In one of his first letters to his mother he told her that Perry's mother, Aunt Mary, had asked Perry for the dimensions of their rooms and had said she would send them two rugs—which would be most acceptable in place of the matting that Miss Prescott had provided. In about ten days, which, considering the length of time it took for letters to make their way back and forth, had given Aunt Mary less than a week for action, he wrote his mother again: "I haven't heard anything of that carpet which we were to have, have father and Aunt Mary given it up?"

Since this brought no response, he touched on the subject the following week: "By the way, what has become of those rugs we were going to get? This matting is all coming up and is so dusty everything gets coated with it." This time he waited nearly three weeks but when the rugs still did not arrive, he sent another, stronger plea—this time to his father: "What has become of that rug we heard of sometime ago? We have a terrible time with the dust which rises off this matting. Everything is just covered with it in the morning. My last bottle of ink got so full of it I had to buy another which is rapidly being spoiled. I have to stand up in a chair when I put on my pants in the morning for if they touch the floor they get covered with matting dust."

This did the trick. Whether his father couldn't bear the thought of the wanton waste of ink or the picture of his son standing on a chair to put on his pants, we do not know, but on the 13th of November Harvey was able to write his mother: "This week has made a big improvement in our room. We have got the rugs down and I wish you knew how much we enjoy them. . . . We have great times with our rooms and the boys downstairs have taken a brace and have got their room fixed up fine."

Harvey, being slower than Perry at grasping things, had to spend more time studying but twice during the autumn he managed to get to New York to attend football games. Such opportunities did not come as often in a student's life as they do now, and the Yale-Princeton game at the Polo Grounds was not only Harvey's first visit to New York, but his first big college football game. As he said, "a person would have to see one of those big games to understand the excitement." When word of his second excursion reached home, his father interpreted it as evidence that Harvey was straying somewhat from the path of duty and wrote him accordingly. The outraged and hurt amazement in his son's reaction must have amused even the strict Dr. Kirke:

Dear Father: I was very sorry to have received such a letter from you as I did last week. . . . I don't know as you have any reason to think that I have not been studying, and do not intend to study faithfully, I am sure you know I always did at home and I don't see why you should suspect I have not here. As for repenting that you sent me here I am very sorry if I have been the cause but if you are afraid I won't study here I don't see why you should suppose I would elsewhere. I went up to N.Y. to spend Thanksgiving with [Tom] Young but did not go up expressly to see a football game although we did go to see the game, and I am sure from the accounts of one of the boys who stayed here that the excitement in New Haven was as great as at New York, if not more so, with bonfires and so forth. I believe you went to college once, and although one has to grind the greater part of the time, there are times when one doesn't. I don't know whether I will make the first division or not as there are a great many remarkably bright men in our class but I have studied hard for it. I hope I haven't said too much but I was surprised and disappointed very much. . . .

Despite his father's disapproval, Harvey continued to be deeply interested in all college sports; and the number of programs of track meets, football and baseball games pasted in the two scrapbooks he kept during his four years testifies to his frequent attendance. These scrapbooks were evidence that he had inherited in full measure the family tendency to save all manner of things. Neatly cut newspaper clippings accompany the programs, along with such mementoes as railroad tickets from New Haven to Lake Saltonstall where the crew races were held, a piece torn from the shirttail of some luckless spectator at a football game, and a photograph of the muscular figure in shorts of Amos Alonzo Stagg (rear view), Yale's famed varsity baseball pitcher.

There were evidences of other interests, but not many. Occupying second place were memorabilia about various societies—clippings, dinner programs, and mysterious summonses to meetings. He always attended the concerts of the Glee and Banjo Clubs and he was in the dress circle at the midyear Hyperion when the freshmen were successful in showing their class numerals (despite the vigilance of the sophomores), first by dropping a shower of cards from the balcony, then by lowering a banner on the stage, and finally by loosing a flock of pigeons with '91 flags tied to their legs. There was an account of a meeting of the Western Reserve Republicans, of the sad decline of the moral and intellectual tone of Harvard men, of how the city attorney in New Haven had retrieved 187 glass street signs from the rooms of Yale students, and, finally, there was the mid-term examination schedule dated December, 1887 and, sewed to it, the pen point with which he wrote his answers.

Shortly after Harvey returned from Christmas in Cleveland, he had letters from his father and mother that were typical of each parent. His father congratulated him on attaining the first division, told him to join a new eating club since he was ready to meet all expenses that would contribute to his comfort and advantage. "But," he added, "I must expect that you deny yourself as much as possible superfluities of no lasting value and which I am told amount to a good deal in a term." His mother cautioned him about taking proper exercise, expressed concern over his persistent cold, and then continued: "I hope all is right between you and Perry. Here is a little private word for my darling boy. May I say it without offense?

You know that you have a propensity to scold. Watch against it, my dear; remembering that your mother's anxious love prompts the suggestion. 'A word to the wise is sufficient.' . . . Goodbye my darling, I wish you could get rid of that cold. Always your loving mother, Bessie M. Cushing."

His mother's letters continued to be placid and cheerful although her strong-minded husband and her impetuous and equally strong-minded youngest son were shortly engaged in a battle of wills on two major issues that went on during most of the spring term. Indeed, it was probably her influence and sense of humor which prevented an open break between them.

After the excitement of the famous blizzard of 1888 (which descended on New Haven on March 12) had subsided, spring weather arrived and with it the questions of sophomore societies and baseball. When Harvey had set off to college he had promised his father he would not smoke, drink, "be guilty of any immoral conduct, or join a college ball club or boat crew." In Cleveland this had seemed easy, but he had reckoned without the lure of competition when the freshmen went out for baseball in the spring. He not only loved baseball but he wanted the excitement of matching his prowess with the others and of making the team. He began practice in February but when he mentioned this fact in his letters home he assured his father it was only because he needed exercise. He broached the matter of joining a society first.

Here there was even more competition, for the two sophomore societies, and the junior and senior societies likewise, would elect only fifteen men each out of their class of around two hundred. In the spring, when elections were made, excitement ran high. *The Horoscope*, published annually at this season "to give a just and impartial summary of the candidates for the senior societies," had this to say about the permanence of societies at Yale: "Deep rooted as they are in the very foundations of our alma mater, it is simply absurd to assert, as we occasionally hear, that they will or should be abolished. Their objectionable features may be abolished, but many a moon will wane ere the ruling spirits of the University—Corporation and Faculty, so many of whom were society men themselves—will permit any radical change. Yale is pre-eminently the home of secret societies."

Skull and Bones, founded in 1832 "so mysteriously that the closest study of half a century has failed to lift the vail [*sic*] surrounding its origin," took in the "solid," thoughtful men, while Scroll and Key supposedly selected the "genial and the popular." If, in addition to being an agreeable gentleman, a Keys prospect was also "a scholar, a writer, and an energetic worker," so much the better. What went on within their windowless marble walls fascinated Harvey, as it had many a man before him. The aura of exclusiveness and mystery surrounding all the activities of the various societies appealed strongly to his sense of the dramatic, and since he very much desired to join, he prefaced his letter with a statement calculated to put his father in a receptive mood. He well knew that this was one of the "superfluities" which he had been asked to avoid. "I am very careful not to run in debt and I never get anything charged and I don't know of anything that pays as well. It is bad enough having a washing bill come in every now and then but some of the boys are always dreading the end of the month because of the bills which flock in." After this righteous beginning, he got down to the point: "I want to talk to you about a matter which I would like to have spoken about before but could not very well for a good reason." (He hadn't yet been asked to join!) Knowing that his father relied on the judgment of Frank Herrick, an older Cleveland boy, Harvey assured his father that Herrick had advised him that to get into one of the sophomore societies (spelled "sophmore sociatys") was a great honor. He finally admitted that having been offered a pledge, he had accepted it—"with your permission that is."

Dr. Kirke countered with a long letter, concentrating more on Harvey's opening paragraph than on what followed. He even went so far as to endeavor to enlist his son's sympathy with a rare mention of his own problems: "When this term ends, I can say that the aggregate years of college life my boys will have had will be twenty-three. In all that time their monthly allowance has never failed. It has not always been easy to do this, for the family at home has had to be kept going, and taxes, repairs, and insurance kept up." He then continued:

Please buy a dictionary and consult it as you write. In almost every letter I note misspelt words. In the last for instance you omit the middle "o" in sophomore giving it thus "sophmore."

At the end of the letter he came to the important matter.

I do not know what to say about the Soph. Society, but am glad that you consulted Frank Herrick. . . . Society influence is either good or bad . . . A man gets rated at his best rather slowly, unless he is a very uncommon chap; but one inclined to be fast gets his character very quickly. . . . Take all the time you can have before deciding the Society matter, and whatever you finally do I will acquiesce in.

Nothing more was said on the question until June, when Harvey wrote:

You remember, Father, what I said to you sometime ago about the Sophomore Society? Well, there was finally no question with me which way you would want me to go and I would want to go myself, and so last Friday I was taken in. The initiation fee was $35 which I won't have to pay till the end of the term. . . . The boys are all manly and studious and mighty nice boys in every way. I was thinking this morning that there are 10 out of the 16 in the first division while in the other society only 2, which I think is illustrative of the two. I hope you will sanction my choice.

Since Harvey was already initiated, there seemed little else his father could do, but he replied: "I trust you will critically examine your Society relations and calmly judge if you do not think the price asked for its blandishments is not large for their worth. At any rate I am glad that you speak so well of your classmen in your Society. You might mention its name." Harvey closed the subject quite definitely in his next letter: "I *had critically* examined my society friends as I promised you *before* I entered the society, and the price charged for its blandishments, as you term them, is smaller than I had expected."

Baseball was not disposed of so amicably. Dr. Kirke was opposed to intercollegiate athletics on moral grounds. He deplored the emphasis placed on them, the excitement which attended them, especially for the players, and the money wasted on betting. Harvey, then, when he asked his father if he had any "serious objections" to his playing shortstop on the freshman nine, innocently gave the impression that it was something which had come unsolicited, and laid more stress on what an honor it was to try to win the Fence for his class— for the freshmen were not allowed to sit on the Yale Fence (the original rail fence around the first building) until they had beaten Harvard at baseball. The Fence had become an institution, a place where the classes gathered, separately, between recitations and after supper to talk and sing. "I suppose it does more social work in the College than anything possibly could." It occupied such a vital part in the life and memories of Yale men that alumni all over the country protested when it was to be torn down to make way for a new recitation building.

Dr. Kirke, in reply to Harvey's letter, firmly reiterated his position on college athletics but did not forbid him to play. However, when he discovered that Harvey was going to Cambridge with the nine, he gave way to restrained anger: "I will try to reply to your letter calmly, though I do feel sore and disturbed over the unhappy position you have brought us into. . . . It looks to me as if in the glamour and excitement of College sentiments and surroundings, you have reasoned yourself into the feeling that if you only kept in the first division it was none of my business what else you did. . . ." This was indeed precisely how Harvey *had* reasoned and he had no intention of withdrawing from the team since a *Y* was one of the surer ways of being "tapped" for a senior society.

He told his father that there was general interest in this particular game throughout the College and that to withdraw would place him in a most awkward position. Dr. Kirke replied by pointing to a New York *Tribune* account of the Yale-Princeton game when the seventy Princeton men left $1,000 (largely in bets), besides their expenses, at New Haven. "College games seem to me to be rapidly taking their place side by side with horse racing and professional ball playing. Can you wonder that I feel concerned at seeing you inching toward such a vortex?"

This made Harvey highly indignant: "I understand perfectly your full acquaintance with the evils of college life for you have had enough boys in enough colleges to know, but I do think that you place too much belief on some of the accounts of college evils which come out in the papers, especially about Yale. . . . But I hope you have enough confidence in me not to suspect my doing anything of the sort [betting] and if you have not, I don't know what I can do about it." His father answered this letter coldly: "Yours of the 13th rec'd. I cannot reply at this moment to your views as therein set forth, but will send the money as it is needed, while my advice and wishes do not seem to go for much." So the battle continued.

In the meantime the *Yale News* was reviewing the possibilities of a Yale victory and objectively estimating the abilities of the team. "Cushing, ss., is a very good fielder, but often throws wildly and loses his head." This must have caused Harvey some chagrin, but he had solace from another quarter. At the spring indoor track meet it was reported that "the work on the horizontal bar was unusually good and quite exciting. Cushing '91 proved the best man."

The Yale freshmen lost the game in Cambridge, but when Harvard invaded New Haven, Yale was victorious. The freshmen had won the Fence. His mother expressed her pleasure and added philosophically: "I am glad you enjoy 'the fence.' If it must go, perhaps some substitute may be found where the boys may foregather, as they have done there. It may be the fate of your class to discover such a place, which though it may not have the charm of antiquity, may have that of novelty. . . . All things, great and small, must have a beginning. Is there no other *fence* at Yale? At all events, *the* fence was not always there." To this heresy Harvey did not reply. After all, his mother could not be expected to understand these things. He ended his freshman year with a telegram to his father: "Please telegraph thirty dollars for secondhand furniture."

UPPERCLASSMAN

Chapter IV

IN SEPTEMBER OF 1888 HARVEY was back in New Haven writing home with all the superiority of one who is no longer a freshman: "Work has started in earnest by this time and we have five new teachers. We have Tracy Peck in Pliny and like him very much but the rest of them I don't like very well. There are Mr. McLaughlin in Rhetoric and English Lit., which is going to be hard for me, Mr. Moore in Tacitus, Mr. Kitchell in Isocrates, and a new German teacher, Mr. Strong, whom I have sized up to be a regular chump, if I may be allowed to speak plainly."

This autumn the loss of the Fence was keenly felt. "Last night four of us went and sat on the steps of the new building [Bingham, still standing at the corner of Chapel and College Streets] which run way around the corner and are quite high. It just shows what a longing for the old fence there is for we hadn't been up there more than a few minutes when there were 10 or 15 fellows up there and we began to sing quietly and before half an hour there must have been about 200 men seated on the steps. It was pretty cold comfort sitting on the dirty stones which don't fit as well as the old rails. The new building is very imposing but one can't help wishing for the fine old trees, the grass, and most of all for the fence."

There was less mention of his room this year; also less emphasis on food, but this did not mean he wasn't still interested. He wrote his mother: "Tell Johanna she won't lack for someone to eat when I get home. In one of the college papers the other day there was a blessing for the eating clubs who are in the clutches of the New Haven landladies which I think is very appropriate. It goes:

> Oh Lord be merciful
> And keep us all alive,
> There's ten of us at dinner
> And grub for only five."

Social activities played a larger part in his life this year. His well-filled prom card showed a wide diversity of interest, with concentration in no one direction. "I never saw so many pretty girls before in my life or met so many nice ones." At these functions he frequently met girls from home because several of the crowd he had grown up with—Katharine Crowell, Ray and Reba Williams, Melanie Harvey, Mary Goodwillie and her sister "Harry," and the Boardman girls, Josephine and Nina—attended the Farmington School or had brothers at Yale and often came down for parties and football games. Harvey liked to dance and was a graceful dancer, but at Yale, as at the country club dances during Cleveland summers, he usually went with a group or joined the stag line.

In March he shared in the general indignation aroused in the College when some who had stayed overlong in a local tavern had unseated the statue of Benjamin Silliman on their way home. In his scrapbook is pasted a cutting of the announcement that Mr. Carpenter, the night watchman, had been dismissed because of laxness in his duties.

His father had laid down the condition that after the Yale-Harvard game of the preceding June, he was not to play baseball again. This did not prevent Harvey from broaching the subject the next year—this time with even more determination, for he was now on the Varsity team. He wrote his father a sincere and very appealing letter. Dr. Kirke tacitly admitted defeat, and Harvey played throughout the remainder of his college career. His "press notices" were now generally gratifying—as after a game in Philadelphia in which Yale had been badly beaten when it was reported that the only redeeming feature of the game was the playing of Cushing and Graves. At the Brown game the following year he showed extraordinary restraint for one of his quick temper when a Brown player, whom he had brushed against in trying to make third base on a fumble, had attacked him on third and struck him sharply in the chest. The papers announced that "Cushing's self-control tied his hands to his sides and kept him silent before Sexton's exasperating jeers," and after the game the entire Brown team apologized to him. He again made the headlines in Cambridge when the score was 3-2 in favor of Yale with Harvard at bat. With the bases full, the batter up hit a long fly and the headline read: "An exciting game of ball at Cambridge yesterday—Cushing's great sprinting for a long fly starts 10,000 persons cheering."

Information of this sort did not find its way into his letters home. With his father he continued to discuss the more serious things of life—the ever-present need for funds and occasionally the political issues confronting the country. Being a staunch Ohio Republican he expressed satisfaction that the Republican Presidential candidate, Benjamin Harrison, defeated Grover Cleveland in the election of 1888.

His needs for clothes were also discussed with his father. "I went down yesterday to see if I could find any trowsers [always spelled with a *w*] that would do for me as my thin ones belonging to my gray suit have about got on their last legs, or rather upon my legs for about the last time." But if it was underclothes he needed, he spoke to his mother, and in very delicate terms—shorts he described as "p. of d." (pair of drawers) and undershirts he called "unmentionables."

In some of these letters home, Harvey complained that there were so many boys in their rooms (he and Perry Harvey had continued to room together) that he had difficulty writing. His and Perry's popularity was also evident in the invitations extended by classmates when vacations came around. "Sam Colgate, the son of the big soap man, asked 'Tot' and me to go down to their place in Orange, New Jersey, on Thanksgiving after Tom Young had asked me. He is a mighty nice fellow and has had three brothers down here." Later he wrote of a

visit to Shinnecock Hills, Long Island, where he was the guest
of another member of '91, Grosvenor Atterbury, who was to
become one of his lifelong friends.

From the Atterburys he went with another classmate, Starling Childs, to visit the Robert Chapins in Lenox, Massachusetts. "The Chapins are in mourning for an uncle which has
prevented them from entertaining, which latter fact I don't
regret much for I prefer the drives and watching the tennis
tournament to the formality of these balls which begin about
the time when a Christian should go to bed and end about as
he should get up."

At the end of his sophomore year Harvey had been elected
to Delta Kappa Epsilon and at the Thanksgiving Jubilee of
the fraternity in November of 1889 he had opportunity to
display his histrionic ability. The program announced "The
Beautiful Melodrama, Pocohontas Powhatan," in which Harvey played the part of Pocohontas—"that cute, coy coquette,
a Bar Harbor rosebud in her second season, and a terrible
example of the effect of Female Seminaries." He made his
entrance with a flourish of trumpets and a double back handspring into the middle of the stage—such a handspring, apparently, as he was accustomed to doing off the gymnasium
steps with a lighted cigarette in his mouth.

Then came the greatest moment of his college career—Tap
Day. "Thursday were the senior society elections and they are
very exciting things to watch. First a Bones man comes from
their hall onto the campus and without saying a word to anyone or without recognizing anyone he walks around till he
finds the junior he wants in the big crowd assembled there
and then slaps him on the back and tells him to go to his room
where he receives his election. Then a Scroll and Key man
comes and selects his man from the anxious crowd of juniors
and so on till the 15 are taken each way." Harvey, to his great
joy, was "tapped" for Scroll and Key as were Tot and Grove
Atterbury. "I won't attempt to tell you what fine things the
Senior Societies are acknowledged to be," he wrote his father,
"what a position they hold in the College World and what
good they do a man, for if you don't already know something

about it, it would make too long a story." Some twenty years
earlier, Dr. William Welch, who was to be his friend and colleague, had written to *his* father of his election to Bones, "the
honor is more agreeable to me than any other in college could
have been."

In the fall of 1890 Harvey faced his final year with anticipation mingled with regret that his college days were so soon
to be over. In his first letter home he bemoaned the fact that
"one more week of this precious year has gone. I don't know
how or where. My time is so taken up from morn till night
that the days pass by like the ticks of a pendulum. We have
begun to feel at home by this time, you may imagine, as dignified seniors. Dignified however is not a very appropriate
word, for I never saw men less so." He himself gave little sign
of it in the description of his rooms that his mother had
asked for.

> B marks the place where our twin bureau stands
> While S marks the place where we wash our hands,
> In D we have dreams of far distant lands
> While I at my desk do obey your commands.
> T is the sofa on which Tot does snore,
> While R are the rugs which lie on the floor.
> C is the chimney down which the winds roar,
> And on this same subject I'll write you no more.

He was happy about his courses, enjoying Marlowe in English and the study of the French Revolution in history. He
reported that he thought the latter course would be very interesting "especially as the man himself, Prof. Wheeler, is very
much so. I wish I could say as much for Geo. Ladd," he continued. "It was all I could do to even translate the first 25
pages of his book. I have got to go down to the sloughter
house and get a calf's brain to explain to the class. Being the
only one in class whose name he knew, I suppose he spotted
me."

Harvey had taken chemistry, physics, and physiology the
previous year and this year was studying zoology and physiological chemistry. These science courses fired his imagina-

tion as Greek and Latin never could, and although he grumbled about the amount of time he had to spend in the laboratory and at getting his assignments, he had at last found something to get his teeth into, subjects on which he willingly spent many extra hours of study. He was particularly keen about his course in physiological chemistry with Professor Russell Chittenden in "Sheff"—the course which had the reputation of being the hardest in college.

The matter of his future was beginning to concern him. In his sophomore year he had written his father: "I will have a talk with Prof. Ladd as soon as possible and see what he says, more definately, about those chemical courses. There is no doubt about it that if I am going to study medicine it is an opportunity not to be lost as I can't take them next year." However, he later wrote: "I don't know whether you have any desires of what you want me to do after I leave college or not. I have thought about it a good deal and can't come to any determination at all." Now, in his senior year, he vaguely had two thoughts in mind. His artistic propensities had given him much in common with Grosvenor Atterbury, who planned to study architecture, and he considered joining Grove and later opening an office with him. The possibility of postgraduate study with Professor Chittenden also had strong appeal. But on a visit to the Atterburys in New York, he had met their family physician, Dr. Henry Stimson, who had offered to take the boys on ward rounds with him the next morning at New York Hospital. Grove turned pale when a bad fracture case was being examined but Harvey was fascinated by everything.

In the spring his senior society brought him the opportunity to hear prominent members of various professions, among them Dr. Bryson Delavan, of New York, who spoke on the history of medicine and surgery, and to whom Harvey listened "mighty interested" for an hour and a half, although he often complained about the "forty-five minutes of wind" he was compelled to endure in chapel from "Prexy," George Ladd, or some outside speaker. These extracurricular contacts added to the interest aroused by his course work. In addition to the calf's brain which he had to explain to the class, he mentioned dissecting the spinal and cranial nerves of a frog, and the dissection of a dog. Thus by the end of his senior year he seemed headed for a career in medicine and the other plans began to lose their substance.

A new interest was uncovered when, apparently for the first time, he visited the library: "I went over to the library to try to look up something for a composition . . . but got so interested looking at other books and relics that I forgot all about the composition till the librarian rang his bell for closing." He mentioned the library a second time in connection with a visit of Katharine Crowell and her mother. "I was luckily free for half an hour and we all went to the library. . . . Mrs. Crowell seemed to enjoy it. I hope she did at any rate for it is a part of the campus to which visitors don't often go, as it probably never occurs to the men that they want to, but I think it's the best place by far to take them and show them it's not all play here. Besides, the reading room in the New Library with the Tiffany window is a remarkably handsome one." [1]

Finally, "the old man with the hour glass and scythe who seems to hustle along with unprecedented speed" began to catch up with him. On April 26 he wrote his mother: "The time of year has come around for the prospective seniors and juniors to pick out their courses and nothing has happened which has seemed to shut us out in the cold as much as to have no courses to pick out for ourselves for next year. All we can do is to receive calls from and advise these illustrious underclassmen as to what paths they should tread. I have persuaded some prospective physicians to follow the same studies I have in 'Sheff'—which courses and Prof. Chittenden I am prepared to swear by."

Harvey did not make Phi Beta Kappa as his father had hoped, but he finished in the first division (in the upper third of his class). Clearly it was the social contacts of his college

[1] He used a cut of this window as the frontispiece for the 1891 *Pot-Pourri*, the Yale yearbook edited by Scroll and Key, for which he and his friend G. Beekman ("Deacon") Hoppin were responsible that year.

years that most endeared Yale to him, and he kept in close touch with many of his classmates throughout his life. During his busy postgraduate years he wrote in rotation to a Keys man every second week.

He was on the committee for the Senior Prom but somehow did not manage to preserve a program and kept his dances on a piece of cardboard. Elizabeth Le Bourgeois and Katharine Crowell appeared twice each, and for one of the intermissions, Mrs. Crowell's name was entered. But Ed Williams, his cousin, took Kate to the class german. Harvey still showed no inclination to lose his heart to any one girl, or indeed to lose his heart at all—even under the Commencement moon.

His father came on for the festivities but was able to stay only a brief time. To his mother, who remained at home, Harvey reported: "We went this morning to hear the President's Baccalaureate sermon in which he managed to tell us in 60 minutes that the past was behind and the future before us and not much more."

On June 24, 1891, Harvey Cushing received his degree from Yale College, and it was a very sad boy indeed who, on the last evening as he was packing to leave, heard the voices of some of his classmates singing in harmony as they made their way across the campus.

> See the full moon, rising, weaves
>   Robes of light o'er tower and hall;
> Thro' the slowly lifting leaves,
>   Silver lances flash and fall.
> Louder yet the chorus raise,
>   Friendship lasts when youth must fail;
> Jolly, jolly are the days,
>   'Neath the Elms of dear old Yale.

MEDICAL STUDENT AT
HARVARD

Chapter V

LATE IN SEPTEMBER OF 1891,
Cushing started for Boston to enter the Harvard Medical
School, following in the footsteps of his brother Ned—a decision he apparently arrived at while with his family during
the summer. It had been an especially gay and carefree holiday
with his old crowd—probably the last vacation they would all
be together. He had begun for the first time to devote his attention to a particular girl—Katharine Crowell, whose summer
home, Breezy Bluff, was a favorite meeting place for the young
people. Kate, as she was called, was a gay, high-spirited, popular girl, not only beautiful, but a good match for Harvey when
it came to things of the mind.

Cushing stopped off at New Haven with several of his classmates, among them Starling Childs who was on his way to
Harvard Law School. He saw Professor Chittenden and many
other friends, and the warmth of their welcome made his arrival in Boston forlorn in contrast. He spent his first, rather
lonely night at the Tremont House and the next day set out to
find a room, but after "walking 10 miles and climbing a 1000
feet of stairs," he had only acquired a composite picture of a
landlady whose name was legion and whom he did not admire.
"It seems to me I never saw so many people before who were
all utter strangers and it's most depressing."

Then to his joy he ran into a "Keys" man on the street—
Henry Sage, of the Class of '89, who was at the Massachusetts

Institute of Technology. With Sage's "invaluable" help he settled in at 32 West Cedar Street, on Beacon Hill, and acquired a lamp, a desk, a "washer-lady named Duffy," and a map of Boston with which he soon learned to find his way like a native.

And if he had been dismayed by the demands upon his pocketbook at Yale, he was even more startled at the cost of graduate education. "How medical books do cost! . . . They are beautiful books though—the Quain [anatomy] especially." But he was lucky in the lot drawing for the last microscopes, so did not have to buy one. He was also fortunate in securing a seat in the classrooms, for there were not enough chairs to accommodate the hundred members of his class (although this was considered a small class), and late-comers had to stand.

It had been over a century since John Warren (younger brother of Dr. Joseph Warren who fell at Bunker Hill) had walked, when weather made the water-crossing precarious, the seven circuitous miles from his home in Roxbury to give his lectures to the Harvard seniors in Cambridge. It was with his appointment to the chair of anatomy and surgery in 1783 that the Harvard Medical School had come into existence. He was the first of many outstanding physicians and teachers who brought honor and prestige to the Medical School. There were his own descendants—John Collins Warren, Jonathan Mason, J. Collins; the James Jacksons, father and son; the Bigelows; the Bowditches—Henry Ingersoll, Vincent Yardley, and Henry Pickering; and Oliver Wendell Holmes.

Nearly all of these men had supplemented their education with study abroad in the great clinics of Europe, and the Harvard Medical School had felt the influence first of the English and Scottish schools—of men such as John Hunter, Charles Bell, and Astley Cooper in London, James Syme and Robert Liston in Edinburgh—and then of the French, especially of the founder of medical statistics, Pierre-C.-A. Louis of Paris. But Charles W. Eliot, when he became president of Harvard in 1869, found that, despite the undeniable prestige of the faculty, many aspects of the medical curriculum were outmoded and he brought about far-reaching reforms and innovations. J. Lothrop Motley, the historian, wrote: "Our new President, Eliot, has turned the whole University over like a flapjack. There never was such a *bouleversement* as that in our Medical Faculty." The so-called "course" was adopted, the student body divided into classes, and an experimental physiology laboratory set up, where, for the first time in this country, students could do their own experiments. Endowment funds were increased, and in 1883 a new building was opened on the corner of Boylston and Exeter Streets. This building, which had seemed very spacious at the time, was in 1891 already inadequate—so great had been the increase in enrollment.

At 32 West Cedar Street, Cushing found a variety of interests among his housemates. He was somewhat alarmed when he discovered that the brother and sister who occupied the two front rooms were musicians and that the sister was planning to give violin lessons. "They are very nice, however, and if they must play I'm glad they play well. I get a good deal of exercise out of it too as I unconsciously beat time with one part or another of my anatomy, whichever is most convenient —foot, hand or head. This is difficult when the man above is playing college songs on his banjo but it can be done."

He saw a good deal of Henry Sage during the autumn— they went together to football games, to visit their Yale friends at the Law School, and occasionally to the Boston Symphony. In a letter to his mother he described his first experience: "Thanks to Sage I made my acquaintance with the Boston Symphony last night. He is a regular attendant and having procured an extra ticket next his, he presented it to me. . . . I enjoyed it all hugely, especially the last number, the Heroic, during which I wept and laughed alternately."

His courses kept him well occupied, but it was mid-November before he had an experience which stirred an intense interest in medicine. It happened on the first day the class in anatomy began dissections. He was assigned a table near the window—an advantage in the days of gas lights—and his first "part" was a right upper extremity. As he concentrated on his work, the rest of the room retreated into the background. The perfection of the human body and the intricacy of its structure fascinated him. His facility in using a scalpel and handling the delicate tissues seemed to be instinctive—it was far greater than might have been expected from his small experience at Yale. So remarkable was his skill that soon his classmates and his teachers began coming in groups of two or three to watch him. This day not only set him apart from his fellows but offered him a challenge from which he could never escape. From this time forward medicine filled his life. He decided to be, in his words, a "leper"—to forego social activities and devote all his attention to his work.

Already he had appraised his classmates and picked out those who would offer the most competition. Elliott Joslin (Yale '90) and C. L. Mix he thought would lead the class, while Edes, White, and Painter he marked as "good men"—something his class abounded in, he told his father. But it was Joslin who set the pace for him.

E. Amory Codman, who became a particular friend, revealed in his letters, when he went abroad in the midst of their course, that he knew of this silent competition. "Now, Harvey, old man," he wrote from Berlin, "I really could not read a part of your letter and if you really wish to get ahead of Joslin you must brace up in that direction. Leave the girls alone or you will be rising at ten in the morning as I do. May the achievement of your ambition be the reward of your virtue."

But not even his growing absorption in medicine or his competition with Joslin could keep Cushing from making the most of every opportunity to revisit Yale. Even at this early date he had only to step off the train in New Haven and his concerns would drop away and his heart lighten and he would be transported again to the idyllic atmosphere of his college days. Late in November he attended the Yale-Harvard football game with some of the Yale-Harvard Law group, Henry Sage, and Dr. Charles Scudder (Yale graduate, friend of his brother Ned, and demonstrator in anatomy).

Harvey now had lost his fear of approaching his father for funds. Dr. Kirke, after his initial letter of caution and advice (Harvey had designated it "a Chesterfield letter"), had begun to write him more as man to man. And he sent money more freely and with little or no mention of the need for thrift. "I am sorry you waited until you were penniless before calling my attention to the propriety of a remittance. So many demands gravitate my way all the time that I do not keep track of the weeks and months as I might do."

Kate Crowell and Mary Goodwillie visited Boston in March. In his letters home Harvey was very offhand about it, saying he was so busy he found it difficult to change his clothes and go to see the girls; but when Kate left, he took her to the station and was so engrossed, he was nearly left on the train. He admitted to his mother that if he had had the time and money, he would not have minded at all!

In April he and Amory Codman, having already been marked as promising students, were honored by election to the Boylston Medical Society. The spring vacation he spent in Boston doing extra dissecting, except for another brief visit to New Haven "to renew his youth."

With the change in seasons his letters became filled with his pleasure in the flowers and trees of Boston. In every one he described some aspect of the spring's awakening, and the Public Garden, "a joy forever," was a favorite subject. His interest in the Garden, which continued throughout his years in Boston, was shared by some of his classmates:

On pleasant evenings Painter, White and I usually take a small stroll through the gardens for about a half hour as they are a particularly pleasant spot at that time, being about deserted. We usually spend our time betting on the names of trees, which are of every imaginable variety. As I am extremely ignorant on such subjects, I was o'ercome with glee to find that they did not know the gentle Catalpa with which I had become acquainted, thanks to Father. White knows all the foreign trees and Painter the New England varieties. I hitch names onto the trees they don't know and swear that they are indiginous to Ohio with whose vegetation I alone am familiar.

At the very beginning of the examination period in June he slipped away to New Haven. "I had no idea of coming till Saturday night but could not stay away and can only say it has been worth it a thousand times over. Would that Perry could have been here! I go back tonight for the final grind."

On June 25 he wrote his father what came to be a familiar letter—he had a chance to do some extra work (substituting at the Massachusetts General Hospital for a few days) and he thought he had better accept it although it would delay his home-coming.

SECOND YEAR—1892-93

In the autumn of 1892 when Cushing returned for his second year at medical school, he began his clinical work on the wards of the hospital. Early in the nineteenth century it had become apparent to several members of the faculty of the Harvard Medical School that a hospital was needed both for the care of patients and for the instruction of students. Accordingly, the Massachusetts General Hospital, the first permanent hospital in New England, had been built in 1821, largely through the efforts of James Jackson and the first John C. Warren. Charles Bulfinch, the Boston architect who did so much to influence American architecture, designed the building with the simple Doric columns and the central dome characteristic of his style.

In the amphitheater in the dome America's greatest contribution to humanity—painless surgery—was introduced to the world in October, 1846, Warren himself performing the operation while W. T. G. Morton, the Boston dentist who had been experimenting with ether, administered the anesthetic. Here had been introduced by the second John Collins Warren, grandson of the first, the aseptic methods of Joseph Lister, in whose surgery at Glasgow he had learned them in 1869. This Warren, the fourth in his line to be actively identified with the Medical School, was now teaching surgery to Cushing, who often administered to Dr. Warren's patients the anesthetic which the latter's grandfather had helped to introduce.

The close contact with patients, sickness, and death on the wards of the hospital caused Harvey Cushing to approach his work with increased seriousness and concentration. He had

moved this year to 89 Charles Street, inhabited largely by men
from Technology. "My room is on the top floor and is much
more pleasant than last year's despite the fact that my outlook
is nothing but brick seen through a tangle of wires and the
front wall has a round-shouldered aspect, unmistakably attic."

His program included therapeutics, advanced anatomy,
pathological anatomy (which he hoped to like—"have a splendid teacher, at any rate, in Councilman of the Hopkins"), and
theory and practice of medicine. (For this he had purchased
Osler's Textbook of Medicine, which he reckoned cost nearly
$5.00 a pound.) Partly through interest and partly because of
the security that extra knowledge gave him, he accepted an
opportunity to assist Dr. Charles Scudder in the out-patient
department, an assignment which, though exciting, was dis-
tracting because it conflicted with regular lectures and forced
him to copy notes from one of his classmates in order to keep
up with his work.

Because his days were so filled, he particularly enjoyed the
relaxation of occasional hours away from the hospital. A week
end in the open always afforded something special to enlarge
upon in his letters home and gave free rein to his powers of
description. In mid-September he visited Annisquam with
Henry Sage and gloried in the sail to Gloucester, the sunset
from Squam Rock after their arrival, and a tramp through
swamp woods bright with autumn color. He was chagrined
but amused by a joke Sage played on him when they got off
the Gloucester train:

Was nicely taken in by Sage last night. Being in a hurry we
left the car before the other people who were about fifteen in
number (though I am not sure now that there were less than a
hundred) all of whom were going in our direction towards Annisquam. We passed in a moment a fine old farm house garden
and Sage said "Did you ever see a Chinese plumb tree?" pointing
to a curious shrub near the house and on which was the most
curious white fruit. I was all interested in a minute and on asking if they cared if people looked at it, Sage said "No, we can go
in and I think the fruit is about ripe." We pushed open the gate
and not till we were at arms length from the tree did I discover

that the "fruit" consisted of a lot of nicely blown egg shells placed about on the small twigs of a young pear tree. Sage roared, as did the people following up the hill, for it seems that the "egg tree" is a standing Annisquam joke. All I could do was to acknowledge the corn and take off my hat to them. I shall not forget that plumb tree till I have a chance to revenge myself on somebody else.

This autumn his father had given him money for his own microscope, which pleased him very much because he could do extra work without fear of keeping the equipment from another student. In addition to assisting Dr. Scudder, he welcomed the opportunity to perfect his skill in dissecting by acting, with Amory Codman, as prosector for Dr. Maurice Richardson who taught anatomy.

Although these extracurricular jobs added interest and experience, they took time, and he became concerned about his marks. In November he sought out his physiology professor, Henry P. Bowditch, to ask about his "Phisiology" mark. "He seemed rather bored to be asked [and] was still more bored when he found that they had made a clerical error and that instead of being 77.5 it should have been 87.5%. I don't know what impulse took me in there but am very glad that I enquired."

He described his weeks as a rush in the middle and a gradual slowing up toward Sunday, when there was a breathing spell and a chance to think about something except pills, then a rapid descent to the middle of the week, gaining momentum with which to pass the next peak. Nevertheless, Sundays were often used for reading papers, bandaging imaginary injuries, and tying ligatures with Painter, Dolliver, Codman, or some of his other friends. But at times he used these "breathing spells" for something besides studying and once admitted: "I have been under the spell of the majic pen of Nathaniel Hawthorn all this afternoon and have just finished reading for the third time *The Scarlet Letter*. After lunch I carelessly picked it up from the table downstairs and opened it. That was enough— I finished the last ten pages at supper which was consumed between the lines. Its a powerful book."

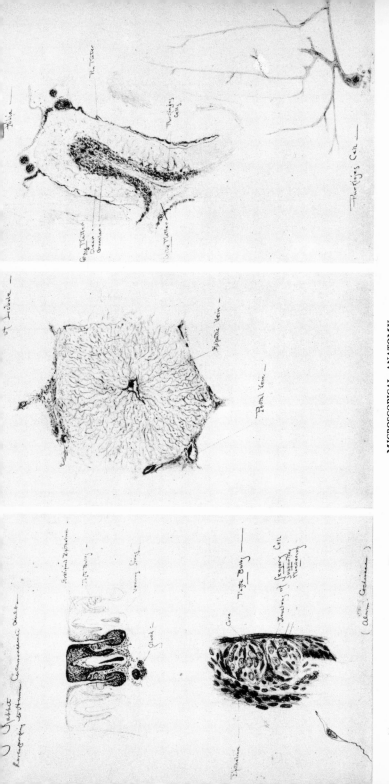

MICROSCOPICAL ANATOMY

Drawings from Cushing's histology notebook kept during his first year in medical school

PLATE 3

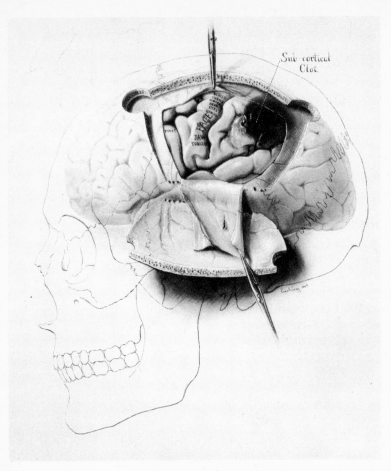

A HUMAN CRANIOTOMY

One of Dr. Cushing's own drawings showing a brain clot and motor area (on which he has indicated the foci governing movement in certain parts of the body). The inner covering of the brain (dura mater) is held back by the two clamps.

PLATE 4

An early interest in books was stirred by being able to browse in such places as the old Archway Bookstore, where he once ran into a Yale friend, "Wint" Noyes, who "told me that he got a Macauley's History of England which he wanted for himself—5 volumes very nicely gotten up, good paper and type for the magnificent sum of *one dollar*."

On November 24 he gently broke the news to his mother that he might not be home for the holidays. "What do I want for Christmas? A MINCE PIE packed in a box and sent to 89 Charles Street for I fear, Ma dear, that the present outlook points to my Christmasing it here though this is not absolutely final." On the same day he wrote his father that he had definitely settled his fate as far as the vacation was concerned and had accepted an opportunity to work in the medical out-patient department for December. The following week he reported on a little out-patient work of his own. "I have a patient here at 89 Charles. One of the Technology boys who has hurt his foot. I poulticed it and sent him to bed last night. Today it's worse. It's a glorious profession all the same."

His first Christmas away from home was not too unhappy. He got a box "as big as a piano" from home and there were several people still at 89 Charles for company—Gary N. Calkins, "Professor of Low Life" at the Massachusetts Institute of Technology, better known as "Bacillus," two young Technology boys, and Dr. Sears, who had his office in the house.

On New Year's Day, his out-patient engagement over, he confessed to his father that he didn't know what he had learned except to ask people with more or less grace how their bowels were. Anyway, it had made him feel a little more at home with a stethoscope in his ears and less like a creature with a formidable proboscis prodding innocent people here and there. He hoped the experience would make materia medica, which he despised, a little more interesting.

In a small diary which had been a Christmas gift, he began to jot down the principal happenings of his days, and here, rather than in his letters, was recorded his complete absorption in his work—here also were revealed moments of uncertainty and inadequacy that rarely found their way into the cheerful notes he sent to his father and mother. "Still working over the poisons. Contemplate taking some myself," and "HARD luck again etherizing. . . . Dr. P. must think I'm a clumsy dunce." On January 10 an incident occurred that plunged him into deep despair; indeed, it was nearly the cause of his leaving medical school.

He had been asked by one of his classmates to take his place at the Massachusetts General Hospital for a week. One of his duties was to administer ether to a woman who was being operated on for a strangulated hernia. He had given ether only a few times before and he was nervous because he had never been adequately instructed in its use. In fact, there seemed to be no formal instruction about anesthesia, the other men usually using enough of the volatile liquid to make the patient insensible quickly and to keep him so a long time.

On this particular morning, Dr. Charles B. Porter, Professor of Surgery, was operating and since he, like all the professors in the Medical School, had a large practice by which he earned his livelihood, he was in a hurry to get the operation over with. When they began calling for the patient in the operating room, Cushing hurriedly finished his job and wheeled the woman in. Dr. Porter had no sooner opened the abdomen than the patient died. Cushing was stunned. He was sure he had killed the woman with too much ether. He left the operating room by himself and wandered out of the hospital. All afternoon he walked the streets of Boston, oblivious of the cold and the city about him. A few short hours before there had been life in another human being—life he had snuffed out with his stupid bungling. He must leave medical school and a profession where life and death were so often in a doctor's hands, for where he had failed once, he could so easily fail again.

In his anguish his thoughts turned to his brother. Had Ed, when he was in medical school, known what it was to lose a life that might have been saved? And his father—had such things happened to him? He seemed suddenly to feel closer to his father, to see him in a new light—his quiet ways, his uncompromising severity with himself and his children, his dedication to his profession—and he longed for that solid anchor of comfort and strength. He thought then of his grandfather Erastus, who had had the courage to leave the home of his forebears and start life anew so close to the wilderness that wolves had often chased him as he returned from a night vigil. And what of David, his great-grandfather? Had he known doubt and fear and uncertainty as he drove long miles through all kinds of weather to bring the comfort of a doctor's hands to the scattered families of his New England practice? Must he, Harvey, be the first to break the pattern that had been so long in the making?

In the early evening he presented himself at Dr. Porter's house and announced that he was going to leave medical school and do what he could to assist the patient's family. To his surprise, the surgeon told him that the woman was in such a condition that she would have died anyway, that such occurrences were not uncommon, and that he would advise him to get a good night's rest and forget about the whole matter. After a time this satisfied Cushing to the extent that he decided to go on with medicine, but he dedicated himself more passionately than ever to his work.

He and Amory Codman began to investigate a means of safeguarding the patient by recording pulse and respiration during operations. They started a competition to see who could give the best anesthesia. The wager was a dinner, and the test was the patient's behavior on the ward—a perfect anesthesia being judged one in which the patient was sufficiently conscious to respond when left on the ward with the nurse and did not subsequently vomit. With the help of a suggestion from Dr. F. B. Harrington, they later devised some charts which were put into use at the Massachusetts General Hospital. This was the first attempt to record the patient's condition during an operation and was an important step forward in reducing the number of deaths during and after surgery.

Cushing continued to administer ether for various members of the staff, sometimes at the hospital, sometimes in their offices. On Friday, January 13, he noted in his diary: "Encysted hydrocele at 38 [Commonwealth Avenue] with Dr. Porter—

A. K. Stone assisted. Promised later to help in a bandaging course with policemen." On the 14th: "Big operating day. Etherized well but don't seem to hit it off with the house officers." On the 16th: "Etherized 3-4 times and pretty poorly. Couldn't study in evening and went to bed early. I fear for the Chemistry exam." And again in March, "Etherized this noon for Dr. Porter who removed a dermoid cyst from a young girl's neck. Beautiful operation. Assisted him till Alex came." On the 22d: "Shattuck told an old hypochondriac to remember the Eleventh Commandment—'Fret not thy Gizzard' & forget all the others if necessary." On the 30th: "Walked out to park with Codman. Saw first robin. . . . Bandaging class with policemen."

Early in the year he spent a week end at Gloucester with his friend Dolliver. "I was much interested in the fishing departments," he wrote his father, "which in fact are the mainstay of the place, as you know. We spent the whole morning and afternoon gadding about in sail lofts, junk shops & on the wharves and I still have a feeling as though my hair was full of sea weed and my mouth of salt halibut, for they have a custom in the smoke houses of offering the visitors appetising pieces to chew which must be done with as much good grace as possible. I consider the habit on a par with that of the good German anatomist—his name I forget now—who is said to chew connective tissue while dissecting. A disgusting thought but it always amused me nevertheless."

Word pictures of such excursions revealed the maturing of his artistic appreciation. For his drawing talent he was finding a practical use in histology and microscopical anatomy, and what he saw in the microscope was recorded with exquisite detail and accuracy in his notebook. He also made use of it in clinic by sketching patients to help him remember them. Even in these small drawings, hastily executed, he was remarkably apt in capturing the essence of a mood or condition—the resignation of a critically ill patient, the labored (Cheyne-Stokes) breathing of a sailor in heart failure, the frightened bewilderment of a foreigner ill in a strange country.

As he made greater use of his own gift, his appreciation

and interest in all forms of art increased. Art exhibits began to
attract him, and early in 1893 he attended one every three or
four weeks. In January he went to see the Massachusetts collection which was to be exhibited at the World's Fair in Chicago. Twice he visited art stores—once to see an exhibition of
Hopkinson Smith water colors entitled "Summer days in
Venice," and again to see the La Farge pictures of Samoa and
Japan. In March, Painter and he attended a loan exhibition of
pictures at the St. Botolph Club. "I am afraid I am not educated
up to Millet but one of Meissonier and some of Corot and
Cazin are fine. The latter gentleman was new to me but he's
a dandy."

He was interested in everything—paintings, etchings, water
colors—even modern art, for he asked his mother: "Have you
seen any of McKnight's impression pictures? I saw a lot of
them here last winter and they are of the most ultra sort. I ask
you because I just ran across this verse which amused me
greatly,

"If you were a sweet potato
     And I were Dodge McKnight,
I'd paint you in colors prismatic,
     So vivid & glowing and bright
That the world would exclaim, 'A Tomato!'
     And damn it, they'd be right
If you were a sweet potato
     And I were Dodge McKnight."

On April 7 his grandfather Erastus died suddenly of pneumonia. The letters from his mother and father touched him
deeply—"What a legacy of an honored name he has left his
grandsons," his mother had written. Depressed by this loss
and overtired from his numerous activities, he decided to accept an urgent invitation from Grosvenor Atterbury, now a
"boy architect," to visit him in New York. He had two enjoyable days there, spending much of the time at hospitals. "The
new Syme operating theater [Sims—at Roosevelt Hospital] is
a wonder, the gentle pyogenic germ is practically unknown
there I imagine," he wrote his father.

Kate Crowell came to Boston to visit Mary Goodwillie in

May. Although Harvey again wrote home that he had very little time to see the girls, he recorded in his diary that he went to Dedham with them ("Beautiful day—dog tooth violets"), on another occasion spent the evening with them reading "The Dove Lady," and also that Kate had mended his black silk umbrella for him. At the end of her visit, there is this diary note: "Have just spent the afternoon with Kate. Too cold & rainy to go to Riverside as expected. She's a fine girl but it's best methinks for me not to see too much of her. Wood's lecture tonight."

During this month he joined the Union Boat Club to get some needed exercise rowing on the Charles River and often after prolonged periods of hard study or before examinations he would go there to cool off and relax. To the announcement that he had joined and also that he had accepted an opportunity to work at Children's Hospital during the early part of the summer, his father replied:

"I can sympathize with you in your blistered hands from unwonted rowing, for I have blisters and soreness which make sitting a solemn business from unwonted devotion to the pigskin (you may or may not know that saddles are made of the porker's integument)." Dr. Kirke expressed approval of the extra clinic and other work, saying that even if his marks suffered, compensation would come in other ways. He concluded: "Jack [Harvey's dog] in spite of all care has had some disgraceful liaisons of late, which have seriously shocked the even tenor of family ways. This is the only piece of news I think of which does not lie in your mother's department."

The month of hard work at Children's Hospital during July was broken by a visit to Plymouth, a trip with Joslin to Wellesley ("which must be a very superior girls college—'as such.'"), and an afternoon (the first of several) with the famous Blaschka collection of glass flowers in Cambridge, "the most perfect things imaginable."

He left for Cleveland early in August, ready for a rest and some relaxation, but his diary revealed that he assisted in an appendix operation at a country farmhouse in Oberlin on the 24th of August and acted as anesthetist at operations at both

Charity and Lakeside Hospitals in Cleveland on the 25th. Kate Crowell's name appeared frequently in connection with his social activities—"making a fool of myself about her" he admitted.

On September 13 he left for Chicago and a week with Ed at the Columbian Exposition, the World's Fair. He was enormously excited by the exhibits from all nations. A "Japanese lady's boudoir" in the Woman's Building is mentioned by name only, but the English nurses' exhibit he described in minute detail. His diary was enlivened by many sketches of things and people that caught his fancy and also by his careful expense account where he listed every beer (sometimes spelled "bier") and "orange cider" and such enigmatic expenses as "crackers and hotbox" for thirteen cents, "M" for five cents, and "W" for one cent. Buffalo Bill cost a dollar.

On the 26th he recorded his "last walk with Kate who had come over to Lunch Club." Two days later he was back in Boston—"my routine of life has been resumed."

THE HALFWAY MARK

Chapter VI

THIRD YEAR—1893-94

At the beginning of his third year, Cushing resolved not to take on so many extra assignments and to attend lectures more faithfully. But he now had more to do with actual patients in the hospital, and he found that if he followed them as he wanted to and during the hours he was allowed to see them, he again had to cut lectures. He also could not refuse the opportunity to do extra work in pathology with William T. Councilman. On the strength of the high mark he later received in the course, Councilman offered him a $250 scholarship. Cushing requested that it be given instead to a classmate "who most certainly deserved it more and, if you will excuse me," he wrote his father, "I think was more in need of the money than I, thanks to your indulgence."

At 89 Charles this year were his close friend from Cleveland, Abram Garfield, who was studying architecture at Technology, and a classmate from Yale, George L. Amerman. During the autumn he spent a great deal of time helping Amerman with his dissecting because he had fallen so far behind in his work that he was threatened with dismissal. While he was thus engaged, the weeks slipped away and suddenly it was time for Amory Codman, who had been his closest companion in medical school (Codman was a year ahead of him), to leave for Europe for six months. An informal "quiz" club, known as the Brownie Club, gave a farewell dinner for him, attended

54

by Charles Painter, Elliott Joslin, Charles Russell Lowell Putnam, Henry Hewes, Frank Denny, George Dolliver, Nathaniel
Bowditch Potter, and H. T. Baldwin. Cushing brightened up
the occasion by bringing ridiculous presents for each one—to
Elliott Joslin, already interested in diabetes, he brought a
wilted bunch of sweet peas. Later he drew a picture of Ye Dis-
consolate Brownie for Kate Crowell's amusement.

*H.C.'s drawing on place cards for the dinner given by the Brownie
Club on the eve of Amory Codman's departure for Europe, 1893.*

Harvey often chid Kate for not writing more often, although his own communications were infrequent. Once he
sent a sheet of paper with nothing on it except a phrase cut
from one of her letters: ". . . I shall answer you promptly—
a perfectly unheard of thing, but you'll see!" Although glad
of her thought and attention, he was very guarded in expressing his own feelings. In his first letters after seeing her either
in Cleveland or in Boston, he usually slipped from his resolve
to keep everything on an impersonal basis, but after a month
or two he might begin a letter like this: "Sunday, Nov. 19 '93
11.45 P.M. Dear old Katy—Guess its about time I wrote you
a letter. You see what time it is and I am going to stop at
twelve to get my beauty sleep, so that you mustn't expect
much. . . ."

He went on to describe a dance he had attended at Miss
Hersey's School where Mary Goodwillie was teaching. The
other gentlemen were in evening dress—H.C. in a wool shirt
and tweed suit. "But that didn't cut any wood, for after the

piano started up, the old leper's heart beat fast and there was no restraining his feet so Mary and he rushed up from the office where they had been chatting and gaily plunged into the merry dance." He also told her about an afternoon with Mary Goodwillie visiting the glass flowers in Cambridge and dining with Yale friends, then ended the epistle with "It's twelve o'clock, Katy. Good night, Harvey."

In November he exercised his prerogative as a citizen for the first time but he told his mother that "although I have registered my name in a dirty book, in a dirtier room, around the corner in this ninth ward of Boston, and on next Tuesday shall cast my first vote, yet things political interest me little."

He went home for Christmas but stayed only nine days because he wanted to be back by January 2 to start Amerman on a new dissection and to begin some extra work in obstetrics. He had been working so hard that he had lost weight and in January he succumbed to a light attack of grippe. This was followed late in February by a more serious bout lasting several days. His father apparently became alarmed, for shortly Ned appeared in Boston, and on March 2 they sailed to Havana for a brief trip.

From New York, Cushing wrote to Kate Crowell (who had been in Boston during February), revealing that her presence had betrayed him into saying more than he meant to. This had been followed by an equally passionate denial, which had hurt them both. He went off, lonely and apologetic, telling her that she meant a great deal to him, and at the same time, that it must not be.

The change in surroundings soon brought him to a happier mood. Strange places, so long as his stay was temporary, always delighted and stimulated him. On the trip down he wrote in his diary:

. . . We have just now struck into the Gulf Stream and the change in the color of the water is remarkable. . . . The wind still holds northerly and against the current makes us roll a little. . . . Ed went to bed with a "headache," and a cracker with some lemon and apollonaris soon demonstrated the etiology of his ailment, for he nearly filled our chamber with his gastric contents and the remark—"It's strange how much a little cracker will do." I never could understand why seasickness should be so mirth provoking. I had no sympathy for him but laughed roundly.

In Havana they visited hospitals, the prison, old Spanish castles, the market. They ate strange and wonderful food, took baths in "the ladies place—the Garçon in holy horror at the idea," and while Ned collected stamps, Harvey sketched. He was fascinated by some beautiful women eating their ices, after the opera, with their knives, he was disgusted at the bullfights—"a brutal event," and his artist's soul was saddened by the passing from beauty of "the old country palace of the Marques de Almendares who 40 yrs ago came over from Spain with a beautiful young wife . . . and there spent many gay years of entertaining &c. . . . The desolate picture of decay of what was but recently wealth & beauty was touching."

The rest and change did Harvey a great deal of good, and he returned to the Medical School with enthusiasm. A letter from Kate Crowell awaited him. "I couldn't forget," she wrote him, "even if you wanted me to."

He was now faced with the decision of whether to take a fourth year. The Medical School had required only three years up to this time, but the requirement was being increased to four. The program for the added year was in a formative stage, and few from Harvey's class were going to stay on. However, his father thought a fourth year would be wise, and Harvey finally decided to take his advice. The race with Joslin was over—"Joslin will easily lead the class."

Planning to make good use of the summer, he accepted an appointment in the women's medical out-patient department at the Massachusetts General (as well as some work at Children's Hospital) for July and he hoped for another out-patient appointment during August; but his plans were changed. Shortly after their return from Cuba, Ned had become very ill with typhoid fever. Harvey's deep affection for his brother, intensified by being so far away, overflowed in his letters home. He implored his mother to write frequently, and his relief was immeasurable when word finally came that Ned was out of danger. When it was suddenly suggested in June that an ocean trip would hasten Ned's recovery, he promptly agreed to go to England with him. They sailed on June 30 with their aunt and uncle, Mr. and Mrs. Edward Williams.

From London, Harvey wrote his father and mother one of the few letters he ever addressed to them both:

I have wished many times that you were along with us. How you would rave over Westminster, the Kew gardens and everything. So much to do and see that it's almost oppressive. . . . Have been nowhere twice except to the National Art Gallery and the Abbey whenever I pass by. We are right across from the British Museum so the chances are we will never go in there, it's so easy. I must see the Elgin marbles sometime however. Saw the Duke of Cambridge review 2-3000 of the Horse Guards at Hyde Park Saturday. It was very impressive to see the long lines of red coats. . . .

The Williamses have decided to go over to Paris Saturday for a few days. We remain here in rainy London. No one seems to mind the wet, however, going about in their frock coats and "toppers" (in which I have not indulged though I should like to) as though it were bright sunshine. . . . It doesn't rain like a Christian sky, but as Ed expresses it, it seems as though there was a sponge up aloft and every few minutes someone comes along and gives it a squeeze.

His diary entries were telegraphic, but he remembered everything he saw. "To Charter-House rich in associations of Thackeray and others . . . saw the corner of the Yard where Thackeray broke his nose. . . . Ed chased a maid into St. James Park which he was prevented from entering by the gate being slambed in his face. Great embarissment followed by mirth from H.W.C. . . ."

Ned, who had once spent six months in London, soon tired of sight-seeing and they left for the "Peak Region." From the Rutland Arms in Derbyshire they made daily tramping excursions, and Harvey, who had departed from London reluctantly, fell almost at once under the spell of the countryside, which was "simply teeming with historic and romantic lore, which has been gathering since long before the days when

"The Rutland Arms" —

Willm Greaves.
The Rutland Arms,
Bakewell

	£	s	d
6 days Board, Bed & attendance	5	8	0
Spirits & Soda		16	3
Beer & Stout		1	9
Books		3	0
	£6	9	0

Received with
Thanks   Allin

*The Rutland Arms and the accounting. From 1894 diary of trip
to England.*

William the Norman gave all this part of Derbyshire to Pev-
erel 'he of the Peak' . . ."

They left Derbyshire regretfully and returned to London.
After a delightful trip to the "tall spires of Oxford" in a
coach and four, they visited London hospitals, where both
found much to interest them. Finally the time came for them
to sail for home. Harvey wrote his father that the trip had
cost $464—$300 for passage and clothes (two overcoats, a
dress suit, and some "trowsers"), and $164 for their twenty-
six days in England. He and Ned had had an "altercation" or
two, but they parted on the most friendly terms in New York
when the boat docked on August 10, and Cushing went immediately to his clinic assignment in Boston.

FOURTH YEAR—1894-95

Cushing's fourth year was preceded by six weeks in the out-
patient department and a week's vacation in Cleveland. On a
typical day in the clinic he was busy from half past eight
until half past three setting fractures, dressing wounds, and
so forth. At four on this particular day, he met Elliott Joslin
(after lunching at the Great American Tea Company on a
cup of coffee with a raw egg in it) and accompanied him on
his rounds in a district near "little Italy." He was appalled at
the squalor in which the poor lived. "We saw ten or twelve
sick families—fathers, mothers, poor meagre infants and what
not with various ills, urgent and otherwise. The ones we did
most for were least grateful and those for which we could do
nothing or perhaps could not recognize the trouble would
overwhelm us with 'God blessing' as is usually the case even
with more intelligent parties in a different grade of society."

Since the clinic was closed on Sunday and since he had no
studying to do, he was able to do some reading. He finished
John Fiske's *Destiny of Man* and prepared to start his *The
Idea of God*. He also became interested during this time in
the new Boston Public Library, not yet open to the public.
The sister of a classmate, Ned Williams, knew the librarian

and had him taken on a tour. In gratitude for this opportunity, Cushing took her paddling on the Charles but was glad it was a cool night "as she weighed in the neighborhood of fourteen stone."

During the autumn he acted as unofficial physician to his cousin Mary Crehore, who had worn herself out getting a master's degree at Cornell, and to her mother, his Aunt Lucy, who was exercised over a date stone which was making itself felt in various parts of her alimentary tract. He often took his out-of-town visitors to the hospital, and their reactions caused him to write home: "I am always a little surprised and shocked to find people depressed by a hospital. I suppose familiarity makes one callous but the Massachusetts General is essentially a bright place."

Having taken on an extra assignment—this time with Edward Hickling Bradford, Professor of Orthopedics—in addition to his classes (he was taking clinical medicine, clinical surgery, legal medicine, operative surgery, bacteriology, operative and clinical obstetrics), he again overworked, and once more Ned arrived to take him off—on this occasion for two and a half weeks in Bermuda. Cushing's diary (the habit was now firmly entrenched) was vivid and enthusiastic and embellished with unique spellings. There were a large number of young people on the island, and the Cushing brothers were popular members of first one party and then another. At one, H.C. sat next to a U.S. Army captain and his "loquacious" wife who told them, to Harvey's considerable amusement, that the "only way to make a donkey go was to rattle nails in a tin can or to stick a hot pin into him." Something of this sort must have happened to Charlie, a donkey whose acquaintance they had made. "As I write this Ed and Miss Morley have dashed by the Hamilton at the rate of a mile a minute, Chas. with ears laid back, Ed. & Miss M. looking very serious."

The equinoctial storms hampered their activities somewhat but gave Cushing a subject for a bit of verse. "Miss Margarethe Morley is a graphologist and has asked me for my writing. Being morbid [about the weather] I gave her the following:

> "This land of lilly and rose
> Is hard upon our starched clothes
> As the clouds are such droppers
> We are limp as the 'floppers'
> And it's almost as bad when it blows."

One of the girls with whom he spent considerable time had her hopes dashed at the end of the holiday when he told her flatly that she needn't expect to see him in Boston because his medical school work kept him fully occupied.

In New York on their return, Cushing was happy to find at his hotel a letter from Abe Garfield saying notice had come that he had passed the examination for his hospital appointment at the Massachusetts General. This meant four months of "extern" service while he was finishing his course work before he started his year's internship, which of course required his living in the hospital. On April 2, when acting as anesthetist for John Homans, he signed his first of the ether charts for recording temperature and respiration during operations on which he and Amory Codman had worked together. This was his initial contribution to general surgery.

During April, also, he witnessed, for the first time, a brain operation on a patient with a compound fracture of the skull. Cushing made no mention of the experience in his letters home, but a keen interest was evident in his careful and detailed case history and the fact that on his own initiative he followed the patient after his discharge from the hospital until he left the convalescent home. The "fearful" hemorrhage from the dural sinuses which he mentioned in the operative note made him aware of one of the most serious problems in any operation on the brain—the control of bleeding. This, he could see, would have to be solved before cerebral operations could be successful.

Abe Garfield persuaded him to take a break later in the month and they went to Salem, whose architecture Garfield had been studying with a class from Technology. Cushing was immediately aware of its peculiar charm. "It certainly is a fine old place, the more attractive because in its prosperity it suddenly ceased to develope and grow but has ever since remained the same old Salem and though no longer the wonderfully opulent center of Oriental trade, it has not degenerated but like a fine, neat old gentleman has simply retired from business."

During his four years in Boston, Cushing attended church spasmodically. Occasionally he went of his own accord, but usually there was some special reason. When he first arrived he was interested in Phillips Brooks (Dr. Brooks died in 1893) and went to hear him with some of his classmates. The music at Easter also drew him, but most frequently it was friends from home who were responsible for his going. He once accompanied Kate Crowell and Mary Goodwillie—"proudly," he said, but he left them before Communion. This spring he escorted his aunt, Mrs. Edward Williams, and his cousins, Ray and Reba, to King's Chapel.

Our pew was not only deep but big as a London "bus" with seats all around it and I was very thankful that there were no more than four of us as I should have had to ride backwards and be stared out of countenance by the rear boxes full of stolid Boston respectability.

We heard a "most Unitarian" sermon of course, some fine music, and after the service by a great effort I managed to reach the lock on the door which was halfway to the floor and on *the outside* and thus let my people out. In so doing I brushed all the "nap" off Abe's silk hat which I had borrowed for the occasion. Vanitas vanitatum.

At the beginning of May he began his extern service with a few days at the convalescent home of the Massachusetts General Hospital in near-by Waverley. He was back and forth during the next four months between Waverley and the hospital. In July he witnessed two more brain operations. When Dr. J. W. Elliot had come back from England in 1889 after meeting Victor Horsley, the London surgeon who had begun to attempt brain operations, he had urged his colleagues to refer to him any cases of brain tumor which they encountered, but the opportunities had not been many.

However, on June 27, 1894 a thirty-one-year-old male, John Maloney, entered the hospital with an obvious growth on the top of his skull. He had been struck on the head some three years earlier, and after two years a tumor had begun to develop at the site of the injury. Elliot operated on July 2, with Cushing assisting. The growth proved to be spongy and deep purple in color, indicating that it had an enormous blood supply. Elliot removed it, but the patient died a few hours later. The tumor was of the type that Cushing was later to name a meningioma, which grows from the meningeal covering of the brain, occasionally as a result of injury, and usually invades adjacent bone. Cushing did the autopsy report.

A second case appeared little more than a week later when a man by the name of Jordan Hunter was admitted to the hospital with severe headache and numbness of his right thumb and forefinger. A diagnosis of tumor was made and Elliot operated, with Cushing again assisting. In his carefully written notes Cushing commented: "Elliot never had less bleeding in opening [a] skull." Although the patient died because of the malignant nature of the growth, there was cause for satisfaction that the location of the tumor had been accurately diagnosed before operation.

During his assignment at Waverley, Cushing spent some time at the McLean Hospital, the psychiatric division of the M.G.H., located close to the convalescent home. It was here that his interest in neurology was first sharpened. The work was absorbing, and the days passed so quickly that he could hardly believe it was time to pack his things. He was reluctant to leave his room at 89 Charles—"this little old top floor room with its retreating frontal bone I have become most attached to. . . . All my belongings are boxed up—and what a lot of stuff one can accumulate in four years—and the bare bookshelves and walls with the litter of packing, a foot thick, make the old place rather unprepossessing on this last night. I've always found it as hard to give up a room as an old shoe. They *are* alike in certain ways." Amongst the "stuff" he had accumulated were the course notebooks which in a way were an index to his medical education. The careful and detailed notes, written in the tight hand which many of his classmates had cursed, and the exquisite drawings were an indication not only of his interest, but of his manner of working—the pattern he was to follow from this time forward.

Hospital duties kept him from attending Commencement, but he received his degrees of M.D. and A.M. *cum laude*—the race with Joslin had not been in vain. He told his mother that had he known what a struggle it was to be, he didn't suppose he "should ever have had the sand to begin."

"*A GREAT PLACE TO GROW HAIR AND WEAR OUT SHOES*"

Chapter VII

Cushing's internship (or appointment as house pupil, to use the M.G.H. term) began officially on the first of August. His assignment to the newly organized South side was initially a source of disappointment because Ned had been on the East side and both East and West had been so long established as to have acquired traditions and an impressive list of interns scratched on the lid of the senior's desk. But the house staff of South—which included a senior and a junior house officer, an extern, and a "pup"—was soon bent on establishing traditions even more distinguished than those of their older rivals. Of their superiors on the service, Cushing wrote many years later: "I look back with an enduring sense of obligation to our four chiefs—to that resolute and picturesque pioneer, John Homans, who twenty years before had been privately advised not to do ovariotomies here, yet persisted in so doing; to C. B. Porter, master of operative technique; to Jack Elliot with his brilliant gifts and uncanny surgical instinct, and to the youngest of them, William Conant, most generous and considerate of his hard-working juniors."

Cushing's new duties made his medical school days seem like days of leisure. He rarely left the hospital—it's a great place to grow hair and wear out shoes, he told his father. But his driving energy sometimes made him a hard person to work with. When he became senior intern, his junior suffered severely, claiming that although Cushing could be one of the most charming people in the world when he cared to be, he

66

wanted to be in the limelight and couldn't tolerate competition. Given a position of some authority, he was thus already showing the strength of his ambition and the impatience he felt when his efforts were nullified by co-workers whose standards were not as high as his.

But it was usually the pleasant side that he showed to his family: "Work prospers. I am ensconced in the out-patient department mornings and do several interesting dressings and a multitude of odd jobs during the rest of the day. It's a great place here with a constant succession of curious and interesting cases." And: "We have been having most wonderful weather with days as balmy as those of May and nights lit up most wonderfully by the Hunter's moon. It is the Hunter's moon, is it not? At all events it makes the old gray pile of the main building stand out like some castle of old if you are far enough away to have the lights from the lower windows shut off and can only see the Bulfinch flat dome with its cupola surrounded by the array of sombre square chimneys. The hospital yard by moonlight makes an impressive sight."

His father and mother paid him a visit in the autumn, and the exchanges after their return to Cleveland indicated the easy relationship that now existed between father and son. Cushing wrote: "I was very pleased to learn of your safe arrival home, for I had visions of fallen bridges, tracks washed away, and other calamities. . . . I wish Mr. J. Pluvious had seen fit to delay or omit that storm. . . . *Five* inches fell in those twenty-four hours according to the weather bureau's bucket. . . . Father came to the M.G.H. the day of your departure and left his umbrella as much as to say 'I shall never need thee more: this must have been the last rain.'" To this his father genially returned: "That umbrella you facetiously allude to was no old one of mine but a brand new one, with an orange wood handle of pleasant form, and with silk which I hope will keep out a Boston rain." And H.C., with the same light touch, replied: "I meant to cast no disparagements on that umbrella even though I did not appreciate its newness. I thought you had sacaraficed your own to your wayward son."

Late in November he managed to get home for a brief vacation and on his return he teased his mother, who had packed one of his trunks, about the number of drawers she had included—"great, long drawers too, 'a world too wide for his shrunk shank,' and such a paucity of undershirts." Christmas, however, brought a possible solution to the problem. It was his responsibility to procure the hospital Christmas tree, trimmings, and a present for everyone. About four days before the holiday, he had not yet had time to do anything about it, but he assured his mother it would be done—even if he had to decorate the tree with iodoform gauze and "sacarafice a pair of those drawers apiece. They will go around everybody, I think, but Painter."

Early in the new year, news reached Boston of the new X-rays that had been described on December 28 by William Röntgen, professor of physics at the University of Würzburg. Cushing was filled with excitement and enthusiasm. "Dr. Röntgen may have discovered something with his cathode rays which may revolutionize medical diagnosis," he wrote his father. He was fascinated by the remarkable and uncanny possibilities of a ray by which one could see "through stone walls" or through the chest to count the ribs and see the heart beat. He contributed some money personally to procure an X-ray machine for the hospital and spent many hours experimenting with it, finding it most useful in locating needles and other foreign bodies.

His letters became more brief than ever, but he occasionally gave a hint of his activities in comments like these: "Things are prospering with us. Elliot is giving us a good service. I think he does the best abdominal work in the house." And again: "Dined with Maurice Richardson the other night with two or three of the house officers—on some Egyptian quail Abbe sent him from New York. Maurice is a corker."

An old patient of Ned's came to the hospital during the spring. "He had a compound fracture of his big toe in Ward 28 under Ned's regime and an injured knee. The combined efforts of the Cushing brothers have now given him a leg that would pull a cork." "Sound as a twenty-dollar gold piece," was the way another patient described his leg. The senior surgeons had said the leg must come off, but two young interns had come along and looked at the leg and had sat down on his bed to discuss it. They were Harvey Cushing and his good friend, C. Allen Porter, and they decided the leg could be saved. Cushing persuaded his seniors to let him operate—with the result reported by the patient thirty-five years later.

In April, Cushing wrote to Kate Crowell to thank her for a birthday present. "You were a good girl to remember me in my senility—few did [he was twenty-six on April 8]. . . . I am much pleased with the *Amateur Emigrant*. Hasn't he written a sequel to it—*Across the Continent* or something of the sort? You introduced me to Robert Louis Stevenson. The *Ebb Tide* was the first thing of his that I remember ever having read."

Throughout the year he had been thinking about the future and had written to several of his friends studying in Europe to ask about professors, courses, etc., in case he should accept his father's offer of a year abroad. He also was considering the Johns Hopkins Hospital. As early as July, 1895, Ned had written him: "I have seen much of Robb in the past three weeks and have been interested by what he has to say of Halsted and the Johns Hopkins. He says that to his mind there is no surgeon like him in the land, that his aseptic technique is perfect, and that the scientific manner of his work, keeping at it from the laboratory side simultaneously with his clinical and operative work, is a revelation to a man. . . . He says strongly that if a place is available after you finish your M.G.H. service, take it by all means—that a year there would be worth five abroad &c &c. Think it over."

While Cushing was in Cleveland on vacation, he and Ned had gone down to Baltimore to have a look at the hospital and medical school. Although the Johns Hopkins Medical School was still in its infancy, the eminence of its faculty and the fine spirit which prevailed there were fast bringing it into a position of prominence. Cushing liked the enthusiasm with which everyone was working and he accordingly applied for a place first with William Osler, the widely known professor of medicine, then, when nothing developed, he approached William S. Halsted, professor of surgery. After negotiations extending over several months, he finally secured the appointment as Halsted's assistant resident in surgery and for the time being gave up his plans to go abroad.

THE JOHNS HOPKINS
HOSPITAL

Chapter VIII

DURING THE FIRST DAYS AFTER leaving Boston, Cushing was lost and desolate. The sudden exchange of the crowded, work-packed hours of his familiar hospital existence for the idleness of vacation days left him restless and ill at ease. However, his cousins, the Edward Harveys and their daughter Melanie, and his brother Ned were in a holiday mood and they had not been long on their way toward Nova Scotia, Prince Edward Island, and Gaspé before Cushing began to be more cheerful.

From Halifax they left for Baddeck where they made themselves at home in the Grand Narrows Hotel. There was much merriment over Cousin Ed's soaking his "trowsers" while out for a sail and over Ned's throwing a soda-water bottle at their landlord when he innocently stuck his head in the room to awaken them—Ned mistaking him for Harvey who had arisen early and taken all the blankets. As always, Cushing was alive to the beauty of the natural scene. He reveled in colors and tones—"The sunset was gorgeous—a fleecy mass of clouds in the West in a great sworl like Elihu Vedder's with reds and pure gold—shifting in color constantly. The contrast of the blue hills at the sides, and the dark green of those under the dropping sun with the darkening water was wondrous."

From Nova Scotia they crossed to Prince Edward Island with "its low shore, red soil, and garden-like appearance." The beauty of the flowers, the antics of the curious-looking sandpipers, fat huckleberries and thick cream, and swimming on a curving beach filled their days with contentment. Next they visited the Gaspé Peninsula: "Early this a.m. we sail into the majestic Gaspé Bay with veils of white mist encircling the rugged tops of the high mounts of the Gaspé Peninsula— the end of the Appalachians." From here they traveled down the St. Lawrence.

Bicycle lesson. From Canada diary, 1896.

At Quebec they visited the Hôtel Dieu where the surgical rooms smelled of burnt-out candles and the chanting nuns at the feast of the Annunciation of the Virgin brought tears to Cushing's eyes and an unexplained sadness. After exploring the city, they traveled overland to Lake St. John through miles of bright goldenrod, tall pink spikes, bluebells, and white yarrow. At the uncrowded hotel that night he and Melanie danced alone in the deserted ballroom.

Two days later, on August 19, Ned and Harvey started from Roberval to Chicoutimi by canoe with two guides. After nine portages and a five-mile ride in a buckboard, they reached the Shipshaw River at dark where a large group of lumbermen made a picturesque scene around a roaring fire. Their guides

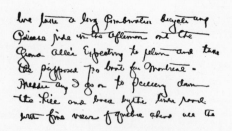

"We Cheer up at the Frontenac." From Canada diary, 1896.

taught them old French songs—"Very old—clean French songs, for there were such things once—peculiar in their pathos and with verses usually of four lines. . . . Some had rollicking choruses in which we joined vociferously, no one but Dame Nature to be disturbed."

A few days later in Montreal he visited the Royal Victoria Hospital, the Hôtel Dieu, and the Montreal General—found that the latter compared favorably with the Massachusetts General. Through Toronto and Niagara Falls they returned to Cleveland. After a month at home, Cushing left for Baltimore to begin the next phase of his career—his residency with the great surgeon William Halsted.

Baltimore in the nineties moved with the studied ease and elegance of an age that was soon to pass. Her dedication to the art of leisurely and gracious living indicated to an ambitious Northerner a lack of initiative hard to understand. In the market place, the contrast between the spineless lack of enterprise of the Southern shopkeeper and the bustling aggressiveness of his Yankee counterpart irritated Harvey Cushing. He also looked askance upon the sumptuous dining habits of the Baltimore epicures and told his mother indignantly that for breakfast they ate griddle cakes and sausage together, and they served their chicken fried! But his disapproval did not prevent him from accepting any opportunity to escape from the hospital meals.

And these were not his only complaints. The townspeople were slow, the architecture uninspired—row after row of monotonous red brick fronts "as like as streptococci" always with three white steps—and the Hospital standards and staff shockingly unsystematic. To complete the forlorn picture, he was alone in a big, bare room with a few lonesome books in his bookcase and no other adornments except a faded photograph of Neddie. The future looked unpromising at best. One wonders whether it was with amusement or exasperation that his father took up his pen once more to suggest patience and a reasonable trial before final judgment was made.

During the difficult days of adjustment Cushing ran across Mr. Goodwillie, the father of his friends Mary and Barney, who had moved from Cleveland to Baltimore. He told Kate: "I should be very homesick here were it not for Mr. Goodwillie. Went to the theatre to see DeWolf Hopper and we are to dine together tonight." Through Mr. Goodwillie he also became acquainted with two of Baltimore's attractions— "Druidill" (Druid Hill) Park, where he was thrilled with the magnificence of the trees, and the great public market with its fascinating array of produce, including "a hundred yards of skinny-skinned rabbits, hanging on a rope with a row of grinning darkies behind them." On his first visit there he found an old friend, the Northern Spy apple, and returning that night munching on one from the bagful he had bought, he began to feel at home.

The Johns Hopkins Hospital had opened its doors in 1889, sixteen years after the death of the eccentric and lonely bachelor, Johns Hopkins, who had left seven million dollars to found a university and a hospital. The university was completed in 1876, and Daniel Coit Gilman, one of the most forward-looking educators of the time (he had been a professor at Yale's Sheffield Scientific School and later librarian of the University), served as president for twenty-five years. He chose for his initial faculty six distinguished professors,[1] and young though the University and Medical School were, both soon took their places beside the best of the older institutions. The hospital was twelve years in the building—under the direction of John Shaw Billings of the Surgeon General's Library who had had considerable experience in the construction of army hospitals following the Civil War. The plans embodied sweeping reforms in hospital planning and construction,[2] but "the real hospital," he told the Trustees, "the moving and animating soul of the institution, which is to do its work and determine its character, consists of the brains to be put in it." Accordingly, the building of a faculty was begun with the appointment of William H. Welch to the chair of pathology.

[1] Basil L. Gildersleeve, Newell S. Martin, George S. Morris, Ira Remsen, Henry Augustus Rowland, and J. J. Sylvester.
[2] There was an amusing provision in the plans which Billings described thus: "If a female nurse is a properly organized and healthy woman, she will certainly at times be subject to strong temptation under which occasionally one will fall, and this occurs in all hospitals where women are employed, without any exception whatever. Something may be done, however, to remove opportunities—and I believe the construction proposed [elimination of large closets] effects this as far as it is worth while to attempt it."

This was the first full-time chair in pathology in an American university, for pathology was a comparatively new branch of the medical sciences. Welch brought to the Hopkins the techniques and traditions of the great German laboratories, where experimental science had been most highly developed. He had spent two years studying under several of the most talented pathologists and physiologists of the time,[3] and after his appointment to the Hopkins in 1884, he returned for a year of further study while the hospital was being built.

The new professor of pathology—a round-faced, jolly young man, always immaculately dressed—combined extraordinary teaching ability with a boundless curiosity that was one of his most winning qualities. In addition to his keen intellect and attractive personality, he had a way of being able to rally people to any cause, an ability that made him peculiarly well suited for the task of organization now confronting him. After his return from Europe, Welch went seriously to work on the problem of a faculty for the Medical School. In the meantime he opened a laboratory, and immediately a number of promising young medical students came to him—Walter Reed, who was to discover the cause of yellow fever, Simon Flexner, long Director of the Rockefeller Institute, William S. Halsted, who remained as professor of surgery, and William T. Councilman, who became professor of pathology at Harvard.

Halsted, an outgoing, cheerful student at Yale (Class of '74), had shown great promise as a teacher at the Bellevue Medical College after graduation from the College of Physicians and Surgeons. Now in uncertain health because of the fact, known only to Welch, that he was fighting gallantly against cocaine addiction,[4] he was reserved and withdrawn. He preferred to spend most of his time in the laboratory, where he could lose himself in thought and research, and there he made many

---

[3] Ludwig, Waldeyer, Hoppe-Seyler, Kronecker, Koch, Cohnheim, Heidenhaim, and von Recklinghausen.

[4] Halsted and three of his New York associates had experimented with cocaine as a local anesthetic using themselves as subjects without knowledge of its habit-forming tendency. Halsted alone was able to fight his way back to a useful life.

original and important contributions to surgery and medicine. His surgery was a work of art, and the example he set—for careful study of each case, exquisite operative technique, and close examination of tissues in the laboratory afterward—was to influence American surgery for many years. It was he who introduced the use of rubber gloves because the delicate skin of his operating nurse, who was later to be his wife, was constantly irritated by the strong disinfectants used in "scrubbing up."

A man of culture and sophistication, Halsted traveled in Europe almost every year, sent his shirts to Paris to be laundered, and was a gracious host or guest on his rare excursions into society, but for the most part he lived the life of a recluse—an enigma to his associates, and especially to his new assistant resident. In the beginning the two men viewed one another with respect but, on Cushing's side at least, with little warmth or affection.

The next appointee to the staff of the Hopkins was the brilliant clinician and teacher, William Osler, professor of medicine at the University of Pennsylvania. A person of medium height, with dark, twinkling eyes and olive complexion, Osler possessed great personal magnetism, for his irrepressible gaiety of spirit and his deep human sympathy and understanding, combined with a sometimes ribald enjoyment of life, drew to him people of all ages. As soon as he entered the hospital each morning, interns, residents, and nurses rallied round him. "Falling in step with his resident, he'd immediately start [with coattails flying] around the great marble statue of Christ standing in the rotunda and make for the long corridor leading to his wards—all others falling in line."

Of his tremendous energy and enthusiasm he gave generously. Osler represented the great English tradition of learning at the bedside (as opposed to the German tradition of learning in the laboratory) of which Thomas Sydenham (1624-89) was the principal modern exponent after Hippocrates. It was Osler who first and persistently advocated that students be brought onto the wards to learn medicine while simultaneously studying it in books. His ward rounds were memorable occasions, for between cheerful greetings and jokes with patients and retinue, he carried on his teaching in a lucid, graphic way that pinned facts securely in mind. His famous textbook, *The Principles and Practice of Medicine*, begun during these years, has been the bible of medical students for over half a century (it is now in its eighty-fourth printing). But in the last analysis his influence as a medical humanist and lover and collector of books will probably outlive his contributions as a physician.

The last of the four Hopkins doctors, immortalized by Sargent in his well-known painting, was Howard A. Kelly, who came in 1889, also from the University of Pennsylvania, to fill the chair of gynecology and obstetrics. He was a sound clinician and an excellent surgeon, far more interesting to watch than his senior, Halsted. He was responsible for many innovations in the operating room, was a man of enormous energy and originality, with a sense of showmanship which attracted students to him by the dozens. Although of a different character from either Welch or Osler, he too had a most attractive personality. Despite his flair for the dramatic, Kelly was a humble man, deeply religious, often calling together staff, nurses, and visitors, if any, for a brief word of prayer before his operations.

With these four men as the leaders, the future held great promise. They were all young when the hospital opened its doors in 1889—Welch was thirty-eight, Osler forty, Halsted thirty-seven, and Kelly thirty-one. The entrance requirements to the Medical School, when it opened four years later, had been set higher than any in the country,[5] and the unique system of residencies which enabled a man to work up to chief resident and then to remain in his job, if he so desired, laid the emphasis where Billings had wanted it. It meant that a few men were trained very well as against many trained for only a brief period, and the system, despite the criticisms of those who were not chosen to reap its benefits, attracted ambitious stu-

---

[5] For the first time in an American medical school, a college degree was required for admission and, in addition, certain specified courses in the sciences and a reading knowledge of French and German.

dents of unusual ability and spirit and produced men of superior stature.

The air was full of anticipation and opportunity—it pervaded the hospital and extended even to Louie Hanselman's bar where medical students, interns, and residents, and sometimes the chiefs, gathered to discuss the cosmic problems of their hospital world over sandwiches and beer. The chiefs did much to foster this atmosphere of enthusiasm and good will by their deep admiration and respect for the special talents of one another and their common desire to further research and set new standards in medical education and medical care. Harvey Cushing was aware of this spirit when he visited the Hopkins—as soon as he had "settled in" as assistant resident, it began to take hold of him and to drive his ambitious mind in many directions.

Chapter IX

ON NOVEMBER 6 CUSHING SAW HIS first case of spinal cord injury when the wife of a brawling bartender was brought into the hospital with a bullet in her neck. From the fact that she was paralyzed on one side and had no feeling on the other he was reasonably certain that the bullet was touching the spinal cord. He put to use an old static machine and with the X-ray tube he had brought with him from the M.G.H. (somewhat to the consternation of the staff there) he ground out the first X-rays to be taken in the new hospital. Sure enough, the bullet was lodged near the sixth cervical vertebra, but since it had only half severed the cord, there was nothing to be done and during the slow convalescence Cushing made a thorough study of the anesthetic areas resulting from the pressure of the bullet. He made it the subject of his first medical report.

At Christmas time he and a newly made friend, Norman B. Gwyn of Toronto, filled some of the big stockings used in the operating room for the children on the ward. "I was surprised that we could fill them so as to make them hang in the proper bulging fashion of the preverbial Xmas stocking." He helped a little girl empty hers and told his mother that when he came to *Alice's Adventures in Wonderland* at the heel he would gladly have been transported back eighteen years.

The letter was written on New Year's Eve and he added reflectively: "It has been rather an eventful year for me despite the sequestered existence I have led. Ten months of hospital life divided between two big institutions means a very narrow and at the same time a very broad experience. Narrow as regards acquaintance with people and things not medical—broad in respect to a little but wonderfully full hospital world. The City bells are clanging away at this moment and I guess the old gentleman is getting ready to slink away with his hourglass and sythe. The noise of the bells is pouring in through my wide open window, for it is quite springlike outdoors, and the twang of a banjo is stringing in to meet it through the open door to the tune of 'Sally in our Alley.' The approach of the New Year is not a serious occasion to everyone."

The first important event of the new year was a visit from Ned and Melanie Harvey who had just announced their engagement. He shared the family's delight in the match but at the same time was somewhat jealous, for he suddenly realized that no longer would he be the principal object of Ned's affection. However, he showed none of this except in telling his mother that he felt a little sad about it for it seemed as if he had lost Ned.

This visit was followed by one from Kate Crowell. To tease her, he had assured her shortly after his arrival in the autumn that yes, the nurses were pretty—a French girl by the name of Miss Mahoney on his ward being especially nice. Perhaps Kate came to see for herself—at any rate she visited the Goodwillies in February. On one occasion Cushing had to break an engagement with her and left a note saying, "You see what sort of a person I promise to be—not to be depended on even for dog shows. We are going to operate at 4 on an emergency case. Will tomorrow do?"

Although closer contact with Halsted had contributed little toward an understanding of the "Professor," as he was called, Cushing had come to respect his ability. At the Massachusetts General where speed was considered important, the surgeons had "operated by the clock," and Cushing was therefore much disturbed when his first patient had not come down from Halsted's operating room for more than four hours and he had prepared a hypodermic of a powerful stimulant; but to his amazement, the patient was in far better condition than the patients whose operations had lasted twenty minutes at the M.G.H. This was his introduction to the painstaking methods of his chief—the careful tying of each blood vessel, the meticulous effort to keep the tissues from drying, the matching of each wrinkle in the closure of the skin.

Despite his good foundation in operative technique, Cushing found he still had much to learn, and he was therefore greatly pleased to have Halsted, in April, suggest that he be advanced to Resident in Surgery the following year. However, Joseph Bloodgood, who then held the post, had not finished his research and wanted to remain another year. Some uncertainty resulted, and Cushing, unwilling to compromise, threatened to resign. But the Professor went out of his way to make things agreeable, offering to create a fellowship in surgery for Bloodgood if necessary and to do anything else that would make the place attractive. Cushing finally calmed down and accepted the divided responsibility without further ado.

Halsted, he had discovered, expected his house officers to make their own bacteriological studies, and although he had had a course at Harvard, he found his knowledge meager when compared with that of his present contemporaries. During this first year, therefore, he spent many an evening hunched over a microscope on the second floor of the Pathology Building with a German book in one hand. This extracurricular activity added to his regular duties, plus the responsibility of the surgical clinics during Halsted's frequent absences, left him in a state of perpetual tiredness—so tired that on visits to the dentist he would fall asleep while being worked on—"to the dentist's amusement and my satisfaction," he wrote his mother.

His letters home consequently were infrequent and brief, while his father's letters, on the other hand, from the leisure of retirement, became longer, and were full of encouragement, humor, and items of interest about books, medical affairs, and such social gatherings as reached his notice. One from which he could not escape was the marriage, on June 9, of Ned and Melanie, and he wrote Harvey: "Please hurry up and get home as soon as you can. The wet, and rather cold, Spring has de-

veloped a rich green of grass and leaf rarely seen. I do not hear
all of the domestic talk [Dr. Kirke had become somewhat
deaf], but from what I do get, should presume that new dresses
and personal adornments were chief subjects. I think Ned is
rather sick of the fashionable prerequisites of marriage, and
will be glad to have it over, though he bears up bravely."

Cushing had a month's leave of absence during June. In addition to the wedding, he attended his sixth class reunion at Yale
where he played baseball with the graduate nine. He then went
on to Boston and the M.G.H. and wrote his father that it was
the most attractive place he knew of and professionally without a peer. He was especially interested in their progress with
X-rays, since he was then doing all of the X-ray work at the
Hopkins.

During the summer his correspondence with Halsted, then
at his summer home in High Hampton, North Carolina, indicated that they were on more easy terms. Cushing reported
on their various patients and suggested certain improvements—
better food and higher wages for the orderlies, a new plan for
handling ether convalescents, and more systematic methods on
the wards. Halsted thanked him for writing when he was so
busy and added: "I am grateful to you for such suggestions &
hope that you will never hesitate to criticise freely what you
consider existing evils."

In September, Cushing himself became one of Halsted's
patients. Late in the month he developed an acute pain in his
abdomen which he diagnosed as appendicitis and he implored
Halsted to operate at once. Appendectomies were then only
ten years old and were undertaken with some reluctance. Cushing had seen the operation in Boston (where appendicitis as a
pathological entity was first described by Dr. Reginald H. Fitz
in 1886) and had done an appendectomy himself just a few
weeks before, only to lose the patient later from peritonitis.
He therefore knew the dangers. However, the operation, performed on September 28, was successful, and his convalescence
not unpleasant. He assured Kate Crowell that he was having a
beautiful time—"am perfectly well, literally living in a bed of
Roses [sent to him by the children on the ward] . . . There

are great baskets of fruit outside each window, a lot of rare old wine in the wardrobe and everything one could wish to read on the table."

Halsted and Osler wired his father daily, and Ned came down to see him immediately, but Dr. Kirke postponed his coming until later. "Very glad to be informed that you can step a little, and can wear, part of the day at least, something besides bedding," he wrote. ". . . I hope to walk in upon you Monday or Tuesday. . . . Probably I shall not have much capacity for sightseeing, but will only want to get my boy and bring him home."

One gathers that during this visit Cushing finally asked Kate Crowell to marry him, although they said nothing to anyone. Two days before Christmas he wrote her: "I have done no Christmasing and will consequently feel very badly when people send things to me because exchange of gifts is one of the nice things about Christmas. So this letter and my love and the picture, when it comes, is my little gift to Katy. I'm afraid the second item is not a gift, however, as you've had it in your possession so long—longer than I knew perhaps."

The year's end brought a warmly affectionate note (in gratitude for a Christmas present) from his good friend Max Brödel, the artist whom Dr. Kelly had induced to forsake his native Leipzig in 1894. To his associates at the Hopkins, Brödel brought a wealth of creative talent, for he was both artist and musician, and they in turn taught him anatomy and surgery so that the medical drawings for which he became famous were superb both in scientific accuracy and artistic beauty. With this simple, jolly, friendly man Cushing had much in common. They exchanged German and English lessons, and Cushing studied drawing with him—a fact which was to contribute greatly to the perfection of Cushing's own medical drawings.

During his convalescence from appendicitis, Cushing had become interested in having a bookplate for the library he was gradually acquiring as textbooks and birthday and Christmas books accumulated. This year he had received a volume on old Virginia from his mother, Dr. Holmes' life and letters, and a biography of the French surgeon, Ambroise Paré, from brother Will. His pride in possessing books was growing, encouraged by visits to Dr. Osler's library. He tried his hand at sketching a bookplate, which he sent to Dodd, Mead and Company in late December. During the early months of 1898 the well-known designer, Edwin Davis French, did a finished drawing from the sketch and eventually the bookplate was printed for the use of the whole family. It was a small rectangle, employing in its simple design the Cushing crest, the Cushing motto (*virtute et numine*—by valor and divine aid), a skull, and a variation of the caduceus of Mercury. It bore the initials of all the Cushing doctors—David, Erastus, Henry Kirke, Ned, and Harvey, together with the dates of their medical degrees—and was so arranged that initials of any future Cushing physician could be added.

Early in January, Cushing was invited to a dinner at the Halsteds—a rare occasion. The Professor was an epicure, and infinite care went into each item of the menu consisting of caviar on thin slices of toast, bouillon, roast oysters, a terrapin stew, asparagus, quail in jelly with pâté de foie gras, an omelette soufflé, an ice, crackers and Camembert, fruit, candy, and coffee which had been roasted that afternoon. All this was accompanied by rare wines from the cellar of Mrs. Halsted's grandfather, who had been a Southern aristocrat of wealth and position.

This evening was in sharp contrast to an afternoon the following month when Cushing took Kate Crowell to call while she was visiting the Goodwillies. On that occasion there were only two grate fires to warm the magnificent stone house full of rare old furniture, and Mrs. Halsted, who had been working with their dogs, met the young guests in a dirty butcher's apron. "They are so peculiar, eccentric, so unlike other people yet so interesting doubtless because of their oddities," Cushing wrote his mother, "that one is inclined to shelve his thoughts about them alongside of those of people from fiction—Dickens perhaps."

Kate Crowell's visit to Baltimore was followed by a letter from Cushing to her mother (her father was not living) saying that he hoped she would give her consent to their marriage. Mrs. Crowell's gracious approval, when it came, filled him with deep happiness and something of this went into a letter he wrote to Kate on March 15—a letter which opened wider than usual the door to his mind and heart:

My Darling Girl—

I have just come upstairs after the usual late lunch of pickings. We have had two very hard days—operations and operations. Yesterday from ten in the morning till half past seven. One of my very best operating room nurses cut her hand and divided some of the tendons so that she, poor thing, had to take her turn on the table and learn what anaesthesia means and all the rest. She has been a good soldier and will look on it some day as I do —a good experience I'm quite sure. That kept us late yesterday.

Excuse this shop talk, Katy, I'm brim full of it. People don't know what it means. Here I am, a youth, doing surgical work that not one of my school confreres will hope to do for years. It frightens me sometimes. The Chief rarely operates. Today I did all his private cases. Everybody seems to do well, however. I've been so fortunate lately that I hardly dare to speak of it lest some day may come a fall.

I think it's all due to you. I'm so happy, I have so many new thoughts and sensations—it seems like a different world to me. I never felt my strength so before—never so confident of my ability to surmount obstacles. I've done more good work since I've had you to help me than ever before. I hope you won't mind these little confessions.

A week later he sent her a printed leaflet entitled "Special Courses for Graduates" which showed that Dr. Cushing was scheduled for the course in surgery at 8:30 a.m. on Mondays and Wednesdays from May 1 to July 1. These courses were "refresher" courses for practising physicians, who often came considerable distances to take them. "What will you say to this schedule, Katy? I am afraid it [their wedding?] cannot be till July. I've got to get up very early in the morning from May 1 to July 1, 1898. Perhaps no one will come to my course, however, and then I can come to yours. Think of my trotting old greybeards about the wards and teaching them surgery."

Besides this graduate course in surgery, the spring brought

several other events of importance to him. In March came the news of a nephew, Edward H. Cushing, whom Ned and Melanie decided to call "Pat" for short. April brought declaration of the Spanish-American War, provoked by the blowing up of the *Maine*, and many of Cushing's friends went off, leaving him feeling somewhat restless, but he occupied himself with a new interest—the gall bladder—doing his experimental work on animals. He also wrote up the results of a study he had begun the preceding autumn. Because of several deaths from improper etherization, he had commenced to investigate the possibility of local anesthesia by injecting cocaine into the proper nerve trunks. The use of cocaine in this connection had, of course, already been largely discovered by Halsted—the discovery for which he was paying so dearly—but the published account of his work was unknown to Cushing and he was a little baffled and disappointed when Halsted was seemingly indifferent to his efforts. He first employed the drug in an amputation at the shoulder. Later he successfully extended his use of cocaine to operations on the hip and for hernia—the latter being the basis of his paper. He presented it before the Johns Hopkins Medical Society on May 8, 1898.

The Johns Hopkins Medical Society, together with the Johns Hopkins Historical Club and the *Johns Hopkins Hospital Bulletin*, were all started the first year the hospital was opened. Welch and Osler were the moving spirits in their establishment, with loyal support from Kelly and Halsted, and their wisdom in thus providing an outlet and a means of encouragement for young men who were just starting was repaid a thousandfold, for all three were powerful instruments in promoting and spreading the vigorous spirit of the Hopkins. Regularly on the first and third Mondays of each month a large and enthusiastic crowd filed into the amphitheater for the sessions of the Medical Society, the Historical Club meeting once a month. These meetings served to make men in different departments of the hospital acquainted with one another and with the work going on within the hospital walls, clinical as well as scientific. Interest ran high, the meetings often exceeding the prescribed limits of 8:30 to 10 o'clock. The faithful attendance of the chiefs themselves in all kinds of weather was a great inspiration, and often they invited men from other medical centers and from foreign lands to read papers and take part in the discussion, on these occasions usually arranging a dinner at the Maryland Club beforehand.

During the spring the days for Cushing flowed into one another, a new one beginning when he had barely closed his eyes on the one before. He wrote his father that he needed a change of scene—a couple of deaths from streptococcus infection, although not among his own patients, had caused him to lie awake seeing chains of "streptococcus devils" on all sides. But it was hard to get away. "When people are sick I have to live with them and when they get well I don't feel like pulling out." However, an attack of bronchitis in April sent him off alone to Old Point Comfort to recuperate, and he had a second respite from his strenuous schedule when he and his good friend Thomas McCrae, a Canadian who was resident in medicine under Osler, went to Fredericksburg, Virginia, for a rest and change.

From July 10 until August 8 he had a real vacation, going first to Boston, where he spent most of his time "hospitaling," then on to Lenox in the Berkshires to visit his friends the Chapins, next to New York to see Grosvenor Atterbury, and finally on July 23 he started for Cleveland where the next day he joined his mother, Ned, Melanie, and the baby Pat, and Kate Crowell on a trip up the Great Lakes.

A week after his return to Baltimore his mother wrote him: "I have learned but *little* of you from your brief communication to *Dr.* H. K. Cushing, and nothing at all from any letter to Mrs. of the same name. I am sorry that you had to exchange this delightful temperature, and these delicious days and cool nights, for the heat of Baltimore so soon." She closed her letter with this: "A lady who shall be nameless, told me last week that she had heard that Harvey & Kate Crowell were engaged —or words to that effect. So you find that you need not be so indignant with your Mother for her insinuations. 'A word to the wise is sufficient.' Your loving Mother, Bessie M. Cushing."

Although Kate was very much a member of the family on the outing up the Great Lakes, Cushing still had not revealed the true state of affairs between them. In fact, Kate Crowell had several years to wait while he pursued his jealous mistress, Medicine.

After the fall of Manila on August 13, and the end of hostilities, the troops began to straggle home. Typhoid had been a more disabling foe than the enemy, and Cushing was sent late in August to Alabama to assist in bringing back a trainload of patients, making several trips for this purpose. Here he had his first contact with typhoid perforation of the gut, and the operations which he performed were the subject of two papers which won for him considerable recognition. Reginald Harrison, a prominent British surgeon, wrote him: "Please accept my best thanks for your reprints on 'Laparotomy for intestinal perforation.' It is a very admirable piece of surgical work & one that is likely to be of great service to the profession. Your first case is unique so far as my knowledge of the subject goes. The whole essay is so well drawn up as to leave nothing to be desired. It makes me almost regret that my field of work in surgery lies almost entirely now in other directions."

His father also thanked him for a copy of the paper, which he had read with great interest, and then went on to describe his progress with the collection of portraits, photographs, etc., of Benjamin Franklin recently begun—"Your mother smiles primly, but it is as interesting to me as mat making seems to be to her."

During the autumn there was admitted to the Hopkins a thirty-three-year-old farmer from Fincastle, Virginia, who had previously come to the hospital in March of that year and been dismissed after observation. On October 26 a presumptive diagnosis was made of bleeding peptic ulcer, and he was transferred to the surgical service for operation. The case came to Cushing as the resident surgeon and he thought the man's symptoms indicated splenic anemia,[1] about which he had been

---

[1] This case got into medical literature as Banti's disease—not once but twice because of the second admission.

reading in his recently purchased Allbutt's *System of Surgery*. With some trepidation he went to Dr. Osler, told him what he believed, and asked whether he might take out the man's spleen if on operating he found no sign of pyloric ulcer. Osler told him to go ahead and do what he thought best.

Cushing the next day made the primary incision on the right side, found nothing, and then proceeded through a new incision to take out the man's spleen—the first splenectomy at the Johns Hopkins Hospital. The patient recovered and two years later wrote to Cushing as follows:

Dear Sir men of good business have advised me to write to the Hospital as it is well known there can be no advertisement put out that will represent the Hospital as well as the scars on my body. I can readily see and know and have knowed for some time that I can send many afflicted people there that never will come until they see what had bin don for me. . . .

Since Cushing did not take advantage of this opportunity to advertise his skill, two years later the man was peddling a patent medicine and attributing his recovery to it!

Cushing's pioneer work on typhoid perforations had further whetted his interest in bacteriology, an interest which was encouraged by Welch and his pupils—Simon Flexner, Norman Gwyn, and Louis Livingood. Indeed, their influence was all-pervasive, for on some notes of this period, Cushing later wrote: "In the old days of the Hopkins everyone was engaged in some sort of bacteriological work and had a pet organism which he was ardently cultivating. Young, I recall, had a strange bug that one day was a bacillus, another day a coccus, either in chains or pairs, and we called it the original Adam bacillus." Cushing himself was interested in a bacillus which he had found in a culture from a young Negro who had been operated on for an abscess of the rib following a prolonged fever, possibly typhoid. He corresponded with such authorities in the field as Theobald Smith and Walter Reed and eventually named his bacillus "O." This work resulted in a paper with a four-line title—and a flourishing friendship with Simon Flexner who was called upon to criticize this and other papers on bacteriological subjects (he later published two more).

In July he teased his mother about dating a letter a week ahead—said it was extraordinary of him to discover it because he rarely looked at dates or knew what the day was.

. . . I am having a dogged hard but very profitable summer privaledged to seek my own ends—unembarrassed by students. Morning rounds, operations daily, laboratory work in the afternoon, littrary work when I can, German lesson every night with Brödel, more rounds, reading and littrary work till midnight and a chapter in Thackery before my light goes out combine to make a busy day and let us hope no emergencies during the night. Since the G'willies departed I have hardly been away from the hospital. . . . I have some very indefinite plans about going abroad in the fall—October or November or Sunday after next —i.e. some remote period.

                                        Aff'y, Harvey.

On September 2 Cushing did his first Gasserian ganglion resection. It had become clear that those who suffered from acute attacks of excruciating pain on one side of the face— trigeminal neuralgia or *tic douloureux*—were victims of irritation of the nerve ganglia which supply the skin of the face. The Philadelphia neurologist, W. G. Spiller, had suggested that relief might be obtained if the ganglion could be surgically excised. Cushing was one of the first to act upon the suggestion, and in his early cases the relief was so dramatic that victims of the condition from many parts of the country were referred to him—indeed the operation proved a source of bread and butter while he was developing less lucrative phases of neurosurgery.

The new year brought a pleasant and flattering surprise— an offer of a post in the Department of Surgery at Western Reserve University. While his mother and father would both have been glad to have him at home, his father, after giving him a suitable interval in which to make up his own mind, finally told him that he believed him to be better off where he was—"it does not matter so much what your title is, or what your relative rank is; the great thing is the opportunity to do good work and to have it recognized." William Welch wrote a warm letter of congratulation but made it very clear that, although he did not know what they could offer in the way of advancement at the Hopkins, he sincerely hoped that Cushing would stay with them—which he eventually decided to do.

Details about his work went to Kate Crowell: "Kate, you are the very best girl that ever lived. I have been very much worretted of late over a man I'd give my right hand to save but am losing him after all and I need you very much." And again late in February: "I have been having a fearful whirl for 48 hours—wrote a long paper under pressure for the Phila' Medical Journal. Had to get it off at 10 o'clock tonight. Stenographer here all day and Tammas [McCrae] correcting manuscript. I'll never be so foolish again even as a favor—nor, I hope, so sleepless."

This constant driving of himself, both to achieve recognition and to accomplish a little more than the next person, often took him well beyond his wiry endurance. Taut nerves, combined with the confidence acquired through his rare opportunity to do so much independent operating at an age when most surgeons were still serving their apprenticeship, resulted in self-assurance bordering on arrogance and impatience, frequently ill-concealed, with his co-workers and even with the Professor himself. Effie J. Taylor, Dean Emeritus of the Yale University School of Nursing, who was a head nurse at the Johns Hopkins during these years, remembers him as difficult to please and not always popular with the nurses and staff. But she also remembers vividly his absolute devotion to his patients and his tender concern for their welfare whatever the cost in time and effort on the part of the staff. Although this did not endear him to his equals, it brought him the unqualified confidence and admiration of those entrusted to his care.

In March he wrote Kate: "I shall certainly leave sometime in June and burn my bridges. The Professor and I do not quite gee. I think I embarass him. He had not been over for ten days and its rather hard work with Mitchell sick and all

the rest. Hence my depression which I will shake off instanter." During this series of bad days when Halsted was unable to come to the hospital, he sent notes to Cushing. On
many of these, all of which he saved carefully, Cushing wrote
comments, several revealing his impatience. The first note
read:

Dear Cushing, Dr. Finney will hold my clinic for me this a.m.
I have caught cold again and think it more prudent to remain at
home. I hope our case of yesterday is not dead.

8:30 Friday
    If any goitre cases turn up, please ask them to come again next
Friday. I will pay their expenses.

Across the top of the letter Cushing had written: "Professor
out at dinner Thursday night at Finney's." At the bottom he
added: "Friday morning, Mar. 16. I explained to the patients
and paid their expenses."
    On Saturday Halsted wrote that he had a splitting headache
in addition to his cold and could not operate. "If my patients
for today do not care to wait until Monday, please operate
upon them & oblige. Yrs sincerely, W.S. Halsted." On this
note H.C. had written: "Mrs. Taylor did not choose to wait.
Femoral hernia with tuberculous peritonitis."
    On Wednesday came yet another note from Halsted, warn-
ing Cushing of the arrival of another patient and giving directions for her reception. Across the top Cushing had penned:
"The Professor operated Monday on a 'wry neck.' Since the
Stomach case (15 March) this is his first operation. We have
averaged six a day since his absence and have almost caught
up." And again: "Dear Cushing, *You* may have the operating
room tomorrow, for I should like to watch the cases which
interest me at present for a day or two longer. P.S. I send over
some papers for the one-armed boy in D." This brought from
Cushing: "Characteristic note of the Professor—not operated
for a week. One-armed boy left hospital a week ago."
    During the spring, plans for a trip to Europe again began
to occupy him. Thomas McCrae, Simon Flexner, the Oslers,
another Hopkins friend, Henry Barton Jacobs, were all go-

ing abroad, and although he was not as enthusiastic about the opportunity as he had been in medical school, the advice of his father and Ned added to that of Osler and Welch convinced him that it was time he went. He knew there was probably only one surgeon in Europe (Kocher in Switzerland) who excelled Halsted in operative technique, so he was not at all certain he could learn more in Europe than he could right at the Hopkins. Furthermore, he wanted to get on with work that would add to the reputation he had begun to acquire through his papers on typhoid perforation, splenectomy, bacteriology, and trigeminal neuralgia so that he could establish himself and get married. But once again Medicine won out, and Kate Crowell loyally went on waiting.

With some fine new trunks, supplied by his father along with letters of credit, and a single letter of introduction from Welch to Victor Horsley, one of the foremost surgeons in London, Cushing sailed for England on June 23, 1900.

A YOUNG PROVINCIAL
ABROAD

Chapter X

"THE MEDIOCRITY OF HUMAN KIND when they have shifted their responsibilities to the sole duty of holding down their respective steamer chairs is depressing." With this misanthropic observation, Harvey Cushing began his journey to Europe. The depression that came over him each time he left familiar surroundings was not long in appearing: "I shall apparently be alone with a few books, some tobacco, my thoughts, and some pretty keen regrets at throwing up the J.H.H. . . . This relaxation from hospital strain leaves one like a bicycle with a collapsed tire."

From the day he landed in Liverpool until his departure over twelve months later, he kept a detailed diary, much of it medical. The journal also records, however, his reactions to people (often astute but often impatiently critical), his visits to museums and to other places of note. But never is there mention of politics or such things as the Boer War, the Boxer Rebellion (which led to Russian occupation of Manchuria and the Russo-Japanese War), the death of Queen Victoria after a reign of sixty-four years, or the growing imperialism of Germany.

On the third of July he reached London and settled himself at 69 Torrington Square in Bloomsbury, not far from the British Museum, with Thomas McCrae. The next day he breakfasted with Victor Horsley, Surgeon both at the University College Hospital and at the Hospital for the Paralysed

and Epileptic at Queen Square, the oldest and most celebrated hospital for patients suffering with disorders of the
nervous system. Horsley was the first surgeon in England to
devote himself largely to the nervous system.

Only twenty-four years earlier, in 1876, William Macewen
of Glasgow had diagnosed a brain tumor in one of his patients,
but permission to operate had come too late—the diagnosis
was confirmed at autopsy. Eight years later, a brain operation
was successfully performed in London on a living patient by
Sir Rickman Godlee, nephew of Joseph Lister; the first in
America was carried out in 1887 by Dr. W. W. Keen of the
Jefferson Medical College of Philadelphia, where the tumor
he removed is still preserved in the medical museum. These
operations—landmarks in the history of surgery—would not
have been possible before the discovery of anesthesia (1846),
the introduction of aseptic methods by Lister (1867), and the
studies of Fritsch and Hitzig on the motor area (1870). These
studies, which indicated what part of the brain governed sen-
sation and movement of various parts of the body, had been
carried forward by David Ferrier, Hughlings Jackson, William Gowers, and other neurologists, and it was on the basis
of the knowledge they had accumulated that Macewen was
able accurately to determine the location of the tumor in his
patient of 1876.

Victor Horsley had performed his first brain tumor operation on May 25, 1886, and the following year had successfully operated on the spinal cord. That same year he performed an operation for the relief of symptoms where
removal of the tumor was inadvisable—a measure Cushing was
later to call a "decompression." Despite discouraging results
in his early attempts, Horsley had persisted until by 1900 he
had performed a number of successful operations. It was therefore with considerable curiosity that Cushing made his way
to 25 Cavendish Square [1] on the morning of July 4. He found
Horsley a dynamic, energetic man of warm personality. Mrs.

---

[1] Previously the temporary dwelling of another great student of the nervous system and predecessor of Horsley's at Queen Square—the French
physiologist, Charles-Edouard Brown-Séquard.

Horsley and the children joined them at breakfast, and Horsley divided his attention between them, his guest, and a male secretary—somewhat to Cushing's discomfiture. At nine o'clock he saw what he had come for—an operation on the brain, and was horrified by the fact that only ten minutes were given to antiseptic preparation. He reported to his father later: "I am a little disappointed in Victor Horsley. His place is in the laboratory doubtless. I have seen him do some interesting things, however—neurological mostly. A spinal case today causing paraplegia and a brain case a few days ago. Monday he operates on the Gasserian ganglion which I will watch with interest. The technique of all of these men is execrable from our standpoint and they must have many septic wounds."

Probably unaware that he fell short of the high standards of Halsted's apt pupil, Victor Horsley went out of his way to be kind to Cushing and help him get established in London and see the people and things that interested him. Osler also saw to it that he met many of the men who were prominent in British medicine—among them Jonathan Hutchinson, Sir William Broadbent, Sir William Gowers, and Sir James Crichton-Browne. It was a rare opportunity for a young man, and he was grateful for it. "It's a treat to go about with Dr. Osler," he wrote his father. "He gets at the meat of things in an extraordinary way."

Sometimes alone and sometimes with his friend Henry Barton Jacobs, he visited the hospitals of London—St. Bartholomew's, founded in 1137; St. Thomas's (1215); Guy's Hospital (1725). The spirit of "the great men of Guy's" hung over the hospital—Richard Bright, Thomas Addison, Thomas Hodgkin, and James Parkinson, to mention a few, all of whom described diseases still known by their names. "It's a fine place, less old fogyism than in our comparatively young institutions as the M.G.H. for instance."

It was at the Hunterian Museum, however, where the past was most vividly evident. As he returned again and again to the great museum with its more than 13,000 specimens of different species—their variations in health and disease—he felt strongly the presence of John Hunter, the colorful Scot who had elevated surgery to a branch of scientific medicine and founded the science of experimental pathology.

Along with his professional activities Cushing began to seek out a little of the flavor of old London. Around the corner from Guy's was the George Tavern—"a delightful old place in which Sam Weller first makes his appearance in Pickwick Papers. . . . This morning I passed 'Bleak House' and the 'Old Curiosity Shop' when coming away from the Royal College of Surgeons which is in Lincoln's Inn Fields." He rode on the top of a bus "through old London once fireswept in the days of Mr. Pepys." And one night he dined alone in Oxford Street for three shillings and was charged sixpence extra for *not* drinking wine, which made him somewhat indignant. He was not a little disturbed at the consumption of wine in England—said the question was always "What wine?" not "Shall there be wine?" However, he admitted that it seemed to enliven a distinguished dinner party given by Jonathan Hutchinson for Dr. Osler. Although he felt "rather out of it," he nevertheless was flattered to have been asked.

After a week end with the Oslers at Swanage, in Dorsetshire, a small village at the head of a bay lined with great chalk-white cliffs looking toward the Isle of Wight, he returned to London to be present at the centenary celebration of the Royal College of Surgeons of England. Physicians came from all over the world for the ceremonies, and Cushing attended the gatherings and demonstrations with eager interest and was overjoyed to see faces from home—Drs. Warren and Richardson from Boston, Dr. Keen, and Dr. Halsted. A few days later he left for Paris, after saying good-bye to Halsted, who had received an honorary degree at the celebrations, the Oslers, and Humphry Rolleston, grandson of Sir Humphry Davy, who had observed the anesthetic qualities of nitrous oxide in 1800. "R's a daisy [his appellation of highest praise]," wrote Cushing, "interesting talk and many fine old books."

At high noon on the first of August he kept an appointment in the Eiffel Tower made six months previously with his Hopkins friend William MacCallum, and together, during the next week, they attended the 13th International Medical Congress. For the second time Cushing saw the pomp and color of a great international gathering—seventy-nine-year-old Virchow, who had promoted the theory that all living matter is composed of cells, was, with Lord Lister (seventy-three) the center of attention. Another picturesque figure at the Congress, Ernst von Bergmann, was of special interest to Cushing because he had achieved prominence for his work on head injuries and cerebral diseases. But the medical meetings in various languages proved somewhat dull, and he escaped one day with William J. Mayo and A. J. Ochsner, a well-known Chicago surgeon, and, on a stone balustrade overlooking the Seine, they planned a society of their own which eventually came into being as the Society of Clinical Surgery.

The Congress over, Cushing moved to the other side of the Seine and found a small room in the Latin Quarter where he would hear more French, and from which he went daily for six hours of "hospitaling" and some sight-seeing around Paris which he loved. The hospitable French were much more like Americans, he thought, than the English.

In the hospitals he was horrified at the careless operative technique, the utter disregard for the feelings of patients— women examined publicly, men bared promiscuously—the lack of histories, the poor, dirty, overcrowded wards, and the indifferent attention to such things as anesthesia, asepsis, and records. His diary became full of detailed notes about operations, equipment, drugs, etc. He noted that interns sometimes held their jobs for four years and rotated, and that they received 100 "franks" a month. Finally, at the Hôpital de la Pitié he saw Henri Hartmann operate. "First really good work I have seen," he commented. He visited Hartmann's laboratory, admired his "scientific instincts," and came away from dining at his home loaded with reprints, some of which he sent immediately to Halsted.

On August 16, Grosvenor Atterbury arrived in Paris, and a week later they went together to the "most picturesque place in the world," Le Puy-en-Velay, a neat village of century-old charm little visited by outsiders. Inspired by the beauty of the countryside and the simplicity of the people, Cushing's sketches on this trip were the most finished artistically of all those which appear in his travel diaries.[2]

After another month in Paris, Cushing left on October 11 for Berne, Switzerland, in the hope of working with Theodor

Avergnat-Romanesque Church at Issoire—Eglise de St. Paul.
From Le Puy diary, 1900.

Kocher, the brilliant surgeon whom Halsted so much admired. Along the way he visited in the clinics of the distinguished physicians of France and Switzerland—Louis Dor, the ophthalmologist, at Lyon; Auguste Reverdin, professor of surgery at the University of Geneva; César Roux of Lau-

---

[2] This diary, *A Visit to Le Puy-en-Velay*, was published in a limited edition (now exhausted) by The Rowfant Club, Cleveland, in 1944.

sanne, who came nearer to being the kind of man he was looking for than anyone he had yet seen.

On October 31 he reached Berne, where he settled himself in a boarding house and began to explore the old walled
town with its seventeenth-century architecture, narrow ar-
caded streets, and curious gates. Kocher lived up to expectations. He was a slight, neat, rather short man, who was shy and
reserved and thus sometimes gave the impression of being
severe. For his work in clinic and operating room, Cushing

"There is more than one way of stealing your own supper."
From Le Puy diary, 1900.

had the greatest admiration. Here at last was what he had come
to Europe for—"careful, painstaking work, elaborate technique, and all the rest which we have in Baltimore. A marked
contrast to Roux who was brilliant, showy, and rapid in his
work." And as for Albert Kocher, the son—what operating!
"The J.H.H. outdone," Cushing wrote his father, "it's easily
seen why 'the Professor' thought so highly of their work."

But his high spirits waned as the days went by and Kocher
did not pose a problem—which, he discovered, was a necessary
formality before he could work in the University laboratories.
Furthermore the weather, which was consistently rainy and
raw, with never a ray of sunshine, began to depress him. His

discouragement led him to the decision to leave Berne and go
to Heidelberg, but before he went he visited the physiological
institute, called the Hallerianum,[3] and was immediately attracted by the friendliness of its director, Professor Hugo
Kronecker. "He is a kindly little man," Cushing wrote his
father, "a great friend of Dr. Bowditch [Cushing's physiology
professor at Harvard]—a leader in his particular branch and
quite a favorite with American physiologists." Kronecker, on
his side, was taken with Cushing and evidently indicated to

*Le Puy from the north. Drawn on a morning tramp to near-by
Polignac. From Le Puy diary, 1900.*

Kocher that he would be glad to have him work at the institute.
The result was a formal invitation from Kronecker and problems from both him and Kocher. With work to do, Cushing
found the world a bright place again.

Kronecker not only made a place for him in his laboratory
but opened his home to him. Mrs. Kronecker and their daughter Charlotte were equally cordial, and their frequent invitations were soon followed by invitations to the homes of other
professors in the University and of townspeople. Cushing
bought a sled which he named the "Gee Whizz" and in an-

---

[3] Named in honor of the great Berne physiologist, Albrecht von Haller.

other month was flying down the slopes outside the town with an enthusiasm and gaiety which caused the heart of more than one Bernese maiden to beat faster. But his own heart was

Wild flowers near the ruins of the chateau at Allègre, 26 kilometers from Le Puy. From Le Puy diary, 1900.

back in Cleveland, Ohio. To Kate Crowell he wrote on November 21:

My dear child, your letter troubles me a wee bit. When your flag is not flying I always feel that I must chase home and marry you instanter. It's wicked in me to have made you wait these long years. If that moonlight night in Baltimore had never been, how different life might have been for you—but oh! how empty and forlorn mine would have been. There could have been no one else and yet how selfish I am in my good fortune.

A month later he wrote again in this same vein:

I have no reason to suppose that there are any professional plumbs [*sic*] waiting for open mouths, or that mine would be

"*Flying Through Snowy Space*" *on the Gee Whizz.*
Berne, 1901.

selected were there any such. It certainly would not be should I stop working and writing now. If after this year I should give up the thought and hope of having a good teaching position and should start in again on a new track, I know that you would be my best help but I don't want you to be put in any such position. I want you to move in with the house furnished and the carpets down and a warm fire burning for you.

Early in December, Professor Kronecker took Cushing and
J. Holmes Jackson, a Yale man who was also working in
Berne, on a mountain-climbing expedition to the summit of
the Niederhorn (6,445 feet). They spent the night in a small
inn at the base and, with a guide, started their climb the next
morning, carrying only some hard-boiled eggs and chocolate
in their pockets. The Jungfrau, the Wetterhorn, and the other
peaks were reflected in the lake at their feet, and Cushing
could not decide whether they were more beautiful by the
light of the full moon or when the morning sun first tipped
them with rose as the blue shadows receded. He sent his father
a glowing account, the letter continuing with comments on
his work and social life.

. . . It's very nice indeed to have the run of the physiological
laboratory and the *Arbeit* is a borderline one of surgery which
will profit me in the collateral reading necessary even if I succeed in accomplishing nothing of any import. The people are all
very kind—in fact now that I have something serious to do it's
difficult to manage the social duties which seems to be expected
on all sides. . . .

Tomorrow night, for example, with Prof. Kocher to a *Sam-
melreferat* of the faculty (medical) at Prof. Zimmerman's; Tuesday evening at the Kroneckers; Friday at the Rector's house
[president of the university]—heavens! By day I am wildly irri-
gating frogs legs via the aorta with various kinds of transfusion
fluids and measuring muscle curves. I think tonight my own
would show marked evidence of fatigue, tested under similar conditions.

But social functions, despite his mild complaints, continued to occupy much of his time. He and Jackson were joined
in January by another Yale man, John B. Solley, and the three
of them learned to wear their gloves until they reached the
dinner table, to dance a curious kind of German waltz with
their dinner partners after they had retired to the drawing
room when the meal was over, how to survive academic balls
lasting from eight in the evening until four in the morning,
with a large repast interlaced with speeches. "Eight mortal
hours—think of it! I wish my frogs legs would twitch that

long." But he felt at home in the friendly atmosphere of Berne and entered into the spirit of things to the extent of growing a professorial mustache. Despite his attempts to curl it each morning, it had a tendency to droop after breakfast and gave him the air of a villain in a rousing comedy.

To Kate Crowell he wrote of his progress: "We busy our-

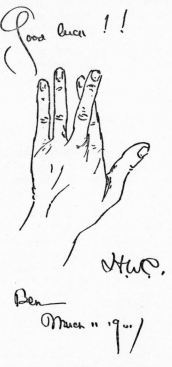

From a letter to Mme. Jeanne Michaud of Berne to wish her good luck in an examination at the University, 1901.

selves in the laboratory and try to make believe that we are scientists which I for one am not and for that very reason think it's good for me to work with those that really are so that I can soak in some of their ways of doing and thinking." To his father he reported that "Kocher seems pleased with my results thus far, though it seems to me that I have hardly learned thus far the best methods or technique for carrying on the research." His problem for Kocher involved finding out what effect pressure in the brain had on circulation and respiration. His experiments were carried out on monkeys, and he conceived the ingenious idea of inserting a small window in the skull of an animal under deep anesthesia through which he could observe the effect of increases in pressure while recording respiration and blood pressure. He discovered that if the pressure within the brain became elevated, the systolic blood pressure rose correspondingly, but if at any time intracranial pressure exceeded the blood pressure, the flow of blood to the brain failed and the animal died.

"In addition to this," he wrote his father, "on off days I am pegging away on a more strictly physiological research for Kronecker with the most extraordinarily elaborate lot of apparatus—clocks and batteries and induction coils and transfusion flasks for all sorts of fluids, all of which focus about a miserable pair of frogs legs sometimes with green sometimes with brown 'pants.' Prof. K. also seems pleased with results though I don't know enough about the subject always to appreciate them myself. In addition I am following Kocher's clinics and the brain and stomach cases which he happens to have—also some other lectures during the week—enough to keep busy and get tired on as you may imagine."

In the back of his mind, as he went on with his work, was the question of his future. In February, Thomas McCrae, to whom he had apparently expressed some of his thoughts, wrote him as follows: ". . . The Chief [Osler] asked me recently what you were going to do. I said that I thought you were uncertain and that you had no very clear idea of what Dr. Halsted thought. ('No,' said the Chief, 'nor has anyone else.') He spoke about your importance to the surgical side as the man who had more '*Geist*' and go than anyone they had. I hope you are not worrying over the future. Things will shape themselves and you are sure of a good niche somewhere. I wish that yours truly had one half the prospect."

From Baltimore came the impetus that prompted his first attempt at historical writing. Osler suggested that he send something about Berne for the Hopkins *Bulletin*, and this encouraged Cushing to write about Albrecht von Haller in whom he had become interested during his first days in the city. "Memories of Haller, the great Swiss physiologist and poet, cling about Berne in many ways. . . . His best and most enduring monuments are to be found on the shelves of Kronecker's laboratory library—12 or so ponderous tomes in Latin of his collected scientific works published in 1755+ and much quoted today." So fascinated did he become with the vast range of Haller's mind and his tremendous energies—which brought him fame as physiologist, anatomist, botanist, bibliographer, and writer of poetry and prose—that the short account suggested by Osler became a full-fledged essay entitled "Haller and His Native Town."

In March, Cushing decided to take advantage of a reduced fare for the "Grand Tour" to visit northern Italy. On March 31 he set out for Turin, where he worked for a month in the laboratory of Angelo Mosso, the colorful Italian physiologist. Here he repeated his Berne experiments on dogs with great success and the beaming approval of Mosso. He wrote Kate Crowell: "I've made a lucky find in some experimental work which won't make me famous but which will help me and some other people understand a little better some things about brain surgery."

A Catholic institution for 6,000 patients on the northern edge of the town also interested him.

. . . I shall never forget those passages—partly underground—full of Sisters, of hobbling patients—of chanting religious processions—everyone seemingly happy and content from doctor to gibbering imbecile—the great dormitory-like wards with sixty-two beds in some of them—the extraordinary kitchen with its low arched ceiling, its brass pots and stirring blue skirted nuns. . . . And most wonderful of all the procession of the idiots from morning service—a few hundred of them following a cross-bearing priest and with grins and mocking laughs and gesticulations they passed under the old gate, crossed the picturesque courtyard and crowded about us while their comrades chattered and mocked from the basement windows behind us. Awful, depress-

ing spectacle—but picturesque to an extraordinary degree—souls
condemned to live in the confinement of the motor and *Sinnes
Sphäre* [motor and sensory spheres] with no association paths
along which they may wander—no glimmer of remembrance, no
fear of a future, simple existence—an enigma. . . .

Throughout his travels, Cushing recoiled from the dis-
plays of the pomp and power of the Church. Yet he could
not help being stirred by the beauty of the churches—the
great columns of black marble, the tremendous silver ornaments and candelabra, the swelling organ, and the high, sweet
voices of the choirboys.

After a month in Turin, he moved on to Genoa where he
attended more clinics and hospitals. Then to Pisa—"a glaring
treeless dead city under a cloudless Italian sky—awaiting what?
But one corner within the old wall had any interest for me
and the Campanile and Battistero are too beautiful to be
seen in broad daylight." But Florence delighted him, particularly the Spedale degli Innocenti with its della Robbia medal-
lions and its "modern *fin de siècle* babes," its cleanness and
modern equipment. The Spedale S. Maria Nuova with "real
operating room apparently beyond criticism," where 150 or
more students could be accommodated—all able to see—
brought forth the commendation that it was "the best model
of an operating room for modern purposes" he had seen either
in Europe or at home. Here he heard Banti lecture on cir-
rhosis of the liver—"a most interesting man who manages his
clinic like W.O. and teaches with the enthusiasm of the same.
Homely—cadaverous—with a marked cast in one of his blue
eyes and a nose which deserves a Cabot behind it."

Next he visited Bologna—"from gay, glittering, beautiful
Florence to dull, homely Bologna—what a change." He was
thrilled with the anatomical theater of the University—"A
room finished simply in wood to which time has given the
richness of color that no learned artificial process can accomplish—a room which, were it not from an artistic standpoint
beautiful and unusual, would still make us stand bareheaded
as though before a shrine, for here Vesalius reawakened the
study of anatomy which since Galen had had a long unques-

tioned period of rest." He was also delighted with some wooden figures supporting the speakers' desk, carved by Ercole Lelli, the professor of anatomy, in 1734. "It is hard to tell," he wrote his father, "whether the artistic beauty of the pose or the perfection of the anatomical details to the very insertion of the tendons is the occasion of delight."

On May 1 he reached Padua, "a fine old walled town." Here again the centuries lay richly on the university buildings which had been the end of a pilgrimage for scholars for hundreds of years. Here Vesalius had also taught, and Fabricius of Aquapendente had demonstrated the valves in the veins by the fitful glare of torches to eager students, among them one William Harvey who later discovered the circulation of the blood.

Venice was a dream city where he thought of Kate and home and became impatient to return to Berne and finish his work. He delayed for a day at Pavia to secure a replica of the apparatus which Riva-Rocci was using to record blood pressure, then went on to Milan, and finally, on May 11, he was back in Berne.

During the rest of the month he worked hard finishing up his experiments and attending Kocher's clinics daily. On Wednesday evening, June 5, he had what he termed "a most extraordinary experience" with Professor Kronecker, who wished to go over Cushing's *Arbeit* before his departure for Glasgow. Cushing's independent spirit underwent baptism by fire that night when Kronecker rolled up his sleeves and, having brewed a big pot of coffee, proceeded to dictate the results of his experiments. Cushing told him that in America things were not done that way—that if Kronecker wanted him to publish the article, he would write it and Kronecker could correct it as much as he liked. After some angry words, Kronecker conceded him the right to do his own paper—recognizing that he had here something unusual in the way of a student.

Cushing's demonstration, on June 3, of his results with Kocher's problem was greeted among the assemblage of professors with unusual interest. The writing-up of the experiments was completed at eleven o'clock on June 14, and so happy was he to be finished that he took the manuscript to Kocher that very night. His friend Asher translated the paper into German for him, and on June 27, after many farewell parties, he left for Strasbourg. To Ned he admitted something that he did not tell either his mother or father: "I was an idiot during my last three or four weeks in Berne and was so anxious to see my work through before leaving that I had little idea under what a tension I was living. I saw them [his papers] through and soon after collapsed."

Strasbourg, Heidelberg, and Bonn passed in quick review. He was fortunate in seeing the leading medical men wherever he went but because of his tired condition he felt no impulse to stay long anywhere. On July 4 he was back in London—spending his first day visiting Guy's Hospital with Dr. George Dock and William Francis, Osler's nephew.

He had written Victor Horsley asking if he might work with him but was later advised to seek out Charles Scott Sherrington, professor of physiology at Liverpool, who was just then beginning a series of experimental studies on the brains of various primate forms—chimpanzees, orang-outangs, and gorillas. He accordingly went there on July 7 and spent the first week somewhat impatiently trying to determine a course of study, Sherrington not having any special suggestions for him. Already eminent as a student of the nervous system, Sherrington was a surprise to Cushing. He found him younger than he expected, almost boyish, "wearing, when he has not lost them, a pair of gold spectacles." He thought he operated well for a physiologist but too often. In fact, he had several criticisms to offer—Sherrington wrote and published too much, went at things too rapidly, and did not take enough notes during his observations—all in all, Cushing put him down as "not quite as big a man" as he had expected. Furthermore, he was surprised to find that almost all physiological observations were open to dispute or to various interpretations, and that experimental neurology was in a most elementary condition and offered vast problems.

It may have been the challenge of these problems, added to the interest in the brain already aroused by his experiments with Kocher and Mosso, that turned Cushing definitely toward neurology and neurosurgery. At any rate, he was soon deep in Sherrington's investigations and was tremendously pleased when Sherrington, taking advantage of his surgical skills, asked him to open the skull of a gorilla and an orangoutang. In his diary he wrote: "It does not come within the realm of everyday experience to be called upon to trephine a gorilla. This happened to me yesterday—the day before an orang-outang and the day before that I saw Sherrington do a chimpanzee. Experimentation on a large scale certainly—and expensive. Mr. Gorilla though ill and unacclimatized (having been in Liverpool only 24 hours) cost 250 pounds."

Toward the end of the month Sherrington left for the Continent and Cushing wound up his work and went to Glasgow to meet Thomas McCrae with whom he had planned to make a brief tour of Scotland. He had come to admire Sherrington and eventually they became close friends. Had he ever gone back to the initial naive appraisal made during his first days, he probably would have been as embarrassed as Sherrington would have been amused.

The Hunterian Museum, left to Glasgow by William Hunter, brother of John, whose museum in London had been such a source of fascination for Cushing, was here also his chief interest. After visiting the Firth of Lorne, Edinburgh, the Oslers at North Berwick, then Leeds, Manchester, and Liverpool, he sailed for home on August 15.

Cushing had approached the Old World with an appraising and somewhat arrogant eye, but he was to return again and again for all it had to offer. From this visit he brought back the definite desire to delve deeper into the mysteries of the nervous system, and with a somewhat vague invitation from Halsted which he had received in June, he planned to return to Hopkins. A Yale classmate, John B. Townsend, meeting William Osler at Old Point Comfort in Virginia that spring, had asked him, "How is my friend Harvey Cushing getting along?" Osler's reply was prophetic of the future: "Your friend Cushing," he told him, "has opened the book of surgery in a new place."

THE CLOSED DOOR

Chapter XI

THE SUCCESS OF HIS YEAR ABROAD and the joy expressed in Cleveland on his return gave Cushing a feeling of security as he returned to Baltimore in mid-September of 1901 full of enthusiasm for the future. But his high spirits were soon dissipated, for upon arriving at the hospital he found all the chiefs were still away and since he had no real assignment—only the promise of one—he had to mark time until they came back. And while there was much to see and to talk over with his friends, his impatience to have his status defined began to mount. Gradually the senior staff began to return. Henry Hurd, the superintendent of the hospital, threw off his customary reticence and gave him a warm welcome. Welch and Osler were genuinely delighted to see him again, Osler immediately inviting him to dinner to see his summer's haul of rare books.

But Halsted, on whom his future depended, was the last to come back and even then it was several days before Cushing was able to see him. He found the Professor cordial but, as usual, reserved and somewhat vague and without any definite plan for fitting him into the picture. Impatiently he poured out his annoyance to Kate Crowell: "It isn't much fun, this marking time and that's all it is; tho' everyone seems to think I am part of the shooting match, I really am not. The surgical side is in bad shape. I finally had a confab with the Prof. two days ago and he made a proposition [that Cushing take up orthopedics] and I told him I didn't want it and in fact got

rather mad. I came very near writing him a letter that night
telling him that he and his people could go to —— that I was
going to Cleveland. Then I thought of you . . . Tonight I
am going to the Hurds to dine. Wish I didn't have to pretend
that I'm chipper any longer."

He had come to the decision that he would like to concentrate on the surgery of the nervous system, despite the
fact that when in his first days in Baltimore he had looked up
some hospital statistics, he had discovered that in the decade
between 1889 and 1899 the diagnosis of tumor of the brain
had been made only 32 times in approximately 36,000 patients
admitted. Of the 32, but 13 had been transferred to surgery
and only 2 of these had been operated upon, both with fatal
results. These figures presented the challenge of a closed door.
He wanted to be the one to open it.

In all fairness to Dr. Halsted, it should be mentioned that he
may have been slow in encouraging Cushing in his determination because he saw no real future for him in the field he
wished to enter. He pointed out that in the hospital at that
time there were only two patients who might possibly have
need of neurosurgery. But Cushing gave him no credit for
consideration. Halsted's lack of enthusiasm only irked him.
Out of his deep pride he admitted: "I knew I could have everything I asked for. What I disliked was the asking. I wanted
offers."

Finally he was able to write his father that the die was cast
and he was to remain at the Hopkins. He and Halsted had
worked out an arrangement that gave him the neurological
side of the surgical clinic, work in the neurological dispensary
under Dr. H. M. Thomas, entry into the wards to see house
cases, one clinic a week with the fourth-year surgical group,
and the opportunity to operate once a week. In addition to
this, he gladly accepted an opportunity to teach a course in
surgical anatomy because he foresaw that if he began to specialize, he would get away from general surgery unless he at
least taught it. This course was to be followed in the spring
semester by an operative course in which he conceived the
idea of using animals as well as cadavers.

With his work in the hospital settled upon, he accepted the invitation of Henry Barton Jacobs and Thomas B. Futcher to join them in bachelor quarters at 3 West Franklin Street, next door to the Oslers at No. 1. The three divided the responsibility of the housekeeping and with the help of a houseman managed to maintain a comfortable establishment. They each solved domestic problems in their own way: Jacobs did his ordering from the grocery by telephone and during his month the bills were high. "Futch" sent William a-marketing, and William consequently fell behind in his household tasks and neglected the brass on the front door and on their name plates. Cushing, to balance things up, decided to do his own marketing, and to Kate he wrote on December 3: "Began housekeeping today. Went to market and bo't roast beef at 15c and chickens and a 'shin bone' for soup and some green goods. It was really great sport and I think I'll go right along, not telephone. It's very domestic and good practice for the days when life will really begin with you."

A later comment on food to his father set Dr. Kirke off on some research. Cushing had said: "My marketing month. Do you know what Chettelings are and corned pigs tails and scrapple?" His father replied: "I have found what the Century Dictionary says about chithelings (intestines of geese), 'corned pigs tails' I can reproduce in imagination, but 'scrapple' is beyond research and imagination. Is it esteemed at No. 3 W. Franklin?"

The residents at this number soon discovered that the best feature of their new arrangement was their proximity to the Oslers. Mrs. Osler had given them all latch keys to No. 1, thus offering them free access to Osler's magnificent library and the informal atmosphere of their home where there was always something interesting going on, centering either around distinguished visitors or the many young friends whom the Oslers like to have about.

It would have been impossible not to assimilate something of Osler's enthusiasm, energetic way of life, intellectual curiosity, and joy of living. Grace Revere Osler played a large part in extending this stimulating and friendly atmosphere. She was as

interested as Dr. Osler in his many students and young colleagues and followed them throughout their careers with
vivid letters full of news about mutual friends, forthright
comments on whatever was current, and amusing accounts
of what they were doing. She was always fully capable of
providing the practical requisites for Osler's generous hospitality—as he once said of her, she was wasted on a house
and should have run a hotel.

When there was an overflow at No. 1, the guests were sent
next door; during most of the year 1901-02 W. W. Francis,
a favorite nephew of Dr. Osler's who was living with him
while attending medical school, stayed with the "Latchkeyers"
and every night at 11:15 he and Cushing finished off the day
with a game of tiddlywinks.

During the autumn, Cushing began work on the preparation of the Mütter Lecture which he was to give in December
in Philadelphia. Dr. W. W. Keen, professor of surgery at the
Jefferson Medical College, had been responsible for his receiving the invitation. Although it was Cushing's disagreement
with Keen on certain aspects of intestinal perforation (expressed in his paper on the subject in 1898) that originally
brought him to Keen's attention, their common interest in
brain surgery was the basis for a continuing friendship. This
was Cushing's first public appearance outside the meetings of
the Hopkins Medical Society, and he wrote and rewrote his
paper several times. He had chosen to summarize the experimental work he had done at Berne on the relation between
intracranial pressure and blood pressure. The published paper
contained a number of his own unusually well-executed drawings, some in color, showing the blood vessels under both
normal and increased pressure as viewed through his impro-
vised window.

When the evening of December 3 arrived, he had worked
himself into such a state of exhaustion and apprehension that
he confessed to his father that he would have courted a railroad accident, a fire, or typhoid fever to escape the ordeal. A
major tragedy did occur—he discovered when dressing that
his dress trousers had apparently been left home—but this did

not prevent his appearance. Dr. Kirke expressed concern as to whether he blacked his legs or borrowed a pair of trousers, but he did not say—he only spoke of his disappointment that illness in Harry's family prevented his father from coming to Philadelphia and said the lecture seemed to go off well.

By now Cushing had become impatient to get married. His love for Katharine Crowell had deepened during his year abroad and his need for her companionship grew stronger with each day. With an eye to the responsibilities of marriage, he accepted every opportunity which came to him to earn money. He had received $200 for the Mütter Lecture and gradually, from papers and occasional private patients, he was accumulating enough so that he began to feel he might be justified financially in taking the step. On one occasion he told Kate: "I stopped writing to you because I'm trying to earn that guinea both with pen and scalpel. Writing a paper—also having some patients."

He decided to go home for Christmas and when his holiday was over, he found leave-taking difficult, as is apparent from a letter sent off immediately after he reached Baltimore: "I found Pa waiting for me with everything packed and we went up to the station and tramped up and down alone and I tried to be cheerful, but don't remember saying much except 'Be good to Kate for me,' and we both blew our red 'Cushing' noses and talked about other things—the Baltimore oyster I believe."

Letters thereafter went to Cleveland almost daily—tender, whimsical letters revealing his loneliness. It was now to Kate that he told his thoughts and the minutiae of his days. "I was very rude to the Professor yesterday. Sorry, but couldn't help it. Some day I will tell him I don't like him and then pack up my duds and go home. . . ." And again: "I have been at the Chief's and dined with a lot of central nervous systems dressed up in clothes. Today I've had a lecture and seen some patients and now must correct proof. Had two fees this past week—$160 and 50—sporadic but encouraging."

In February they announced their engagement and their intention to be married in June—on the 10th, and as June approached, Cushing began counting the days. Once he wrote

Kate: "I'm so afraid we're going to be poor—in money." And "Please don't let people do any 'work' over our wedding preparations. As long as it's fun, why all right. If it savors of 'Arbeit,' stop it. Don't let's have any 'glad it's over' feelings. I want people to wish they could go to another like it every week."

Dissatisfaction aroused by the lack of understanding between him and Halsted evidently prompted him to look into the possibility of another post. He set his sights high and never took his eye off the target. The only place he wanted to go other than the Hopkins was the Harvard Medical School. On February 22, 1902, he had an encouraging letter from W. T. Councilman (to whom he had addressed his enquiry) suggesting that he write President Eliot.

What Cushing wrote to Eliot, we do not know, but it brought forth a cordial reply:

You left behind you at our Medical School and the Massachusetts General Hospital an excellent reputation, and your experience on the surgical staff of the Johns Hopkins Hospital has doubtless added much to your value. There will probably be, as you say, some reorganization of the clinical teaching staff of our School within three years. If Dr. Burrell, Dr. Maurice Richardson, or Dr. J. Collins Warren knows you well, I should advise you to state your desires to any one of the three, or to all three, so that your name may be present in their minds whenever the reorganization shall be attempted.

He followed up Eliot's suggestion, for there is a letter dated March 15 from Herbert L. Burrell in which he says: "In thinking and planning for the School you have been in my mind for a long time. The work that you have done has deeply impressed me and I admire your courageous effort in striving for the highest and best in surgery."

There the matter stood. He must wait. But in June mention of Harvard came from an unexpected source. The professorship of surgery at the University of Maryland, offered first to J. C. Bloodgood, an excellent general surgeon at the Hopkins, was later offered to Cushing when Bloodgood declined. He

apparently considered the offer seriously and wrote about it
to Halsted who was just leaving for Europe. Halsted asked
him to consider the obstacles that would be encountered in an
institution where lack of funds would mean drudgery and less
opportunity for experimental work. "Your position at present
seems to me so ideal that I really envy you. Your time is absolutely your own and your opportunities all that can be found,
at least in America." However, if Cushing decided to make the
change, he promised the utmost in co-operation and assistance,
for, he said, "I have your interests very much at heart." He
closed the letter with—"I wish you good luck in your choice
and great happiness in life. How can you fail to be happy with
such prospects &, may I say, such a wife."

It may have been this letter that influenced Cushing's decision, but it was more likely one he had two days later from
Bloodgood, which said in part: "I feel that you should know
this, which I have learned in confidence, indirectly. Your name
has been considered in Boston—Harvard thinks much of you—
in the rearrangement of its surgical teaching. If you did not
know this—you should—& should consider this possibility."

Whatever the deciding factor, Cushing elected to wait and
he therefore declined the Maryland offer and went on with
his work at the Hopkins. That it was creating interest was
evidenced by the fact that between March and June he was
asked to give six lectures—one before the Johns Hopkins Hospital Medical Society on his nine cases of Gasserian ganglion,
one at Buffalo, New York, where he stopped off after attending a bacteriological meeting in Cleveland, another before the
Medical-Chirurgical Faculty of Maryland, and two evening
lectures at Johns Hopkins University. The last and most important was the annual lecture in surgery given before the
State Medical Society at Milwaukee during its meeting held
June 4-6. He spoke on the avoidance of shock in amputations
by cocainization of large nerve trunks, with observations on
blood-pressure changes in surgical cases.

As soon as the meetings were over, he hurried back to Cleveland and, on June 10, 1902, he and Katharine Crowell were
married. Mrs. Osler in a letter to Henry Barton Jacobs, then in

Paris, said: "I hear that Dr. Cushing's wedding went off charmingly. They were married in the country very quietly. Dr. Barker was there and wrote it was quite ideal." By the first of July they were settling themselves at 3 West Franklin Street. In April Dr. Jacobs had married the widow of Robert Garrett, the former president of the Baltimore and Ohio Railroad, but Thomas Futcher continued to live with the Cushings until they moved to a larger house.

The summer brought a letter of congratulation on the paper describing his work with Kocher from the above-mentioned Lewellys F. Barker, a Hopkins friend now at Chicago: "The *Hirndruck* etc. is *magnificent*. Hearty congratulations. You are showing the world the kind of work that a *real* Professor of Surgery ought to do. The coming profession in the clinical branches must be an entirely new breed. We cannot put the new wine into the old bottles."

In November, Cushing was flattered to be asked to go to Philadelphia to discuss a paper on brain tumors although he had had but two cases himself, neither successful. On this occasion he met for the first time the eminent neurologist and physician, S. Weir Mitchell, who invited him to visit his library and fired his imagination in the direction of literature and poetry.

With occasional invitations of this nature and with hospital work, teaching, writing, and the increase in social activities that came with marriage, the autumn and winter passed quickly. In April, Kate Cushing wrote to Dr. Kirke: "This is supposed to be vacation, that is there are no classes, but we have several patients at different hospitals at different ends of town, and some proof to read and articles to finish. . . . Dr. Osler [who was attending a meeting in Cleveland] will give you a good account of Harvey—he is very well—but there are two questions I have been meaning to ask you—how do you make him take care of himself when he has a cold, and how old is he? I put thirty-three candles on his birthday cake, but he thought there should be more."

During the spring, Cushing had told his father that he might expect a fifth grandchild [1] at the end of July, and late in June he urged him to come to see them before its arrival. "Don't you suppose you could manage it for a week, before the middle of the month, please? After the 20th or thereabouts we prefer to be left alone. I wish you would, on the quiet, hint to Mrs. Crowell that she had better come down after 'the Event.' Futcher is to be away on his vacation but a nurse and an arrival and a mother-in-law in the house at the same time, especially should it be hot, will make matters pretty complicated with our new servants, as well as in other ways."

His father did not feel equal to making the trip to Baltimore, nor was he more successful in postponing Mrs. Crowell's visit, but this may have been due to the fact that the baby did not arrive until the fourth of August. It was a healthy eight-pound boy whom they eventually christened William Harvey. The happiness occasioned by the arrival of a son was, however, somewhat overshadowed by the news from Cleveland that his mother was ill. But since her symptoms did not seem indicative of serious trouble, the family hoped that this illness, the first in her lifetime, would soon clear up. Dr. Kirke's letter of August 3 had been a little more encouraging. "Your mother is spare, and weak, but not more so than would be expected, and puts her best foot foremost mentally and bodily as usual. Great thing if she would retire from business, after the manner of H.K.C., but she will, I have no doubt, go down with her flag at the main. Perhaps her way is best."

The birth of the baby brought a letter dated the 10th from his mother in her own hand. Cushing was relieved to see her writing, even though it was somewhat shaky, but his heart was twisted by her admission "I found myself one day enacting the part of the child who cries for the moon—I wanted so much to see *you*. . . ."

This was the last letter he had from her. She was able to gratify her wish to see the baby when Kate and William Harvey went home at the end of August. Cushing joined them early in September. After their return to Baltimore his

---

[1] Harry had three children and Ned one.

mother failed rapidly and on October 21 she died. Cushing went home immediately and wrote Kate from Cleveland: "Just a big wreath of autumn leaves outside the door and nothing black—just like Mother. But oh! so still and cold. I hardly realized it till I saw her. No one was there but Father. I was glad because I behaved pretty badly. No one knows but you and he and Mother how near the surface lie my emotions. Father is always there—perfectly calm and under control. . . . I don't think he has slept any and looks thin and worn." The next day he sent Kate another letter:

Everything is much the same here. Father is quiet and terribly nice to everyone who comes and very communicative for him. . . . Has a great deal to say of Mother, affectionate things, little incidents of one sort or another. Keeps looking at her pictures with red dry eyes, the old daguerreotype and the rest. . . . I stayed down here until about eleven to try and get him to lie down, as Alice said he walked almost all the first night, and he talked and talked. I wish you could have heard him. He spoke of her hands—how square they were for small hands, shaped like his own and some of the rest of us—how he had never seen them for 50 years a moment idle or unoccupied; often doing unnecessary things to save others—or holding needlessly heavy work like those big carpet rugs she used to make—but always doing something. . . .

I'm glad she saw and held our little boy before she died. I hope that she passed on to him some of her absolute unselfishness and rare qualities of other sorts which his father missed.

Betsey Maria Cushing was buried on the hilltop at Lakeview on October 24, a beautiful autumn afternoon, and H.C. went sadly back to Baltimore. Carolyn Cushing, Will's wife, later wrote to Kate: "We all wished Harvey might have stayed on a little. As Ned says, 'Harvey is the only one of us who can go up and put his arm on Father's shoulder.' The others all minister, and greatly to their father's evident pleasure, but Harvey's way is his own. . . . I am so glad, dear Kate, that Aunt Bessie had the happiness of having you in her closest circle, and of knowing that Harvey was possessed of his heart's desire. . . . Such force, such intelligence and judgment, such patience and courage, and so much love in her big heart—the combination was not a common one!"

Cushing wrote to his father as often as he could, and Dr. Kirke's replies were cheerful but his loneliness evident. "I was glad to get your letter and to have the latest news from you, Kate and the young hopeful. Indeed, anything which breaks in upon the enduring vacancy which fills the house is pleasant. As with you, the weather is mild and pleasant. We pick some flowers from her beds every day. Nasturtiums, dahlias, now and then a rose, with chrysanthemums make up the variety." But the thing that touched Cushing most deeply was his father planting, under Ned's direction, some three hundred bulbs that his mother had ordered. "What the result will be is a matter of the hereafter, like so many others. Some were also put into the grass of the cemetery plot." So under a blanket of crocuses Betsey Maria Cushing rested on her hilltop while those who loved her tried to fill the gap with memories.

"FOR BOOKS ARE NOT ABSOLUTELY DEAD THINGS"

Chapter XII

O N T H E I S L A N D O F Z A N T E , O F F the coast of Greece, there died a physician in the year 1564, whether from an uncommon disease or from exposure following shipwreck, it is not known. But it is known that this lonely figure, dying so far from his native Belgium, was Andreas Vesalius, author of one of the greatest books ever written, the first to picture the human body and skeleton as we know it today.

The story of this man and his great masterpiece—his precocious youth, his impetuous twenties, the unfulfilled promise of his middle age, and his death at fifty-four—was to fascinate Harvey Cushing until the end of his days. It was probably Osler who introduced the two, or it might have been at a meeting of the Johns Hopkins Hospital Historical Club that Cushing first made the acquaintance of Vesalius. Anyway, he was sufficiently interested in him in the spring of 1901 to seek out the anatomical theater at Padua where Vesalius had performed the public dissections pictured in the frontispiece of his book, *De humani corporis fabrica* (On the Workings of the Human Body), published in 1543 at Basel, Switzerland, Vesalius having taken his drawings and manuscript from Venice over the mountains on donkeyback.

Who was this Vesalius who was to lead him into bookstores, libraries, and museums all over the continent of Europe for the next forty years? Someone has called him "a man of wrath";

impetuous he undoubtedly was, and strong-minded and courageous. But such qualities were needed by a physician who was
to break with traditions that had governed the practice of
medicine for over fifteen hundred years. Impatient with professors who sat on a platform reading medicine from a book
while the ignorant barber-surgeons dissected the cadavers for
the benefit of the students, Vesalius did his own dissections and
soon discovered that what he found and what the book said
were not in agreement. He further discovered that the dis-
crepancies were due to the fact that the anatomy which had
been taught for centuries was based on dissections of dogs and
pigs and not on the human body.

So at the age of twenty-eight he published his celebrated
Anatomy, and because he had the assistance of artists from
Titian's studio, perhaps even of Titian himself, his figures stood
forth from the pages as if they were alive. Even the dry bones
of his skeletons had life. Gone were the two-dimensional, flat
figures of his predecessors—gone many of the old errors of
structure and function, and in their place something which
thrilled and shocked his contemporaries and which earned him
through the centuries the title of "Father of Modern Anatomy." His figures are still used as examples in schools of art,
and his contribution to the advancement of medical knowledge never fails to stir the admiration of students and historians
of medicine.

Although the storm of criticism which greeted his revolu-
tionary work caused Vesalius in a fit of wrath to burn all his
manuscripts and retire from teaching to become a court physician for the rest of his life, this only seemed to highlight the
phenomenal activity of his earlier years. Many before Cushing had found Vesalius a challenging and provocative figure
of great strength, imagination, and stubbornness, but few followed his trail so long or so diligently.

Just how it all began is a matter of conjecture, but we do
know that on May 31, 1903 Cushing wrote his father: "Dr.
Osler has started me on a Vesalius essay. He has turned over
to me pro tempore a stunning copy of the 'De Corpera [Cor-
poris] Humanis [Humani] Fabrica' with the famous plates

etc. I want very much to collect photographs of the various portraits and as many engravings of V. himself as possible so if you run across any of them in your perusal of catalogues or see a notice of the sales of any of his books I wish you would let me know."

But his ambition soon extended beyond photographs and engravings, and we find William MacCallum writing him from Paris during the summer: "As to Italy there was nothing unusual except that I got you a Vesalius like Dr. Osler's tho' not in quite as good trim—it is the Basel edition of 1543." Fuel was added to the fire when Osler came home from Europe with *four* copies of the *Fabrica*.[1]

The paper on which Osler had started Cushing was given the title "The Books of Vesalius" and presented before the Book and Journal Club of the University of Maryland on December 16, 1903. The day after this meeting, Dr. Kelly left on Cushing's doorstep a handsome copy of the second edition of the *Fabrica*.

Dr. Kirke's mention, sometime later, of his own copy of the *Fabrica* caused Cushing to enquire immediately: "What was the Vesalius which you were getting bound? If I make some money this year I am going to try and purchase copies of all of his writings to go with my Edns of the Fabrica." Two years later came the opportunity to fulfill a part of this desire: "A good doctor man on whom I recently operated for epilepsy has sent me a check for $200 for books!" he told his father. "I hope therewith to complete my Vesalius collection." And other gifts came to him, for the Biblical phrase "to him that hath shall be given" is true of no one so much as the book collector: "Dr. Pilcher of Brooklyn came down to give us a paper on Mundinus [2] at the Historical Socy—he stayed with us for a few days which meant dinners &c, but I feel well paid for the time as he has sent me a Vesalius Fabrica, Edn 1568, which helps fill out my collection of Vesal's works now reaching some proportions."

---

[1] Which he presented as gifts to individuals or medical school libraries.
[2] An anatomist of Bologna who wrote a popular anatomical textbook two centuries before Vesalius was born.

It was from these beginnings that the greatest existing Vesalian collection was brought together. Although Cushing rashly thought in 1906 that with $200 he might complete his collection, he was still adding to it until the day he died.[3]

Although the most engrossing, Vesalius was only one of Cushing's interests. And Osler, although he gave much impetus to Cushing's collecting by stirring up his enthusiasm, adding to his knowledge of the men who had made medical history, and by passing along book catalogues, was not the only one who was responsible for his growing library. David Cushing, it will be remembered, had collected a library which Erastus had carried with him when he left New England. And such small amounts as Dr. Kirke could keep for his own use during the growing-years of his large family had been spent on books. It was his father who offered him the earliest encouragement by gradually transferring to him the books the Cushing doctors had accumulated. Early in February of 1899 Cushing wrote him that "the books came safely this morning and I am delighted to possess them. My library groweth apace. I must have some 250 volumes." A year later it was Dr. Kirke who wrote: "Just as soon as I am able to do anything, I will send off some of the old books we spoke about to you. How about the five vols. of the International Surgery in the little case in your mother's bedroom? You can have them if you would like, or anything else that will help or comfort you."

And books *were* a comfort. What they meant to him, Milton had eloquently expressed when he wrote "For books are not absolutely dead things, but doe contain a potencie of life in them to be as active as that soule whose progeny they are; nay they do preserve as in a violl the purest efficacie and extraction of that living intellect that bred them." And during Cushing's year abroad, as he had walked the streets where Milton

---

[3] Four years after his death another book was added—the *Bio-bibliography of Vesalius* which Cushing himself had partially completed and which friends and his literary executor, John F. Fulton, finished so that it might appear, as was Dr. Cushing's intention, on the four hundredth anniversary of the publication of the *Fabrica*. It was published in a handsome edition by the firm of Henry Schuman of New York.

walked, had seen the lifework of John and William Hunter spread out before him in their museums, passed the site in Leicester Square where "goodnatured Charlie Bell" had set himself up in practice in a ramshackle house that proved "a heavier burden than nine bastard children"—as he had wandered in these places of rich memory, the history of medicine had beckoned to him and never let him go.

In Berne the ancient clock, around whose tower the mechanical bears march solemnly every hour, had told the passage of time to the great physiologist Haller as it did to him. At Padua he had stood in the amphitheater where Fabricius of Aquapendente had demonstrated by torchlight the valves in the veins to William Harvey who was to return to England and eventually discover how the blood circulates through the body —a riddle that had baffled the imagination of men since thousands of years before Christ.[4] These men, and others like them, who had labored and suffered through the centuries in their search for truth came to life again as Cushing gathered together their books and information about their friends and colleagues, their predecessors and their followers. It was a game which became an unending source of pleasure and relaxation during the difficult years that lay ahead.

From a modest beginning (his book bills from December 31, 1902 to January 1, 1907 amounted to $854.07), his collecting grew to an expensive pastime. As long as his father lived, Cushing continued to receive treasured volumes from the library in Cleveland and gifts of books in which he had expressed an interest. Rarely did a letter pass between them without some reference to their mutual interest—references such as the following:

FROM H.C. TO H.K.C., FEBRUARY 28, 1900
In spite of press of work I have had time to peek into the fine

---

[4] Cushing in 1907 had an opportunity to buy the memorable book in which Harvey made known his discovery to the world in 1628—*Exercitatio anatomica de motu cordis et sanguinis in animalibus*—but he did not have in ready cash the $200 purchase price. Since there are only forty-six copies of the book known to exist, the next time he had a chance to secure a copy, the price was $3,000.

old volumes you sent on. The Chas. Bell [5] as a book is of course far the most valuable but the associations with the others make them doubly interesting to me. I found in one of D.C.'s [David Cushing] the appraiser's mark. . . . The old *Lancet* is fine. This volume is one of the most active of any in the crusade against the "Hole and Corner" surgery of the day.

FROM H.C. TO H.K.C., OCTOBER 12, 1902

Many thanks for the Chas. Bell. I now have three of those thin volumes and would like the other. I will give away no such books for the present at all events. Kate and I are very proud of our book shelves. Twenty fat volumes of Walpole—letters, essays, etc. came as a wedding present from Mrs. Tracy. Our "End of the XVIIIth Cent." Collection is getting strong—Mrs. Piozzi— your Johnsons—"The Spectator" etc.

FROM H.K.C. TO H.C., MARCH 12, 1903

Last week there was a sale of part of the library of Harold Price, of Philadelphia, a non-resident member of our Rowfant Club. It was rich in Americana. I was fortunate in getting Dr. John Morgan's "Discourse [upon] the Institution of Medical Schools," Phil. 1765, with this inscription "For Dr Whytt Professor of Medicine at Edinburgh from the Author." . . . It bears the imprint of Wm Bradford (By Dr Thomas Cadwallader—Wm Bradford the Second). At the Exhibition of the Grolier Club, New York, Apr. 14, 1893, of Books printed by William Bradford and other printers of the Middle Colonies there *was no copy* of Morgan's Discourse.[6] . . . I do not know as this sort of back talk will interest a man busy daily with practical affairs of life, and your paternal may seem a bit musty, or at least hard up for materials for writing.

FROM H.C. TO H.K.C., JUNE 30, 1903

Kate and I are feasting ourselves on book catalogues of which from the Osler supply we gain several a week. We have picked up some interesting things in our present line of reading—Lord Wharncliff's "Lady Mary Wortley Montague" 'par example' from the Shepard Book Co. of *Salt Lake City*, Utah. Strange place for

---

[5] Bell was the leading British anatomist of the nineteenth century.
[6] John Morgan's 'Discourse' led to the founding of the first medical school in America (at the University of Pennsylvania in 1765). Dr. Kirke was a graduate of this school.

a large book (old) Emporium n'estce pas? Very (comparatively) cheap books. . . .

We would like to have you come down if you can and care to and we would like to have you bring your 'Kit-Cat Club' book as we are continually having tantalizing references to it and its members. Lady Mary Wortley Montague was the youngest 'toast' of the club. . . . Do you remember, by the way, that she brought back from Constantinople the inoculation against smallpox scheme in 1717? Dr. O. mentions it in his text-book.

In January of 1904, Cushing wrote his father: "Much interest was excited yesterday by the reception of an installment of books which I had ordered sometime ago from Blackwell in Oxford. They turned out to be from the library of Sir Henry Acland with his bookplate etc. One of them was a presentation copy of Gross's essay on 'John Hunter and his Pupils' and in it was pasted Dr. Gross's note in which he refers to a prospective visit to England of Dr. S. Gross and his 'sweet and beautiful wife'—the present Mrs. Grossler,[7] as Dr. O. calls her. Curious that the note should have boomeranged back so near to her after all these years."

Another association of interest was found in the gift of the *Statical Essays* published in London in 1733 by the Perpetual Curate of Teddington on the Thames, Stephen Hales. Hales was a fascinating character, a contemporary of Isaac Newton's at Cambridge, who not only performed his clerical duties most zealously, but in addition contributed much to the scientific progress of his time. He was the first to measure blood pressure by an experiment on a mare in his parish yard, the first to invent a ventilator and insist on its use in prisons, slave ships, and hospitals. His books were read widely, and the copy which came into Cushing's hands bears the bookplate of Patrick Henry and was in the library at Red Hill, his plantation on the Staunton River in Virginia, when he died. The book came to Cushing through a descendant whose husband had been one of his patients.

---

[7] Mrs. Osler had been married to Dr. Samuel W. Gross of Philadelphia, the eminent son of an eminent father. Three years after his death in 1889 she had married William Osler.

From collecting books it was easy, with Osler's example, to drift into writing historical essays. His interest in the Kit-Kat Club, for example, resulted in a paper which began: "In the reign of Queen Anne, a pasty-cook, one Christopher, or Kit for short, 'immortal made by his pyes,' kept a tavern near Temple Bar at the Sign of the Cat and Fiddle. Here was wont

SIR,

YOU *are defired to Accompany the Corps of Mr.* John Dryden, *from the College of Phyficians in* Warwick-Lane, *to* Weftminfter *Abby*; *on* Monday *the* 13th *of this Inftant* May, 1700. *at Four of the Clock in the Afternoon exactly, it being refolved to be moving by Five a Clock. And be pleafed to bring this Ticket with you.*

Dyd April 30th

From facsimile of card to Dryden's funeral.

to gather a group of the most distinguished men of the time . . . [among them] the subject of this sketch, the popular, the generous, the companionable Garth."

Samuel Garth was a physician-poet whose rhymed history (*The Dispensary*) of the attempt to have drugs dispensed by physicians rather than apothecaries was enormously popular in its time. It was Garth who saved his friend John Dryden from ignominious burial, arranged for a proper ceremony, and saw to it that he was buried in the Poets' Corner in Westminster. Cushing searched for years for the invitation which was issued on this occasion:

Sir, You are desired to Accompany the Corps of Mr. John Dryden from the College of Physicians in Warwick-Lane to Westminster Abby on Monday the 13th of this instant May, 1700. at Four of the Clock in the Afternoon exactly, it being resolved to be moving by Five a Clock. And be pleased to bring this Ticket with you.

He finally had to be content with a reproduction of the only copy he ever located. The original had been bought in a London auction room by an American collector just a short time before he began his search.

But such "misses" were more than balanced by the "finds" and added zest to the never-ending fascination of the game. The word satiety does not appear in the lexicon of a true book collector. The thrill of the hunt, the triumph of acquisition, the joy of possession never diminish. For Cushing, the excitement of his early years of collecting the books that made up the history of his profession continued as long as he lived, even when he became an experienced collector, branching out into other fields of science. And when he shared it, as he did with all who entered his library, there was no one who could withstand the contagion of his enthusiasm. "Books delight us, when prosperity smiles upon us; they comfort us inseparably when stormy fortune frowns on us. They lend validity to human compacts, and no serious judgments are propounded without their help." These words he had found in 1903 in the *Philobiblon* of Richard De Bury, who presided over the See of Durham in the fourteenth century, and, like the colorful, book-collecting bishop, he enjoyed bringing others under "the wondrous power of books" since "through them we survey the utmost bounds of the world and time, and contemplate the things that are, as well as those that are not, as it were in the mirror of eternity."

Chapter XIII

ALEXIS CARREL, THE FRENCH SCIentist who is probably best known to the general public in this country for his work with Charles A. Lindbergh on a mechanical heart,[1] wrote a letter to Harvey Cushing from Chicago in December of 1905. Although his English was good, the letter contained an amusing misuse of a word. "Please tell me when your new laboratory will be established," he said. "Then I will go to Baltimore for a few days in order to admire it, and, if possible, to see you performing some of your splendid nervous operations."

It was an apt word to describe the early brain operations. The story is told that when Cushing, in the midst of a long procedure in which things were not going well, asked for the blood pressure, he was surprised in a few moments to feel someone fumbling about his leg and to discover that the inexperienced student nurse was attempting to take his blood pressure instead of the patient's!

The terrific tension under which the pioneer brain surgeons labored brought Harvey Cushing to every procedure as keyed up as a race horse. He allowed no conversation while he scrubbed up, and insisted on absolute quiet in the operating room. Each patient became his personal responsibility, and the operation a fierce contest between him and the forces that

---

[1] Dr. Carrel received a Nobel Prize for his work on intestinal anastomosis and is also well known for his studies on tissue culture.

threatened life. Eric Oldberg once voiced the admiration of Cushing's assistants for his tremendous courage in the operating room. "Although always meticulous and careful, he, like all surgeons, was sometimes faced with catastrophic accidental occurrences. He always rose to these occasions instantaneously and magnificently, and to be associated with him in such a battle was nothing short of emotionally moving."

It takes little imagination to guess what might happen to an assistant or nurse who was slow in anticipating his needs in such emergencies, or who handed the wrong instrument, or who fidgeted or obviously showed signs of weariness—even though the operation might last from four to six hours. At these times feelings were of no concern to Cushing, the only thing that mattered to him was the exposed brain before him. Such was his concentration that when the operation was over, he himself never appeared to be at all weary. Sometimes he was aware that he had been sharp and caustic and might hunt up a student nurse who had gone out of the room in tears to say that he was sorry. But he did not often make apologies and some of his assistants smarted for a long time from tongue-lashings they had received, deservedly or undeservedly, during an operation.

Nor did he always confine his criticism to operations. Osler, in 1902, felt constrained to write him a note in which he said he had heard that Cushing did not get on well with his surgical subordinates and colleagues. "The statement also is made that you have criticized before the students the modes of dressings, operations &c of members of the staff. This, I need scarcely say, would be absolutely fatal to your success here. The arrangement of the Hospital staff is so peculiar that loyalty to each other, even in the minutest particulars, is an essential. I know you will not mind this from me as I have your best interests at heart." This brought from Cushing an offer to resign, to which Osler replied cheerfully (and effectively): "Do nothing of the kind! Who is free from faults—& failings! It is a simple matter—'Keep your mouth (as the Psalmist says) as it were with a bridle.' Your prospects here are A.1. & we need you."

Although knowledge of the brain was slowly growing through the persistent efforts of a few pioneers and the studies, both physiological and pathological, coming out of experimental laboratories, attempts at tumor removal still resulted in a disheartening number of failures. Only five to ten per cent of the different tumors were considered operable, and only about five per cent of the operations were successful. The studies of Charles Sherrington and his associates on the anthropoid brain had added extensively to the knowledge of cerebral architecture already accumulated and had made possible more accurate localization of tumors. Horsley and his associates, particularly Charles Beevor and Edward Schafer, were continuing their work on the same problem. On the technical side, the Gigli saw had been found to be more effective than a trephine in opening the skull, and the German, W. Wagner, had reported a new method for making bone flaps for the purpose of cerebral exploration. All of those advances reduced the hazards of entering the cranial cavity, but there were many problems still unsolved—the ever-present danger of hemorrhage, the control of increased intracranial pressure, the uneasy question of how deeply the brain might be encroached upon in the removal of an infiltrating growth; and there was the constant threat of postoperative infection.

The story is told of Sir Victor Horsley by one of his graduate students, Dr. Ernest Sachs, that he walked into the wards at the Queen Square Hospital one morning to see a patient at the request of Dr. Charles Beevor. He decided that the patient had a pituitary tumor and announced that he would operate the following Tuesday. Beevor, knowing the usual result of such attempts, protested, "But Victor, if you operate on that man, he will die." "Of course he will die," returned Horsley, "but if I don't operate on him, those who follow me won't know how to perform these operations."

This had to be the underlying philosophy of all who attempted surgery of the brain in the first discouraging years. But Victor Horsley persisted courageously, success occurring just often enough so that he felt justified in going on. His efforts won him the distinction of being called the founder of neurosurgery, although he was not the first nor the only one in the field. Macewen of Glasgow had had favorable results with a long series of brain abscesses, but tumors presented more difficult problems and it was tumors in which Horsley was most interested. The work in France had been summarized by the French surgeon, Chipault, in 1894, and von Bergmann in Germany had published a monograph on cerebral surgery.

After the turn of the century it became apparent that the neurological and pathological knowledge of brain tumors, meager though it was in comparison with what is known today, had surpassed the knowledge of the technical methods for removing them, and it was here that Cushing made his great contribution to neurosurgery. Although Horsley is said to have founded the specialty, Cushing was the first surgeon to devote his entire time to it. His interest was shared in America by a small number of general surgeons and neurologists, notably Charles A. Elsberg of New York, who became the neurosurgeon of the Neurological Institute at Columbia and whose particular concern was the surgery of the spine; M. Allen Starr and Bernard Sachs, New York neurologists who were firm believers in the surgical treatment of tumors, and the men who did their surgery, Frank Hartley and Arpad G. Gerster; and a group in Philadelphia (which S. Weir Mitchell had made something of a neurological center). This group included W. W. Keen, of course, Dr. Mitchell's son John, Charles K. Mills, and William G. Spiller, neurologist, who worked with Charles H. Frazier, surgeon. Together, Spiller and Frazier made improvements in the Gasserian ganglion operation for the relief of trigeminal neuralgia, on which Cushing was also working, and originated the operation of cordotomy—severing the anterolateral tracts of the spinal cord for the relief of unbearable pain.

From the beginning, Cushing pushed to the forefront of the new field, although his early efforts were almost without exception unsuccessful despite careful study and infinite pains. What motivation was behind his tremendous drive is a question that his contemporaries asked many times. Personal ambition, of course, for he was by no means as disinterested in priority as was his chief, Halsted. His confidence that hard work would accomplish almost any desired end was another factor. But there can be no doubt that medicine itself—aside from the strong moral obligation of service to humanity, an obligation he assumed seriously—never ceased to fascinate him from the moment he first began to dissect the human body. He never failed to find excitement and challenge in its problems. His curiosity about what lay behind the closed doors never diminished.

It was well that this was so, for in the beginning there was little beyond his own interest to encourage him in the way he had chosen. The opportunities to learn through experience were few and far between. Not only were patients reluctant to submit to brain operations, but few physicians yet knew enough about the symptoms to recognize them when they were present. It was for this reason that Cushing made a habit of publishing his results. When these were negative, he included his appraisal of his mistakes and the results of the autopsy if one was done.[2] In this way physicians began to be aware of the conditions that might indicate disturbances of the nervous system.

Because Cushing's first efforts so often ended in fatalities, Halsted is rumored to have made the statement that he didn't know whether to say "Poor Cushing's patients" or "Cushing's poor patients." But defeat only acted as a spur. He continued his work in a high fervor of determination and concentration. His service was considered the most strenuous of any in the hospital. First there was the detailed and time-consuming neurological and physical examination. After the long pre-

---

[2] Cushing, from the first, insisted upon autopsies because, although always important, they were particularly important in brain cases where knowledge was in a rudimentary state. Some of the tales growing out of his persistence on this point bear a close resemblance to the stories of "body-snatching" in earlier centuries, when anatomists had to resort to all manner of surreptitious methods to further their knowledge of the human body. In one particularly baffling case, when autopsy was refused, it was reported (with details left to the imagination) that Samuel J. Crowe, his assistant at the time, secured the brain "under inauspicious circumstances."

liminary study, the patient was prepared for the operation. This again was a lengthy procedure—likewise the operation itself, which required an unusual number of instruments and special techniques. Cushing liked to keep his patients absolutely quiet after the operation, and sometimes they were not moved from a small room adjoining the operating room for a day or two. During the day he would slip in as often as possible to see how the patient was coming along and to be sure that no crisis was developing.

When the intern and the nurse finally took over, he would call frequently from his house for a report on the patient's condition, often at midnight and again later in the night, asking in minute detail what had been done in the interim. Woe to the intern or nurse who couldn't say which arm or leg the patient had moved or in what direction the eyes were turned! When they could not, they were often asked why, then, had they taken up medicine if they were not sufficiently interested to watch symptoms closely? It made no difference if the intern had assisted in two or three long operations during the day—Cushing drove him just as he drove himself. But because of the quality of his own work and the standard he set for all who worked with him, he was an excellent teacher of good medicine. And it was the rare student who, even though smarting under some of Cushing's strenuous methods, did not acknowledge an indebtedness to his teaching.

In December of 1901 an undersized and sexually undeveloped girl of sixteen was admitted to the Hopkins complaining of headaches and failing vision. After careful study, Cushing attempted three exploratory operations (on February 21, March 8, and March 17), but none disclosed a tumor, and the patient died of pneumonia on May 1 with her symptoms unrelieved. Autopsy showed a tumor of the pituitary gland located at the base of the brain, where it was then considered extremely inaccessible from a surgical standpoint. During this same year Alfred Fröhlich, the Viennese neurologist who had been a fellow student in Sherrington's laboratory in July 1901, wrote him of a case with similar symptoms. Fröhlich had persuaded a surgical colleague to attempt operation, and the results proved favorable. This success of another in a situation where he himself had failed was a cause of chagrin to Cushing and immediately fixed his attention on the pituitary gland. But his knowledge grew slowly because he rarely encountered such cases.

In the meantime he worked at perfecting the operation for trigeminal neuralgia which had been his first venture into neurosurgery. In May 1903 he wrote his father: "Received (or will receive when the bill is paid) my first fee for a ganglion operation this month—my seventeenth case. Wish I had the nerve of Dr. ——— [a St. Louis surgeon who asked Cushing to attest to the lawyers of his deceased patient's estate that $3,500 was not exorbitant for a Gasserian ganglion operation]. I might in time make some money out of medicine."

He also concerned himself with similar problems—cases of facial paralysis, the virus infection called herpes zoster, and the relation of the Gasserian ganglion to the taste buds of the tongue. He worked, too, on devising technical instruments, among them the cranial tourniquet for the control of bleeding (no longer used, but at the time a distinct advance), and more efficient burrs and saws for penetrating the bony structure of the head.

While he was establishing himself in the field of neurosurgery, he made an important contribution to general medicine. When he had been in Italy, he had made a special journey to Pavia and the Ospidale di S. Matteo because he was interested in the blood-pressure apparatus of Riva-Rocci. Here he was given a model of the inflatable armlet which they used at the bedside—a much more practical means of taking blood pressure than the instruments then available in the United States.

Upon his return he immediately had blood-pressure readings added to the charts on which pulse and respiration were recorded. He made an initial report on his studies before the Wisconsin State Medical Society in June of 1902. A year later he and his friend George Crile of Cleveland were invited by W. T. Councilman to report on their blood-pressure studies in Boston. Cushing's paper was published a few months later under the title of "On Routine Determinations of Arterial

Tension in Operating Room and Clinic." Because of the interest aroused, a committee was formed at the Harvard Medical School to consider the importance of blood-pressure determinations in surgical diagnosis. After some deliberation, they came to the conclusion that the skilled finger was more accurate than any pneumatic instrument and dismissed the matter as of no importance. Despite this conservative Boston judgment, blood-pressure determinations became routine in medicine and surgery throughout the United States, and Crile's book on *Blood-pressure in Surgery* (1903) became widely used. In it he acknowledged that most of the interest in this country had been aroused by Dr. Harvey Cushing.

But although his work on blood pressure was important, it was only a by-product of his main concern—surgery. In November of 1903 he wrote his father: "I have been very busy all week. Have succeeded in getting my operative course started—no doghouse yet but still hopeful. Also have operated nearly every day, a baby with an occipital meningocele, removal of a thyroid for exophthalmic goitre, a brain tumor, etc." Later in the month there occurred a real event in his surgical career. A case of spinal cord tumor was admitted to the hospital and he not only diagnosed it correctly but made an accurate localization of the tumor and was successful in removing it. "It's the first case of the kind hereabouts," he told his father, "and really only happens about once in an operative lifetime."

Six months later, however, he had another spinal cord tumor. When the report of the case appeared, Cushing received a letter which pleased him so much that for years he kept it in his desk. It was still there when he died. The letter was short—"My dear Dr. Cushing: Just a line to tell you that Charlie and I have gone over your case in the Annals [of Surgery] for June with great interest. The Cleveland case—cerebral haematoma in the child which Dr. Crile told us about—is also great. It is evident that painstaking work will produce results, and an American Horsley has been found. Sincerely, W. J. Mayo."

The reference to cerebral haematoma was to a new operation that Cushing had been attempting. In making some investigations on cerebrospinal fluid, the increased pressure of which was such a hazard in brain operations, he had asked Dr. Kelly, head of the department of obstetrics, if he might perform autopsies on babies that were stillborn or had survived only a few days. He found in many instances that the cause of death had been an intracranial hemorrhage from birth injury —a cause, incidentally, of many of the spastic deformities in children who survive such hemorrhage. This fact was known, but many physicians thought an infant only a few days old could never survive a brain operation. Cushing proved this was not true. In 1905, at the annual meeting of the American Neurological Association, he gave a paper entitled "Concerning Surgical Intervention for the Intracranial Hemorrhages of the New-born" in which he summarized his experience with four cases.

In the autumn of 1904, Cushing wrote his father: "Very busy here. Was out of town yesterday operating on a cracked head—football injury with hemorrhage. Tapped the clot very luckily. Today a cerebellar tumor in a child. The successes are so far between in cranial work that when they come life is quite easy—the failures are very depressing." The Puckish sense of humor of a certain young reporter on the Baltimore *Sun* did not help matters either. He was wont to insert notices about people who had come long distances for operation, a few days later recording their death without comment. The fidelity of this reporter in following Dr. Cushing's efforts finally brought a protest from the Hopkins authorities.

But the publicity at least had the effect of making him known to the public as a brain surgeon. He stayed in Baltimore during the spring holiday in 1904 in the hope of getting some work, but none was forthcoming, and he told his father somewhat ruefully: "People have begun to think me a neurologist and the ordinary run of simple money-making things doesn't come my way. A lamentable condition which I am endeavoring to face without chagrin."

Although it didn't provide him with much of an income, his work was bringing him invitations to speak and calls to other university posts. There had been the University of Maryland professorship in 1902, and in 1904 Dr. W. W. Keen invited him to become his successor at Jefferson Medical College. Cushing considered the matter for two years—he was fond of Dr. Keen and there was much interest in neurology in Philadelphia—but he finally declined in 1906, just a few weeks before he received a letter from President Arthur T. Hadley of Yale asking him to come to New Haven to discuss a professorship of surgery in the Medical School.

If it had been difficult to come to a decision about the chair in Philadelphia, it was much more difficult to decline the post at Yale. In doing so he set down his convictions about medical education—convictions that were little altered as time progressed: "So far as I could see during my brief visit, the one pressing need of the School is a hospital with a continuous service for those occupying the clinical Chairs. Without a hospital in which they have clinical and teaching privileges *the year round*, clinical professors are as destitute of opportunities for instruction and investigation as a chemist or a physicist would be without a laboratory. And without such a hospital a medical school can hardly expect to develop."

He further pointed out the advantage, in furthering the reputation of a hospital, of the publications of a teaching staff. He advocated higher entrance requirements to ensure more mature students—students who in their fourth year could safely be given the freedom of the hospital wards. Until these conditions were present at Yale, he did not feel justified in giving up the opportunities offered at the Hopkins.

Although he elected to remain in Baltimore, such recognition was gratifying, as were the invitations to present papers at local and national meetings; they always meant hard work and long hours of preparation but gave him a chance to arouse interest in neurology and neurosurgery. He discussed the relation of the taste fibers to the trigeminal nerve before the American Physiological Society in Washington in December of 1902; reported on the surgical treatment of facial paralysis by nerve anastomosis at a meeting of the Philadelphia Neurological Society in February of 1903; spoke on "The Special Field of Neurological Surgery" at the Academy of Medicine at Cleveland; and was invited to address the Montreal Medico-Chirurgical Society in February of 1904. At this meeting he reported on his results with his first twenty Gasserian ganglion operations.

While in Montreal he was asked to operate on a cerebral tumor. Although he never liked to operate away from his own familiar surroundings, he reluctantly consented—fortunately with successful results. His return via Boston was hastened by news of a devastating fire which destroyed much of Baltimore's waterfront. Their own house was out of the path of the flames, but at one point the danger was sufficient to force Mrs. Cushing, who happened to be alone, to take young William to the Goodwillies and return for their precious Vesalius volumes.

In the autumn of 1903 there materialized the idea that had originated on a balustrade overlooking the Seine during the International Medical Congress in 1900, when William J. Mayo, A. J. Ochsner, and Cushing had decided that it would be profitable to form a small society of surgeons in the United States. This became known as the Society of Clinical Surgery and met twice yearly. "The Society is a sort of peripatetic one, the towns visited being supposed to furnish the entire program and to show the members what is being done in a teaching way, in research, in the matter of records and new things in a clinical and operative line. . . . They are all young and enthusiastic and I think we ought to make a good thing out of it."

Even though he now had a wife, a son, and a home, Cushing's absorption in his work kept him occupied almost as much of the time as it had before he assumed these responsibilities. On June 11, 1904 he wrote to Mrs. Cushing, who was in Cleveland visiting her mother with young William: "Isn't it awful to have forgotten that yesterday was our anniversary? Except that every day is a sort of anniversary with you and none seem particularly different. Still it would have been pleasant of me to have sent you a message at least. Will you forgive your thoughtless boy?" But it is probable that Kate Cushing, although she did not always find it easy to accept, guessed before they were married what pattern their life together would take.

KATHARINE CROWELL
From a daguerreotype of 1892

HARVEY CUSHING
His Christmas card in 1900

WILLIAM OSLER
Reproduced from a snapshot in H.C.'s 1904 diary
under which he had written "The Spirit of research"

PLATE 5

DR. CUSHING ON THE STEPS OF THE AMBULANCE AMERICAINE
Paris, 1915

PLATE 6

In July, Cushing and "Tammas" McCrae sailed for England with Dr. Osler to attend the Congress of the British Medical Association. The footworn steps at Oriel College in Oxford where they were being put up for the meetings brought back nostalgic memories of New Haven to Cushing. That evening the president of the British Medical Association welcomed them in the Sheldonian Theatre. It was a gorgeous spectacle, the fine old hall making a perfect setting for the white dresses and brilliant robes. Cushing and McCrae were surprised to discover their friend William MacCallum among the colonial delegates, and as the Association filed out, they "paralyzed MacCallum by shouting in unison 'MacCallums Carriage' like a lot of freshmen as they were calling the carriages of the distinguished guests."

The next day, again at the Sheldonian, degrees were conferred on several distinguished physicians, among them Osler. "I do not know when I have seen a more impressive ceremony, one which was so associated with ancient formalities that seem rightly to belong to a past generation of people." The candidates all wore flamingo gowns with slate gray sleeves and all received a great ovation but "nothing like that accorded Dr. Osler who showed his emotion by a pair of bright red cheeks as he took his seat."

Cushing attended two sessions of the Congress at which Victor Horsley spoke, for in the four years since his first encounter with Horsley he had come to appreciate something beyond his operative technique. "Very interesting talks," he recorded in his diary. "Horsley is a daisy." The rest of the week he explored Oxford, "doing" fifteen of the colleges, visiting bookstores and libraries. At the Radcliffe he told the Librarian he could not leave without seeing the first edition of William Harvey's *De motu cordis* (1628) and was promptly shown ten editions! Later he visited the Merton Library, "where many books are still chained to the shelves and where are old astrolabes and globes and beautiful carved oak shelves —'twould make in color and design and proportion an ideal library for a modern bibliophile who like these books would gladly remain chained to a shelf of such a room." His last commentary on Oxford was: "It is a despair to see such a place and ever to leave it; for it would take a life time, and more than one, to comprehend and enjoy it satisfactorily."

Back in London, after a hurried trip through the Midlands, he visited a few hospitals and followed the trail of the "Kit-Kat" poet, Dr. Garth, through bookstores, graveyards, and the British Museum. On August 5 he sailed home with Dr. Osler and McCrae. Although it had been a most stimulating holiday, he and McCrae returned with heavy hearts, for Dr. Osler had been offered the Regius Professorship of Medicine at Oxford. The suspense they were in as to whether he would accept was ended one day when Cushing picked up several sheets of paper that had fallen from Osler's berth and read on the first the scrap of a sentence: "The story of my acceptance of the Chair at Oxford may be briefly told."

Cushing's research during the summer on Dr. Garth took shape in December when he introduced the "Kit-Kat" poet to the Johns Hopkins Hospital Historical Club. When the paper (already described in Chapter XII) was published, it brought him a letter from Worthington C. Ford, the historian: "Many thanks for the copy of your essay on Dr. Garth—as good in substance as in dress, and with the flavor of a true critical biographer. I congratulate you upon possessing this literary taste and upon your use of it, for it means much fine essence for sweetening the drudgery of a professional life."

Next door, the man who had given Cushing the inspiration to do this kind of writing was preparing to withdraw his influence to a greater distance. Talk of books and medical history now had to be sandwiched in between patients (for everybody in the country wanted to come to Osler before he went), his sittings for a portrait, speech writing, and the many functions given in his honor. The tempo of the Osler household, always brisk, became hectic. But Osler remained his merry, cheerful self, and every time the Cushings slipped through the fence for a few minutes when the coast was clear, they went back carrying books and journals from Osler's shelves—gifts that would have delighted them were they not reminders that the happy days of living next door to the Oslers were numbered.

During the first months of 1905, Cushing spent from one to two hours a day writing for contributions toward a suitable tribute for Dr. Osler. He and Henry Barton Jacobs had taken the lead in the project and had received some $30,000 in pledges, but Dr. Osler's valedictory address, in which he made joking reference to Anthony Trollope's suggestion (in *The Fixed Period*) that those over sixty, having fulfilled their usefulness, should be chloroformed, was taken seriously by the American press and given such publicity in the newspapers that many of the pledges were subsequently withdrawn.

Furor, excitement, and sadness were thus mingled in Osler's last months in America. He was deeply distressed by the reaction he had unwittingly caused and in his last address, given at a large farewell dinner at the Waldorf-Astoria in New York, he said: "I have made mistakes but they have been mistakes of the head, not of the heart."

The Cushings bade the Oslers good-bye on May 16. The next day a demolition crew arrived to take down the house, and the hole in the fence was boarded up.

THE DOGHOUSE

Chapter XIV

ABOUT THE TURN OF THE CENTURY a Baptist minister in Montclair, New Jersey, was introduced to Osler's *Principles and Practice of Medicine* through a medical student who had formerly been in his congregation in Minneapolis. He was fascinated by the style and led on to read the whole book in detail, but he was at the same time appalled by Osler's frank admission that physicians could cure only four or five diseases, that in many instances about all that could be done for a patient was to give him good nursing care and alleviate his suffering as much as possible. He began to realize how neglected had been the scientific study of medicine throughout the world, for places such as the Koch Institute in Berlin and the Pasteur Institute in Paris were very rare and yet Pasteur's discoveries had saved a greater sum for the French nation than that spent on the Franco-Prussian War.

This man was the Reverend Frederick T. Gates, philanthropic adviser to John D. Rockefeller. On the basis of his reading of Osler's textbook he made recommendations to Mr. Rockefeller out of which grew the Rockefeller Institute for Medical Research and eventually the Rockefeller Foundation; and the movement thus started in medicine led to the founding in 1902 of the Carnegie Institution of Washington which Andrew Carnegie endowed with $10,000,000 for "the support of biological and chemical investigation of great importance to medical science."

While these great philanthropic institutions to support science were being set up, schools of medicine were facing the fact that the laboratory sciences—pathology, physiology, bacteriology—had developed to such an extent that they were now the strongest part of the curriculum. And the gap between the scientific discoveries of the laboratories and their application on the hospital wards was rapidly widening. It was clear that the clinical teachers must take the lead in bringing about changes in the hospitals which would ensure that the advances of the laboratory reached the sick patient. Lewellys Barker put it into words when he wrote Cushing: "The coming profession in the clinical branches must be an entirely new breed. We cannot put the new wine into the old bottles."

Harvey Cushing, who, for all his firm belief in the value of laboratory experimentation, never lost sight of the fact that the primary concern of all medicine was the good of the patient, approached the problem in a most realistic way. In May of 1902, very early in his teaching career, he addressed a memorandum to the Committee on Schedules in which he set forth his ideas for preparing a student to practise medicine by integrating his theoretical and his clinical work. The most important of his several suggestions was that the course in operative surgery (application of bandages, dressings, etc.) be started at the beginning of the third year to give the students practical work on animals and cadavers in preparation for their work in minor surgery in the out-patient department and operative clinic. He proposed that the course be given one entire afternoon a week ("possibly Saturday") throughout the year and that it be an elective. This memorandum brought a reply straight from the desk of the president, Daniel C. Gilman, who wrote: "Your suggestions are entitled to great weight," and asked that he stop in to discuss the matter with him.

The important points in Cushing's plan were adopted, and in October forty out of the forty-four men and women in the third-year class elected Cushing's course in operative surgery. Kate Cushing reported the general reaction to Dr. Kirke:

"Harvey has begun his clinic today with a new set of students. People say the nicest things about that course he gives. They all want to work in his laboratory." Cushing admitted to his father that he was much pleased with the response but that a smaller number would be easier.

The work involved in teaching a large group was well re-paid at the end of the year when he received a letter from G. Lane Taneyhill, Jr., W. R. Kellogg, and John B. Carr of the third-year class, saying that they had been asked to convey the class's appreciation of the value of the course—for the origi-nality in methods of teaching, the close personal attention, and the clearness of presentation of the underlying principles of operative surgery.

After struggling with the large group in inadequate quar-ters, Cushing began to agitate more actively for a project he had had in the back of his mind for some time. In June he wrote his father: "I wish to the devil they would build an animal house. A real good one such as we need would cost about $10,000 but I am inclined to plea for a shanty pro tem-pore which they could afford. We need a good animal *hospital* where the animals necessary could be cared for like patients and also where veterinary work could be done." His father replied promptly: "Anent the Dog Shanty business, if a few hundred dollars will avail in helping it on, why I think you can safely talk to me about it." When in the autumn Cushing reported: "Have succeeded in getting my operative course started—no dog-house as yet but still hopeful," his father again offered assistance: "On what are your 'hopeful' hopes as to the dog house founded; if upon H. M. H[anna]., I hope his brother Marcus has come out ahead in the Ohio voting today. Remember I asked to be kept informed so that I could help a little perhaps as I am quite sure your Mother would have liked to do it."

The following year he was "still hopeful" but still waiting. "I have had another spinal cord tumor case since writing you —cases come in duplicate. Also a dog, a large grey greyhound with a goitre which I removed Friday in the operative course. Much pleased thereat as it is the beginning of the '*comparative surgery'* work I am anxious to inaugurate. Oh! for an animal house. I have in small amounts raised $2400 and need $1200 more. Would this be a very inappropriate time to approach Mr. Hanna again?"

The great fire in Baltimore which caused such extensive financial losses to the University (because much of their income came from real estate which was destroyed by the fire) ended his hope for receiving any assistance from University sources, but H. M. Hanna, Robert Brewster of New York, and other interested friends finally subscribed $5,000, and with this amount as a nucleus, the University in 1905 constructed a laboratory at a cost of about $15,000 which would serve Cushing's needs and also those of the pathology department. After much thought and consideration the "doghouse" was named the Hunterian Laboratory after John Hunter, whose studies in comparative anatomy were unequaled.

In August the building was nearing completion. Cushing and MacCallum had decided to put the radiators on the ceiling to save floor space and because working next to them was often uncomfortable, and he asked his father what he thought of the idea. "It's an experiment of course, but then it is to be an experimental laboratory!"

Dr. Kirke was finally given an opportunity to make good his offer of financial assistance. They needed money for a microscope [1] and pictures of John and William Hunter—"to hang in the hall and to be an example and stimulus." A check for two hundred dollars arrived in the next mail from Cleveland. By December, Cushing was able to write him that "everyone is showing great interest in the new laboratory and I think we have started a new and original kind of place."

The name, Hunterian Laboratory, misled the public into thinking it had something to do with hunting dogs, but this was all to the good because it brought dogs to the Laboratory, and the surgery done on the canine population of Baltimore

---

[1] There is an amusing exchange in 1912 between H.C. and the superintendent at the Hopkins, for Cushing took the microscope with him when he left the hospital. He explained that since his father had given it, he had always regarded it as more or less his own!

was no less expert than that which their owners might receive in the hospital itself. The building was anything but beautiful architecturally, it reeked of carbolic, and under the hot Baltimore sun even less desirable odors became apparent, but the building was kept neat and clean by a small, wiry man named Jimmie who managed with equanimity to keep the various departments of the school supplied with experimental animals of the right size at the right moment. He managed the dogs with the same effective complacency, thus preventing complaints from people living near the laboratory. Cushing's word was law to him and if he said no work was to be done on Sunday, Jimmie maintained the edict no matter how urgent the requests.

Cushing now had the facilities to carry on the course as he wished. Surgical experience on cadavers was quite a different thing from experience on a living animal under anesthesia. Even before he had the laboratory in which to expand, he had begun to have the students write up histories, keep an ether chart during operations, make operative and postoperative notes and histological studies of tissues, and do a complete post-mortem examination if the animal died. The whole procedure, therefore, was carried on as if the dog were a human being. They usually began with a consultation of the "family physicians," in which the history of the patient was discussed and the diagnosis made. This was followed by the operation. The students worked in groups of four, one acting as operator, three others as first and second assistant and anesthetist.

Cushing followed the same plan in his course in operative surgery for graduates, held in May and June of each year. He often had in this class one or two of the local veterinarians with whom he had established cordial relations. He limited the number to sixteen and charged one hundred dollars for the course. This gave him sufficient income so that he could offer his university stipend of five hundred dollars to an assistant who could take some of the routine of the laboratory off his shoulders.

The first surgical assistant at the Hunterian was Philip K. Gilman, a graduate of the Class of 1905. He was followed by

J. F. Ortschild, Lewis L. Reford, Samuel J. Crowe, Emil Goetsch, Walter E. Dandy, and Conrad Jacobson. After a year in the Laboratory, several of these men became Cushing's assistant residents in surgery. Each year a report was published under the title "Comparative Surgery" and the first work of many of the men who were later outstanding in their profession appeared in these reports. It was here that Lewis H. Weed began his classic studies on cerebrospinal fluid, later carried on at Harvard. Walter Dandy, who was to rival Cushing as a neurosurgeon, did his first experimental work in the Hunterian, as did Herbert M. Evans, the discoverer of vitamin E. After 1908 almost everyone working there was engaged in research on some phase of the pituitary gland in which Cushing had become engrossed.

Interest in the work of the Hunterian spread. Dr. James C. Munro of Boston wrote Cushing: "I want to congratulate you on the new pathway you have broken in your work on comparative surgery." The *Sunday North American* of Philadelphia (July 23, 1905) carried a full-page article with pictures under the headline: "Pet dogs replacing human bodies in surgical demonstration: Some curious, humane experiments at Johns Hopkins." The text announced:

No longer will the dead human body, or "cadaver," be the main reliance in teaching operative surgery to medical students, if experiments recently made with success at the Johns Hopkins Hospital, Baltimore, are followed by other schools.

This departure is nothing less than the substitution of dogs or other animals for human bodies in surgical instruction. By operating upon living instead of dead bodies the student is enabled to observe the effect of his work upon normal tissues and nerves, and to control hemorrhage from arteries filled with flowing blood instead of coagulated masses. He is also impressed with the absolute necessity of asepsis, or surgical cleanliness, which otherwise he might fail to regard.

At first stray dogs were employed in the operations, but so favorably known are they becoming in Baltimore that the owners of valuable, though afflicted dogs, sometimes pets, are taking them to the hospital.

The reputation of the Hunterian for an interest in the treatment of pets had both its comical and its tragic side. One day one of the medical students returned to the Laboratory after lunch to find a small boy with tears streaming down his dirty face clutching a badly wounded dog. The student, recognizing that the dog was almost dead, gently tried to take it from him, but the small boy would not let him. He wanted Dr. Harvey Cushing—he wouldn't trust his dog to anybody less.

Letters like this from Dr. Hurd also came to Cushing.

My friend Mr. Kurtz (Jno. D. Lucas & Co.) has become very anxious about his cat and asks me to inquire if you will not take up her case. He seems to feel that while she may have but *one* life to live now, she may have *nine* eventually if the surgical operation is a success. I do not know what the trouble may be but I hope in the light of experience it may be a phantom hair ball. Please pardon me for my pernicious activity.

In Britain the work of the Hunterian Laboratory strengthened the hand of those fighting the antivivisectionists. Leonard Hill, a prominent London physiologist, asked for information on teaching operative surgery on animals to present to the Vivisection Commission, which had a bill before Parliament —"the information will be of great value to our colleagues in their up-hill fight." Victor Horsley, one of those who was constantly working for animal experimentation in England, also appealed to Cushing. "If you have *another* copy of your paper on your Surgical Laboratory would you let me have it. I want to refer to it at the Vivisection Commission." He later wrote: "I thought of you the other day & your class. If you want a cheerful exercise in the surgery of the cerebellum, I recommend the common duck, on whom we are doing some experiments at the present time, as calculated to break the proudest spirit."

The example set by the Hunterian was followed by other medical schools. The Surgical Laboratory at Harvard (administered by the Arthur Tracy Cabot Fellow) was patterned after it. In an account of the Hunterian Laboratory written in 1920, Cushing paid tribute to Halsted: ". . . Dr. Halsted

always had a problem on foot and came to the laboratory frequently during its early days. His custom . . . of giving his
juniors free swing with their own projects was what really
made the laboratory a possibility."

Cushing felt that the most gratifying tribute to the work
of the Laboratory was the recommendation by Abraham
Flexner, President of the Rockefeller Foundation, that $100,-
000 of the Rockefeller funds given to the Hopkins in 1912
be utilized for the enlargement of the Hunterian. That its
contributions were of inestimable value to the advancement
of medicine, there can be no doubt, and Cushing had a right
to be proud of the large part he played in its inception and the
early years of its growth to international recognition.

THE PATH BROADENS

Chapter XV

IN DECEMBER OF 1905, DR. WELCH
had written to Cushing: "I dare say that I should have known
that Mrs. Cushing is not going out, but no one ever tells me
anything of real, vital, human interest. I am sorry that I must
lose the pleasure of Mrs. Cushing's company, but I am glad
that there are such prospects awaiting your family." The
"prospect" arrived on January 27, 1906, and was christened
Mary Benedict.

A month after her arrival, her father was offered a post at
the University of Virginia and six months later one at the New
York Hospital, but again he decided to remain at the Hopkins,
where the new Hunterian Laboratory offered ideal opportunities for teaching and research. And in the back of his mind
there was still the thought of Harvard. Each time an invitation
came and he looked over the possibilities, he compared the
opportunities in his mind's eye with those in Boston, and each
time held off in the hope that what he desired would eventually
be offered to him.

In January the Oslers returned for a visit which Cushing
described in a letter home:

The Oslers are here—have been to luncheon in fact. It's very
good to see them again. They all look very well and even Dr. O
has a touch of English high color. He says it's port—not health.
It was very interesting to hear their tales of English—rather Oxford life—Rhodes Scholars, convocations, his rooms (John

Locke's) at Christ Church, the Ewelme Alms House and I know not what all. They are very funny about it all—Sunday service at Christ Church, for example, where the most tardy of the dons has to read the service. Dr. O consequently very prompt—usually calls a carriage and hustles the family up—scrabbles into his cap and gown and marches in to sit with the Fellows on the front bench, with a wink at Mrs. O as he passes by. She hopes to make him late enough some day to have to officiate.

When life returned to normal after the Oslers' departure, Cushing began work on two major papers which he had been invited to give at the meetings of the American Neurological Association and the Surgical Section of the American Medical Association, both to be held in Boston in June. At the first he discussed the causes of sexual infantilism and at the second, cases of spontaneous intracranial hemorrhage associated with birthmarks. In addition, W. T. Councilman had asked him to prepare a special exhibit for the A.M.A. meeting on the work of the Hunterian. These preparations, together with his concentrated operative course for graduates, a meeting of the Society of Clinical Surgery in Baltimore and another of bacteriologists and pathologists with the attendant entertaining, plus examinations, made almost everyone, he told his father, come off with poor digestions and fretful tempers.

Meantime Mrs. Cushing was struggling with the problem of getting two children, baby carriages, trunks, and servants ready for an escape from sweltering Baltimore to Westerly, Rhode Island, where she was to spend the summer. When the Boston meetings were over, Cushing and William MacCallum spent two days there sleeping, eating, and enjoying the country air before returning to their jobs.

Reunion in New Haven—Cushing's fifteenth—renewed body and spirit and was more of a vacation than the month he later spent at Westerly, for a manuscript on the surgery of the head, which Dr. Keen had invited him to contribute to his five-volume *System of Surgery*, was hanging over him and he spent most of his days working. "The life of an editor, I presume, must be a troublous one," he wrote his father when he had returned to Baltimore, "certainly that of an author is. Few do it so well and are so favored as Dr. Osler. I had a notice from Appleton to the effect that they have sold two printings (17,000 copies) of the present [*Principles and Practice of Medicine*]—the 6th Edition—and are going to set up another for the fall. Dr. Osler, too, had a good bargain with them—a dollar or more—perhaps two—a copy. They must have sold 117,500 copies since the beginning. Pretty good for a text book is it not? . . . There is little of news here. Futcher and I are keeping house together. . . . One of our neighbors has bought a talking machine (Edison) and another has married one, which is worse as the machine runs down and she doesn't."

December brought another visit from the Oslers—they having come over to celebrate W.O.'s mother's hundredth birthday. The Cushings gave a large reception and tea in their home. Over four hundred guests were invited, including almost everyone on the university, medical, and nursing staffs, as well as local Baltimore friends and out-of-town guests such as the Secretary of the Navy and his wife, Dr. Simon Flexner of Philadelphia, Dr. George Crile from Cleveland, and Dr. Charles Mayo of Rochester, Minnesota.

During the following year (1907), Cushing began imperceptibly to take Osler's place in the Johns Hopkins Historical Club. Welch was still a guiding spirit, always arranging dinners and taking a prominent part in the discussions, but he was coming to be so much in demand outside the Hopkins, particularly in his role as adviser to the Rockefeller Foundation, that the leadership fell more and more to Futcher and to Cushing, who served as president during 1907 and 1908. Little by little, too, they began sharing with the chiefs the responsibility for entertaining, in the Baltimore tradition, the distinguished guests who came to lecture at the University.

Early in January of 1908 the Cushings moved from 3 West Franklin Street into a house of their own, at 107 East Chase Street, which had electric lights "even in the cellar" (thus making furnace tending less of a chore), a large, sunny nursery, and the space they needed for their growing family. On May 18 a third child was born to them—a daughter, who was named Betsey after her grandmother. When she was but a month old, the family went on its annual pilgrimage northward. This was the second of many summers the Cushings were to spend at Little Boar's Head, situated on the short stretch of New Hampshire which borders on the ocean.

During the month of August when Cushing joined the family, he endeavored to sit still long enough for Edmund Tarbell to paint his portrait. In March Dr. Kirke had written: "I want a likeness of you, in oil, by the best artist in Baltimore, Philadelphia, or Washington, and will pay cash for same on demand. I will leave it to Kate after I am through with it." To this Cushing replied: "I'm afraid it's an awfully expensive business getting an oil portrait. Wouldn't a pastell satisfy you? I am at such a nondescript age and so whiskerless that I cannot imagine being portrayed even for your sake. If I was an infant or had reached a dignified old age and could wear an academic gown whose folds would be depicted, it would be different. However, I promised Kate to submit and we shall see what can be arranged."

The summer sittings were the result. Cushing told his father that since he could not combine them with reading, the time would have passed slowly had Tarbell not been amusing. Tarbell, however, found Cushing difficult to paint. Between sittings they played golf. Mrs. Cushing had interested him in the sport, for she had been before her marriage an excellent player, but although he enjoyed the game, he did not have a great deal of time for it in Baltimore during the school year. He reported to his father: "We are all brown and fat. Betsey and I are racing in matters averdupois and I think she leads. Furthermore, she is very good and cunning, which is more than I can say for myself."

He worked during this vacation also on his section for Dr. Keen's textbook (surgery of the head). On one occasion when Keen had enquired as to when he might expect the manuscript, he apparently had received a peppery reply, for we find him writing a soothing letter in return: "I shall feel very badly if I have been the cause of your being 'swearing mad.' I am sure when you have written the chapter and see it in print, you will be so proud of your baby that you will be 'swearing glad.' "

He went on to tell Cushing that his drawings were as good as any he had ever seen and that he would be glad to have as many as the article required.

When the manuscript was finally delivered, it was Keen's turn to be disturbed, for instead of the 80 pages he had asked for, Cushing had delivered 800 with 154 illustrations. After his first concern, Keen was appeased by the excellence of the manuscript. It was published in 1908 in a monograph of 273 pages.[1] The book stands as Cushing's first systematic treatise on brain surgery and definitely established him as the leader in the new specialty. Sir Victor Horsley congratulated him "on presenting a succinct & yet thorough account of such a complex subject. I hope and feel sure it will do a large amount of good for it is extraordinary what lack of knowledge of common methods still persists."

Cushing's growing reputation brought him both students and an increasing number of patients. His surgical load had now become so heavy that he was compelled to ask Halsted for an assistant of his own in neurosurgery. He first approached Ernest Sachs, a promising young graduate of the Hopkins who was interested in entering the field of neurosurgery, but he was in England at the time, studying with Horsley, and felt he could not leave the work he was doing. Finally Halsted let him have his own assistant resident, George Heuer. Two students who sought him out at this time were John Homans, a young surgeon of unusual ability whom Maurice Richardson had sent down from Harvard, and Robert M. Yerkes, a psychologist, also from Harvard,[2] who was interested in learning surgical and aseptic technique.

During this year two more chairs of surgery were offered Cushing—one at Rush Medical College in Chicago and the other at the Bellevue Medical School in New York, but Cushing declined both because he had begun some research in the

[1] During the First World War the book was reprinted by the Surgeon General and used as an Army handbook on traumatic surgery of the head.

[2] He later became the distinguished professor of psychobiology at Yale whose primate laboratory at Orange Park, Florida, is well known.

Hunterian Laboratory that was too engrossing to interrupt. In April, Professor Edward Sharpey-Schaefer, the eminent Scottish physiologist who had worked with Horsley on a number of experiments, was invited to Baltimore to give the Herter Lectures. That he should have come into Cushing's orbit at this juncture when Cushing was beginning to meet with some success in his brain operations was of considerable significance in his subsequent career. On four evenings Sharpey-Schaefer spoke on different aspects of the pituitary gland, and Cushing's interest in the gland, hitherto unexplored because of more pressing problems, was intensely aroused. Indeed, he could think of little else.

He began to delve into the literature on abnormalities of growth—to be interested in acromegaly and gigantism and in dwarfs and the sexually undeveloped. Acromegaly, a disease of the pituitary associated with enlargement of the bony structure of the hands and feet and with coarsening of the skin of the face (as opposed to gigantism which is abnormal growth in adolescence), was first described in 1884 by the German pathologists, Fritsche and Edwin Klebs. Two years later Pierre Marie, the French neurologist, named the condition acromegaly, and it was he who expressed the belief that it was caused by a tumor of the pituitary gland.

Adiposity and sexual immaturity (called Fröhlich's syndrome because of the case he had described in 1901) were also thought due to an enlarged pituitary, since, at operation, Fröhlich's case proved to have a tumor of the gland. Cushing immediately started research in the Hunterian. He set John Homans and his surgical assistant of that year, Samuel J. Crowe, to removing the pituitary gland from dogs. Most of them died, but one day when Cushing was looking at a particularly fat, logy, sexless animal that had survived the operation, there flashed into his mind that here was Fröhlich's asexual adiposity—caused by *lack of secretion* from the pituitary. Acromegaly and gigantism, therefore, must be due to oversecretion of the gland. This fact was beginning to be recognized, but the asexual adiposity had been confusing because it likewise seemed due to enlargement of the hypophysis, or pituitary.

Homans was with Cushing when he made this observation. "It was Cushing's quickness and insight in connecting the hypophysial adiposity of the dog with the Fröhlich syndrome which straightened out the confusion and made Cushing the leader in this field. I remember well how quickly his imagination leaped from the hitherto overlooked fat, asexual dog to the whole picture of the hypophysial disease." The door was now open to a new understanding of pituitary disorders and to the whole field of endocrinology. Cushing began to turn his energies and ingenuity to devising a feasible surgical approach to the gland. On December 30 he gave an address before the American Physiological Society for which he chose the challenging title: "Is the Pituitary Gland Essential for Life?"

Cushing was not the only member of the family who was attracting public attention at this time. Late in November a new laboratory of experimental medicine, made possible through the generosity of Mr. Howard M. Hanna and Colonel Oliver H. Payne, was dedicated at Western Reserve University. It was named the Henry Kirke Cushing Laboratory of Research. Dr. Welch gave the principal address, and Cushing attended as an official delegate of Johns Hopkins University. Kate Cushing wrote Dr. Kirke: "Harvey has just left. Tomorrow will be a proud day for the Cushings! I wish I might have gone with him on this great occasion—nothing but Betsey would prevent."

In January of 1909, Dr. Arthur Tracy Cabot of Boston wrote Cushing about a personal friend on whom he had operated four years previously and who was now having a return of symptoms. Cabot wrote guardedly because his patient was the popular and prominent Major General Leonard Wood, well known to the public for his outstanding service during the Spanish-American War and his subsequent governor-generalship of Cuba, during which he had virtually eliminated the scourge of yellow fever from the island.

In 1898 General Wood had struck his head on a low chandelier, and a few years later a tumor had begun to develop at the site of his injury. The area of bone containing the tumor had been removed by Dr. Cabot, and since the present symptoms were a weakness in the arm and leg of the opposite side, Cabot was loath to believe that it indicated a return of the tumor. Cushing, however, diagnosed it as such, but since it appeared slow-growing, he decided to proceed cautiously and recommended that operation be postponed.

Early in January W. T. Councilman sent him suggestions for his paper before the Harvard Cancer Commission: "It is very important that we should have represented here what the intracranial tumor means; the gradually increasing pressure within the brain; the variations in rapidity of growth; the whole clinical phenomena. . . ."

The Oration in Surgery for the American Medical Association to be delivered at Atlantic City in June on "The Hypophysis Cerebri" kept Cushing rushed during May. He wrote to Mrs. Cushing, who had by then taken "the caravan" to Little Boar's Head, that "the Oration went off O.K., I think, though I do not believe many of them knew what I was talking about. There was a large crowd and they kept coming in and I had to wait several times for quiet so that it was rather disjointed. Still it was a good paper, wasn't it? And some day they will find that 'Sam' [Crowe] and 'John' [Homans] and I helped straighten out the hypophysis question in the winter of 1908-09." To his father he said: "I think of little else than the pituitary body nowadays—a poor solace, however, for an empty house."

But he found some solace in daily, or almost daily, letters to Kate Cushing, a few of which follow:

June 14, 1909. My ganglion case went badly today—3 hours— all tied up in the scars of the previous operation. Will have to try again in a few days. Much exhausted and a German Geheimrath Prof. looking over my shoulder all the time. . . . That washerwoman!! My shirts were simply eaten to pieces—great holes. Says she used the "gold dust" which you have always allowed Susie to use. Found it in the laundry indeed! I gave her a good scare and will buy some new shirts.

June 15, 1909. Hospitaling all day and a lady to tea. Fear not. She's a suffragette—friend of Allie Porter's—M.D. Glasgow—over here studying osteopathy!! Which she intends to practice. Rather like Mrs. Porter and quite able to take care of herself. I sicked her on to Miss Sabin—only took one cup of tea.

I can't remember our anniversary nor when Betsey was born but I know your birthday.

June 24, 1909. It's my turn to be depressed. I lost a little boy today with a brain tumor—most unexpectedly—and his poor people are terribly broken up. This is only one of many troubles. I never had such a lot of bad cases at one time before. I guess it's because my judgment is not very good just now. . . . Much love from your most lonesome H.

Baltimore about the hottest in the country 90-94, but I stand it well.

July 2, 1909. Hotter'n Tophet again. Glad you are having some tennis and swims. You'll be feeling very sturdy—good preparation for our jaunt abroad.

It's a good thing you stirred up Tarbell. These artists are procrastinators. Alice probably won't have it in the house. I know she thinks it was a shocking expense and I hope the Pater has not told her what it really cost.

What are you knitting? Good thing. You may have to teach me some day. We will spend our evening years on the back porch ruminating on the past—knitting side by side.

July 6, 1909. I'm just hustling off to the dentist's—teeth full of cloth and all askew—very cross. Age 40 and need repair—much porcelain. You can't drop me now or I'll break.

Still cool weather. The writing goes fairly well. Hope to have the first draft ready by the end of the week—then the going over which takes much time.

July 24, 1909. A check from your Mother for "sidesteps" abroad. I will deposit it in your acc't at the bank where it will do most good, I judge. I'll pay for the sidesteps. . . .

Gen'l Wood wants us to spend the night at Governors Island —will send us to the Lusitania in a gov't tug with a brass band.

Glad that his operation has been postponed; for everyone dies that I touch. Have had a dreadful tumor mortality this month. Another case today—again tomorrow. Are you keeping your fingers crossed?

In another letter, written in an injured, husbandly tone (called forth because Mrs. Cushing had apparently overdrawn her bank account), he revealed himself to be, beyond the shadow of a doubt, his father's son.

You know how I hate this sort of thing. I don't see how you could have mistaken your bank acc't to this extent. If there is one thing in the world to be punctilious about it's the *prompt!* payment of debts. . . . Whenever you are behind you can come to me and get funds as you know but this pushing off of settlements until the last minute when there is no wherewithal to meet them is paralyzing and destroys your and my credit with banks and trades people. . . . So you see it's poor economy as well as a bad principle. It's one of the things I want firmly grounded in the children's minds as they grow up.

On July 27 Dr. and Mrs. Cushing embarked on the *Lusitania* for Liverpool, after a gay send-off by Grosvenor Atterbury, his father, and the Atterburys' guest, Mr. J. P. Morgan, which included dining at Sherry's and attending the Follies of 1909. This was their first trip abroad together, and they made a point of visiting many of the places that Mrs. Cushing knew from H.C.'s letters of 1900 and 1901.

Cushing's first duty was the William Banks Memorial Lecture at Liverpool, for which he had chosen the title "Recent Observations on Tumours of the Brain and their Surgical Treatment." He wrote his father that "the lecture went off well enough and they ceremonially dined us and toasted us, to Kate's embarrassment." This over, they hurried to Oxford.

At the Bodleian Library they studied the six anatomical plates which Vesalius had issued before he completed his book, the *Fabrica*. Only two original sets existed, and this copy, which Osler had borrowed from Sir John Stirling-Maxwell, was one of them. Both men were of course greatly excited, and Cushing took two rolls of film of the various pages.

On August 11 the Cushings went up to London, and while

Mrs. Cushing went to art galleries, H.C. visited hospitals, the Hunterian Museum, bookshops, and the tailor. At the Hunterian, Cushing was impressed anew at the extent of John Hunter's collections—"John's collossal industry is paralyzing when one sees his things spread out." He was also much taken with Sir Arthur Keith, the Curator: "The new Conservator, Keith by name, is a daisy—a fit successor to those gone before." One evening before they left for the Continent they dined with one of Britain's foremost neurologists, Henry Head, and Gordon Holmes, who was on his way to similar distinction.

On their way to Berne the Cushings traveled through Holland and from The Hague H.C. wrote home: "We got here this morning [August 15] at the unseemly hour of 7 having been routed out of our steamer at the Hook at 5 A.M.!! It was a fine cold misty Dutch morning full of cows and dykes and sabots and windmills." He spent an hour studying Rembrandt's School of Anatomy:

> Tulp's hands are the most wonderful part of it to me though I dislike even more than in the familiar prints the way he is holding and apparently crushing the muscle with a heavy pair of forceps like modern clamps. The whole composition is of course marvellous and it's curious how inconspicuous the cadaver is in spite of its ghastly greyish blue color—actually the lightest part of the whole picture; more so against the black coats of the graduate onlookers.

When they reached Berne, the Kroneckers, the Kochers, the Michauds, and many others gave them a royal welcome, and they spent several happy days there resting up for their next objective—the International Medical Congress in Budapest at which Cushing was to give a paper. They went by way of Munich, where they were met by Dr. MacCallum, and thence to Vienna, where Alfred Fröhlich entertained them.

The opening session of the Congress on August 29 was a "very gorgeous but piping hot affair" where there was too much noise and too many people to hear and see very well.

But the pomp and ceremony, the color of elaborate uniforms and academic gowns, and the distinction of the vast gathering was fascinating. Here were collected the most eminent names in medicine from every country—in a half-professional, half-holiday mood. Cushing's own paper was read on September 2 —late and to a dwindling audience because he had been detained by Sir William Macewen, who insisted on eating a leisurely lunch.

When the Congress was over, the Cushings went to Venice, whose enchantments H.C. had so longed to share on his first visit there in the spring of 1901. They spent the first sunny, cloudless day in and out of gondolas, ending with a swim at the Lido and return by sunset. The next day, while Cushing looked for Vesalian items, Mrs. Cushing went to find the Bellini portrait that had reminded her husband of her when he had first seen it. They then went on to Florence, where the Uffizi, bookshops, Vesalius, Titian, the National Library, lunch on spaghetti with chicken livers, chops, cheese, and Chianti left them "worn but courageous." The next five days were spent in Milan, the Italian lake country, Bellagio, Lausanne, and finally Paris, whence they sailed for home. They parted in New York, Mrs. Cushing returning to her family in Little Boar's Head, and H.C. to Baltimore.

Chapter XVI

Early in 1910 Cushing went to Cleveland to speak again on "The Special Field of Neurological Surgery." Five years had passed since his first paper, and he had encouraging progress to report. In all, he had had up to that date 180 patients suffering with some type of brain tumor. Of the last one hundred cases there had been eight operative deaths in the first fifty, and only three in the second. This was partly due to the fact that patients were beginning to present themselves before the outlook was completely hopeless, since early signs of tumor were being recognized more readily. Patients less frequently arrived at the clinic already blind, because ophthalmologists had become aware of what conditions indicated pressure on the optic nerves. Mortality statistics had also been reduced through increased knowledge of the factors important for surgical success:

They are ticklish performances, these operations for tumor, and demand not only a rigorous regard for detail, such as the patient's position on the table and the choice of the anaesthetic, coupled with the highest skill in its administration, but also a thorough knowledge of the diverse tricks of controlling haemorrhage from scalp, meninges and brain, with a full understanding at the same time of the cerebrospinal fluid circulation under states of tension; for this latter is really one of the keynotes of success in these difficult problems.

While in Cleveland, Cushing received a telegram from Mr. Abraham Flexner, then head of the Carnegie Foundation for the Advancement of Teaching, asking him to come to New York. His object was to offer Cushing the chair of surgery at the Washington University School of Medicine in St. Louis, which was to receive an endowment of two million dollars for reorganization on the Hopkins model. It would be a challenging opportunity, offering free scope for his ideas and with ample resources for implementing them. It was a real threat at last to his long-held thought of Harvard.

While he was considering the matter, the problem of whether or not he would operate on Major General Leonard Wood again confronted him. The General's symptoms had gradually grown more severe and it seemed as if the time had come for surgery if he were to improve. He strongly urged Cushing to operate, but the possibility of losing such a prominent man and servant of the country filled Cushing with apprehension. Nevertheless, he made up his mind to go ahead and on February 5 made what proved to be a first attempt, for the bleeding was so profuse that it was thought wise to replace the bone flap and attack the tumor itself at another operation.

The second stage was scheduled for February 9. The day before, Arthur T. Cabot, General Wood's close friend and former surgeon, arrived in Baltimore at Cushing's suggestion to be on hand for the procedure. This time by slow dissection a large tumor was carefully tilted out. The patient stood the four-hour session well, the wound healed without complication, and eleven days later General Wood was walking about his room. Dr. Cabot was most favorably impressed. "He had never seen an operation of the kind," Cushing wrote, "—no more had I." It was his first successful experience with a meningeal tumor—the most difficult to remove because they are so vascular—and his first complete (or so he thought) removal of a tumor. Because General Wood's illness would have caused national concern, his presence in the hospital was kept as quiet as possible and he was able to leave shortly thereafter with only a brief mention in the newspapers of the fact that he had been hospitalized for repair of an old wound.

Cushing's elation over the success of the operation was dimmed immediately by word from Cleveland that his father was ill. Dr. Kirke had felt poorly during the first days of February and on the 8th was confined to bed with anginal pain alternating with light cerebral attacks which caused temporary loss of speech and paralysis of his right hand. On the 9th, the day of the second-stage operation, Harry Cushing wrote H.C.: "I read father your letter half an hour ago. He had another attack this noon, longer and more severe, it seems to me, than the one yesterday, from which he has rallied however. He insists that I answer your note, telling you not to come unless sent for, and giving you all his love, and I therefore do so, as instructed."

On the 10th there was a telegram from Ned: "Fair night. Rather more comfortable. No return of anxious symptoms. Demurs at your coming but I know will be very glad to see you." Cushing arrived on the 11th, barely in time, for his father died that night shortly after midnight. His affairs proved to be in perfect order, as he had endeavored to keep them all of his eighty-three years, and his children discovered that although most of his suits were well worn, he had saved one to be buried in.

The esteem with which Dr. Kirke was held in Cleveland was expressed in unreserved terms that his own reticence would have forbidden during his lifetime. The tribute of his eldest son, William, in reminiscences written for the family, would have pleased him, especially the statement that "he remained, up to his brief final illness, in full command and control of himself and of his affairs." But the tribute that would doubtless have moved him most deeply came from outside his family. It was a memorial adopted by his fellow members in the Rowfant Club.

. . . To us he was the cultured booklover, the collector of portraits, and the lover of Cleveland's quaint and historic scenes. . . . He had an affection for the last Indian, the old names, the founders of our institutions; he remembered the Ohio City, the bridges in the hollows, the boys' old trysting places on the flats, the trignale, the Ark, the early civic and social discouragements and triumphs, in many of which he participated. . . .

We were the privileged ones. To us he was the charming raconteur, to others, the austere and learned physician. While others may have profited from the fruits of his labors, we had the aroma of his life. He loved these rooms when empty and when full. He enjoyed their charm alone or at the board. Even when his eighty years weighed heavy on him and the grasshopper became a burden, and his ear dull, his erect form, draped in his great gray cloak, sprinkled perchance with snowflakes, would come in past the candle, and he would take a place amongst us, be one of us, and grow young again. . . .

Toward the end of March, Cushing had a letter from Mr. Lowell, President of Harvard. It was not an offer of the coveted chair, but it announced the fact that it would be offered to him. Arthur T. Cabot was a member of the Harvard Corporation—apparently his visit to Baltimore and news of the developments in St. Louis had finally stirred Harvard to action. In the meantime the people at Washington University were bringing all possible pressure to bear. "Things moved along pretty actively for a while," Cushing wrote some years later, "But I wobbled a little owing to Edsall's final withdrawal [he had been offered the chair of medicine]; father's death upset me greatly, and St. Louis seemed very far away."

In his moment of triumph, Cushing sorely missed his father's counsel, and Ned took his place as confidant. On April 23 he wrote: "I think your letter to the Brigham Hospital people is good and ought to help them see the light, whatever the outcome of your personal problem. I have gathered that they are a pretty conservative group of folks and very positive in their conceptions. . . . I wish I could thrash over with you all the pros and cons of the St. Louis-Boston propositions."

On April 12 Cushing received letters from A. Lawrence Lowell and Alexander Cochrane, President of the Board of Trustees of the Peter Bent Brigham Hospital, offering him the position of Surgeon-in-Chief of the Hospital and a professorship in the Harvard Medical School. He was to be appointed to the senior chair in surgery, the Moseley Professorship, then occupied by his former teacher and long-time friend, Maurice Richardson, upon Dr. Richardson's retirement.

The Harvard Medical School had never had a teaching hospital under its control (as did the Johns Hopkins) until the Peter Bent Brigham Hospital became affiliated with it. An informal arrangement with the Massachusetts General Hospital and the Boston City Hospital had filled this need. In 1872 Peter Bent Brigham, a merchant who had peddled fish on the streets of Boston when he had first come from Bakersfield, Vermont, left $1,300,000 to be held in trust for twenty-five years and then used for founding a hospital for indigent persons in the County of Suffolk. When the hospital was begun in 1911, the estate had grown to $6,250,000, of which $1,250,000 was to be used for the building, leaving the balance for endowment. The clinical material in its wards was to be available to the students of the Harvard Medical School, which was to have a voice in the control of the hospital—sometimes a larger voice than the Board of Trustees of the Brigham deemed appropriate.

The land for the hospital had been bought in 1907 on Huntington Avenue near the Harvard Medical School, and John Shaw Billings had been consulted about the plans for the building. Cushing himself at one time had met with Dr. Billings and Dr. Welch at the Maryland Club to discuss the plans. However, it was not expected that the hospital would be open to the public until 1912, and Cushing in the meantime would remain in Baltimore, carrying on by letter arrangements for the hospital organization and the planning of the building with Henry A. Christian, who was to be Physician-in-Chief and Professor of Medicine. Christian was a Hopkins graduate of 1900 and had had his later training under Osler. He and Cushing had thus acquired many of the same traditions.

A flood of congratulatory messages poured in on Cushing when his decision became known. Along with those on the Harvard appointment, the Cushings also received congratulations on the birth of a second son, on May 22, who was named Henry Kirke Cushing. Because of young Henry, Mrs. Cushing did not accompany her husband when he sailed for England on June 22 with the Society of Clinical Surgery to visit hospitals and clinics in Liverpool, London, Edinburgh, Newcastle, and Leeds. They attended demonstrations arranged by Sir Victor Horsley, spent a day at Oxford with Osler, and dined with the Royal College of Surgeons in Edinburgh.

September at Little Boar's Head was largely devoted to a paper on controlling bleeding in cerebral operations by the use of silver clips. This was the first description of the clip Cushing had devised—a valuable aid in brain operations which is still used today. He also did some preliminary work on a paper on disorders of the pituitary for the Harvey Lecture to be given on December 10—his tenth paper during the year.

In March of 1911 Cushing had word from Cleveland that Ned Cushing was seriously ill. It was discovered that nothing could be done, for he had an inoperable carcinoma of the bowel. While waiting helplessly for the end, H.C. wrote in agony of spirit: "In a short while I shall be the last of the Cushing doctors. A little more than a year ago there were three of us. Now Neddie is dying in a near room in a most beautiful and ecstatic euthanasia." Death came on the 25th, bringing deep grief not to his family alone, but to much of Cleveland, for as professor of pediatrics at Western Reserve and a practising physician he was widely known and greatly loved. Cushing's only comfort was that his father had been spared the knowledge of Ned's premature death.

A month later he was offered the chair of surgery at Western Reserve, but even if his future had not been settled, he would have found it difficult to return to a Cleveland that no longer held his father and brother.

To take his mind off his loss, he buried himself in work. In June he crossed the Mississippi for the first time to give a paper on "Distortions of the Visual Field" at the annual meeting of the American Medical Association in Los Angeles. He stayed with Dr. W. Jarvis Barlow, the founder of the Barlow Sanatorium there, who shared his interest in medical history.

His Harvey Lecture of the preceding year formed the basis of a book for which he had been collecting material since he first became interested in the pituitary. During the summer of

1911 he commenced work in earnest, signing on August 31 a contract with J. B. Lippincott for a book 300-350 pages in length with 150-200 illustrations (the book when published ran to 341 pages with 319 illustrations). He was to have the completed manuscript in their hands by October 7. On September 1 he wrote to Mrs. Cushing at Little Boar's Head: "Still at it. . . . It's going to sell for $4.00 and if they sell 2,000 copies I'll be given 10% on all back ones. I'll give you all my royalties!!! for being so patient. It's foolish to think I can finish it before September 15th but I'm going to pretend that I can. . . . I get up at 7 (when I don't oversleep) and work till eleven, then hospital till 4 and come home and work till eleven. There are about 300 illustrations." These were largely photographs of patients in various stages of pituitary malfunction—fat people, giants, pygmies, bearded ladies, etc. He added, "There ain't nuthin' the hypoph can't do."

The book appeared in 1912 under the title, *The Pituitary Body and Its Disorders. Clinical States Produced by Disorders of the Hypophysis Cerebri*, and was dedicated "In loving memory of three physicians: Erastus Cushing (1802-1893)—Henry K. Cushing (1827-1910)—Edward F. Cushing (1862-1911)." Based on a detailed study of fifty cases, the book was not only an important contribution to endocrinology, but a milestone in the history of American medicine.

Cushing had pointed out earlier that the "hypophysis and the ductless glands in general so influence the function of every organic process that they overlap into every individual specialty." The main contribution of the pituitary volume was the elucidation of this influence, especially the effects of undersecretion of the gland (hypopituitarism), oversecretion (hyperpituitarism), and recognition of the clinical signs of such malfunction. The numerous photographs were most effective in portraying the resultant changes which take place in the body.

It was believed that the anterior lobe of the gland was essential to life and bore close relationship to the disturbances of growth (acromegaly, gigantism, and forms of infantilism). The posterior lobe, on the other hand, was closely bound up with water metabolism. In his microscopical studies, Cushing had discovered that the eosinophilic cells of the anterior lobe (those that stained readily with a dye called eosin) secreted the growth hormone, but the function of the other cells in the lobe, the so-called basophilic cells, still baffled him. Twenty years were to elapse before he knew the answer.

The monograph thus approached the pituitary gland from every aspect—anatomically, physiologically, pathologically, and, of course, surgically. Horsley and others had attempted a few operations on the pituitary, but the results had not been encouraging. After the publication of the pituitary monograph, pituitary operations were undertaken with more confidence and eventually came to be routine.

The book aroused much comment. Halsted wrote: "This morning the book has arrived, and I am greatly pleased to have it. It reminds me forcibly of my shortcomings, of which I have been daily conscious for many years." Osler called it *"a ripper"* which "opens several new chapters in cerebral physiology, to say nothing of metabolism. The figures are excellent. What a lot of work you must have put into it! It is very nice to see the dedication to the three generations but 'tis very sad that poor Ned did not have a chance to live out his days." J. Collins Warren, his professor of surgery at Harvard, wrote: "Please accept my thanks for remembering me with a copy of your splendid monograph on the pituitary body. . . . I am taking the book to the country to learn the new surgery—so as not to get too far behind in the procession. With such progressive leaders as yourself, this is no easy task." Harvey Cushing had indeed opened the book of surgery to a new place.

At the end of the year Osler said to him: "I hope you are going to take a good year 'off' before you settle in Boston. You certainly should do so, as you have had the topsails set and a pretty stiff breeze behind you for a good while." But for Cushing there was never any rest. He had become interested in a variety of subjects, for the pituitary had led him into several byways. With Emil Goetsch, who had been surgical assistant at the Hunterian in 1909-10, he had studied the phenomenon of hibernation, believing that the pituitary was involved. With Conrad Jacobson, who followed Goetsch, he had investigated the absorption of carbohydrates, having become interested in the relation of the pituitary to sugar metabolism because his acromegalic patients frequently had diabetes. This brought him into touch with his former classmate, Elliott Joslin, now a world-renowned specialist in diabetes. His interests ranged over so wide an area that his friends accused him of trying to relate every new clinical entity to the pituitary.

In 1912-13 he had started his current assistant, Lewis Hill Weed (Hopkins 1912), on experiments on the cerebrospinal fluid. He had also engaged another graduate of the Class of 1912, Clifford B. Walker, to work with him on ophthalmological problems. Since tumors often pressed on the optic nerve, causing visual disturbances, he had set up his own darkroom for the study of the visual fields. Their collaboration resulted in a number of papers which stand as classics in the field of ophthalmology.

Some of Cushing's theories about the pituitary and its influence on bodily function were proved erroneous in the light of later knowledge, but they served to set men to thinking and working on the problem. His method of experiment was for the most part based on inductive reasoning. Rather than making deductions from an assemblage of facts, he was inclined to postulate a theory and then set out to prove it. There would have been no quarrel with this method if, when proven wrong, he had been willing to abandon his theories and start on another bent. But Cushing, unfortunately, in pride and stubbornness clung to his ideas and more than once wasted the time of his assistants trying to prove the impossible.

In the meantime the walls of the Brigham Hospital were slowly rising, and letters passed frequently between Cushing and Christian, Alexander Cochrane, President of the Board of Trustees, and John Reynolds, Chairman of the Building Committee. Many things cropped up to mar the serenity of their days. Cushing found it difficult to concentrate on practical details of the building because it was almost impossible for him

CUSHING CHILDREN
*Betsey, Mary, William holding Barbara, and Henry
Christmas, 1915*

PLATE 7

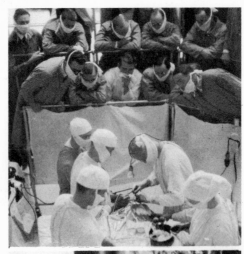

above
OPERATING BEFORE THE HARVEY CUSHING SOCIETY, 1932
below
WRITING THE OPERATIVE NOTE AFTER
2000TH TUMOR OPERATION, 1931
Courtesy of Richard U. Light

PLATE 8

to visualize anything from plans—he only knew (and that quite definitely) whether or not he liked it when it was done. This left much of the burden to Christian who, however, was in Boston so that it was a little easier for him to make decisions. When the work seemed to go along slowly, Cushing badgered Mr. Cochrane, and again Henry Christian acted as go-between —explaining Cushing to Mr. Cochrane and vice versa.

But gradually the difficulties and problems were resolved. The admission of private patients to a hospital intended for the indigent sick was decided on the theory that the indigent would greatly profit by the presence of paying patients. The plan for organization which outlined personnel, salaries, retirement age (sixty-three), and made special point of emphasizing the importance of autopsies to the success of the hospital, was adopted by the Brigham Trustees virtually as Christian and Cushing had drawn it up.

During the summer of 1912, while Mrs. Cushing and the children were at Little Boar's Head, Cushing began to finish off his work in Baltimore. From June to July he was in Europe, again with the Society of Clinical Surgery, this time to visit the German clinics. Cushing left the party long enough to make a hurried trip to Berne for Professor Kocher's *Jubileum*— "it really was fine—the music especially—a great chorus of male voices; and when they sang *Mein Heimatland* it made things run up and down your spine. . . . A great crowd— many notables. Kocher made a gift to the University of $40,000—his Nobel Prize I guess—for the establishment of a research laboratory. Then there was a great banquet at which I sat between Kronecker and von Monakow, the psychiatrist— very amusing time. A lot of people I knew. . . . It really was bully and well worth the wear and tear of two long nights on a German *Schlafwagen*."

Cushing bought a car during this summer which he spelled variously "Cadilac," "Cadallac," and finally, "Cadillac." He looked upon it with somewhat doubtful pleasure—"I enjoy it, but feel as though I had an elephant on my hands. Some day it will step on me and squnch me." His reaction was akin to that of his father when in 1899 he bought his first "electric"—

"Can say of it as Carlyle said of the Emersonian periodical, the 'Dial', 'I love your Dial but it is with a kind of shudder.' "

There were many problems—buying a house in Boston, arranging for its redecoration, getting bank accounts transferred, engaging additional house staff, and much else. On August 7 he sent a clipping which announced that "Dr. Harvey Cushing Buys in Brookline . . . the old-fashioned residential property at 305 Walnut Street. . . . The parcel comprises a handsome colonial house, combination stable and garage, formal garden, beautiful shrubs and trees, and about 121,457 sq. ft. of land." To Mrs. Cushing he wrote: "We're getting altogether too much notice. You'll have to wear a quieter hat, and I'll raise some whiskers and hide myself behind 'em—perhaps some spinach from your garden will do. I suppose you think you're going to drive around Brookline like Mrs. J. Gardner and have a Vermeer on your wall and Gustave up in front and Joseph up behind and vote for vimmen, and lunch at the Chilblain. Not much. I'm going to stay here and take the Preston Street car and read the Journal on the way over."

On August 23 he announced: "I'm beginning to see the end here. Have had about enough. Am winding up pro tem a lot of papers on the J.H.U. material; am closing the lab'ty with Lewis Weed who's about fagged out. Will begin to think of packing next week. . . . Shall I bring the grass rugs in the cellar?" Finally, on September 2, the night before their belongings left Baltimore, he wrote: "Nothing left here but this desk and it goes tomorrow, the last thing. All the reflexes of 5 years +. I look up at the clock—reach for a watch—turn for a book—nothing there. Very funny—rather sad."

RETURN TO BOSTON

Chapter XVII

HARVEY CUSHING RETURNED TO Boston in September of 1912. With him was a group of young house officers eager to begin work in the new hospital. But when they arrived, they found the building still unfinished, and except for Lewis H. Weed and Emil Goetsch, who immediately began the organization of the experimental laboratory, all of them were forced to mark time. For Cushing this was irritating—not only because it interfered with his own work, but because he hated to see anyone whose energies he might command standing idle. What little operating they did had to be done at the Corey Hill Hospital.

During the waiting time Cushing worked on several unfinished papers and in December presented a report with Dr. Weed and Conrad Jacobson (the resident) before the American Physiological Society in Cleveland. This paper, "Further Studies on the Role of the Hypophysis in the Metabolism of Carbohydrates," was an important contribution because it revealed the extent to which metabolic functions were under nervous control.

In the meantime Mrs. Cushing settled the family in the large, comfortable house, painted yellow, with green blinds and a white picket fence that they had bought in Brookline. "What a bully house, what a nice yard & what a solid fence," wrote William MacCallum on receiving their first Christmas card. "I can just see the way in a few years the Boston Jeunesse dorée or cultivée will be sidling along that fence cussing the distance from the house & trying to catch a glimpse of 'the Cushing girls.' " Those who entered the Cushing door were immediately made to feel at home—even the maids had assimilated something of the friendly manner of the family they served. The tea hour, in front of the open fire when the season called for it, or by the tennis court in summer, was a daily ritual, and many a medical student or house officer received a warm welcome from Mrs. Cushing and all the family even though their host, engrossed in a case or experiment, never appeared.

Their grounds and garden were in the hands of Gus, the man-of-all-work who also drove for Dr. Cushing after he was involved in a traffic accident in which, though not through his fault, a woman was killed. Gus was deeply devoted to Dr. Cushing, but his unconventional ways were occasionally a source of embarrassment to the family, and Dr. Cushing was always fond of telling of the morning when, irritable from a night emergency operation, he had pointed out to Gus all of his shortcomings and Gus, quite unmoved, had announced: "Doctor, you got egg on your chin."

The Cushings soon discovered that the social climate in Boston was far more formal than that to which they were accustomed in Cleveland and Baltimore—a fact which doubtless meant more to Mrs. Cushing than to Dr. Cushing, for his life revolved largely around his profession. Their frequent guests were often his—students, house officers, or distinguished visitors—but before the evening was far advanced he usually managed to slip away to his study, and Dr. Weed, who was often there, remembers many a time when he helped Mrs. Cushing put the children to bed after his host had gone to work.

Through the interest and friendship of a neighbor, James Ford Rhodes, the historian, also from Cleveland, Cushing was invited to join a number of select clubs in Boston. He became a member of "The Club," the famous Saturday Club, and the Tavern Club. The Wednesday Evening Club and the Winters-night Club which met on Tuesdays he declined since he was afraid they would interfere with meetings at the hospital.

The Saturday Club, which met the last Saturday of each month for luncheon (an endowed feast which, as Mr. Rhodes pointed out, was a unique feature of the Club), was founded in 1857 and had had among its members James Russell Lowell, Oliver Wendell Holmes, Ralph Waldo Emerson, John Lothrop Motley, Richard Henry Dana, Jr., Louis Agassiz, Henry Wadsworth Longfellow, and Nathaniel Hawthorne. When Cushing joined, he found among the group his friend W. T. Councilman; A. Lawrence Lowell; M. A. DeWolfe Howe, then Editor of the *Atlantic Monthly* (which had been founded by the Saturday Club); Bliss Perry, the eminent professor of English at Harvard; and Harvard's former president, Charles W. Eliot, who was one of his sponsors. But according to Mr. Rhodes, who was Cushing's adviser in these matters, the "Saturday Club is not 'in it' with The Club. Always neglect the former for the latter but don't tell President Eliot I said so."

Bliss Perry was in "The Club" also, and former members had included Henry and William James and Mr. Justice Holmes. Another member, who became a warm friend, was Major Henry Lee Higginson, the financier who had sponsored the Boston Symphony Orchestra. The Higginsons were especially gracious to the Cushings and did much to make them feel welcome in Boston. "The Club" met on Fridays for dinner—"Such good talk!" Cushing wrote, "even if the Civil War did largely figure." The Club of Odd Volumes, of which he had been a nonresident member since 1911, was another place where there was always good conversation and associations which Cushing enjoyed.

The Peter Bent Brigham Hospital finally opened its doors in January. Amongst the medical profession in Boston there was considerable opposition in the beginning to the resident system that Cushing and Christian were inaugurating. The interns in the other hospitals did not have sufficient training to perform major operations, but the residents who had served in the Hopkins system had had sufficient experience to qualify them to carry out surgical procedures on ward patients who did not have private physicians. To counteract this feeling, Cushing selected men from other Boston hospitals for permanent positions on the Brigham surgical staff, and John Homans of the Massachusetts General Hospital (who had worked with him in Baltimore in 1908-09) and David Cheever of the Boston City Hospital carried the burden of the general surgical work for the next twenty years.

Cushing had gone to the Brigham hoping to institute there some of the good features of the Hopkins. He had three particular things in mind: a common instead of a departmental source of animals for experimental purposes, a central library, and a journal for the Medical School that would offer junior men an outlet for their publications. The library was the only one of these projects he ever came near to accomplishing. But the sweep of the new broom touched so many hitherto undisturbed corners that one of Cushing's colleagues on the medical faculty, Dr. F. C. Shattuck, upon meeting a Hopkins man, began quizzing him about Cushing in his Baltimore days and said that at Harvard he was acting like a bull in a china shop.

Early in his career at the Brigham, Cushing became involved in a matter which was to bring him into opposition with the authorities of the University. The question was whether or not Harvard would adopt the so-called "full-time" plan, and the decision was to have far-reaching effects. To understand the issue at stake, one must know a little of the background of American medical education. From the founding of the first medical school (at Philadelphia in 1765), the teaching of the clinical sciences—medicine, surgery, obstetrics, pediatrics, and so forth—had been in the hands of busy practitioners whose first concern had to be the private patients who were their source of livelihood. When Cushing was appointed associate professor of surgery at the Hopkins in 1902, at the age of thirty-three, his salary was $500, which, even for that period of considerably lower living costs, was obviously inadequate for a married man looking forward to raising a family. An outside source of income was essential. On the other hand, chemistry, physiology, and the other preclinical sciences were taught by men who held faculty appointments and whose

salaries were adequate to allow them to give their entire time
to teaching.

Early in the twentieth century there was talk of giving
clinical teachers a salary sufficient to enable them also to give
full time to the medical school, the fees from private patients
reverting, under this arrangement, to the hospital. "Full-time"
men, trained in educational methods, whose entire energies
would be expended under the hospital roof, would, it was
believed, greatly improve the quality of medical education
and result in better medical care for the patient. The General
Education Board of the Rockefeller Foundation therefore offered the Johns Hopkins in 1912 a million dollars to enable
that institution to embark on the full-time plan.

The preclinical and laboratory men were in favor of the
change—it was natural that they should want to see the clinical
teachers on an equal basis, for it was only human for them
occasionally to envy or resent the lucrative opportunities in a
successful private practice. Those clinical teachers who had
no desire to enter into the competition of a general practice
were also in favor of the change. But those to whom it meant
a much reduced standard of living, while they might approve
in principle, were reluctant to join in. Welch, however, was
able to put the plan across at the Hopkins despite opposition.

When the General Education Board offered Harvard a
million and a half to effect the same change, Cushing came
out firmly against it. He agreed that a clinical professor should
have his activities under one roof—his teaching, his clinical
work, and his research—but he did not think that he should
be deprived of the income from his private patients or the incentive which such a practice would offer. His stand was
dictated by principle and not by any personal reluctance to
give up the opportunity to make money from private practice, for he never coveted money for money's sake and,
although he spent liberally on foreign travel and his children's
education, he lived simply and turned much of his income
back into the clinic. Furthermore, he had private means, for
the real estate Erastus and his father had purchased in the
heart of Cleveland had through the years increased a hundred-
fold in value. He himself, therefore, could have managed well

on a "full-time" salary, but he felt that the modified plan, already in effect at the Brigham, was a sufficient departure from the old system and that more radical plans should be deferred until a fair trial had been made. Christian, with certain reservations, would have "gone along" with the administration, but Cushing offered to withdraw if the authorities felt the full-time plan was the best one and should be inaugurated immediately. Harvard, with its eye on the badly needed million and a half, countered with the suggestion, which did not please Cushing, that a younger man might be secured for the post of Surgeon-in-Chief while he stayed on as a consulting neurosurgeon. In the end the Brigham Trustees voted to retain Cushing as Surgeon-in-Chief and to reject the offer of the General Education Board. Mr. Lowell accepted the decision with grim grace and said nothing, but it was the beginning of an aloofness between Cushing and the Harvard administration which was never dissolved.

During the first year of his incumbency, Cushing kept his absences from duty at a minimum. He gave two papers, one with Clifford Walker, at the meeting of the American Neurological Association, on the visual disturbances in cases of brain tumor, and another before the Massachusetts Medical Society on his studies on diabetes insipidus, which at that time, as has been mentioned, he believed might be related to pituitary dysfunction. Percival Bailey and Frédéric Bremer later proved that diabetes could be induced by lesions of the base of the brain which did *not* impinge upon the pituitary. But eventually both were proved right, since the Bailey and Bremer lesions had injured nerve cells controlling the secretory cells of the posterior pituitary, and the ultimate effect was similar to a pituitary lesion.

In April, Cushing planned an impromptu ceremony at the Brigham so that Sir William Osler, who was in America to give the Silliman Lectures at Yale University, might give his blessing to the new hospital. The function took place on the 30th, although Cushing had received a somewhat indignant note of protest from H. B. Howard, the superintendent of the Hospital (prompted by H.C.'s request for some potted palms to grace the occasion), who said the Trustees had wanted the hospital opening informal and informality would be impossible with such a well-known man as Dr. Osler present.

In June, Yale University conferred on Cushing an honorary M.A. degree, and the summer brought other honors—he was elected to Honorary Fellowship in the Royal College of Surgeons in England and was invited by Sir Thomas Barlow to give one of the three principal addresses at the 17th International Medical Congress held in London.

Like all international gatherings of this sort, the Congress was especially brilliant on the social side. There were receptions at the Savoy, at Windsor Castle, at all the London hospitals, at Horace Walpole's Strawberry Hill. There were excursions to Oxford and Cambridge and special services at St. Paul's and Westminster. The most picturesque of all the functions was an evening fete given by Lord Strathcona—the High Commissioner for Canada being then in his ninety-third year—at the Botanical Gardens in Regent's Park. The five thousand guests wandered about by the light of Japanese lanterns, entertained by the music of the Royal Artillery band alternating with Scottish pipers and strolling singers.

Cushing's paper was entitled "Realignments in Greater Medicine: Their Effect upon Surgery and the Influence of Surgery upon Them." It was delivered to a session of the entire Congress at the Albert Hall on August 7.[1] The address was a frontal attack on the antivivisectionist obstruction to medical research and on the British training in surgery (which allowed a student to pass his examinations in surgery without ever having seen an operation) and other weaknesses in British medical education. It aroused several readers of *The Times* to irate protest, with Sir William Osler and Sir Charles Ballance,

---

[1] Dr. O. Hirsch, an otolaryngologist now of Boston, remembers this occasion vividly. The following day, when Cushing came into the section on otolaryngology, the whole audience rose and the chairman acknowledged the honor extended by his presence. Young Hirsch was not then connected with a university but was hoping to become a *Dozent* (lecturer) at the University of Vienna. The fact that Cushing came to the meeting to discuss his paper carried such weight that he received his appointment the following spring.

an eminent British neurosurgeon, entering the lists in support of Cushing against his adversaries.

But there was also much favorable comment. James F. Rhodes wrote: "I have read your brilliant essay and learned from it much that I am glad to know. It is a triumph to prepare so excellent a literary composition in the midst of a busy and exacting life. I do not wonder that you had a large audience eager to hear you in London." William Welch also had warm praise for the address: "I am delighted that you chose the subject you did, and the address was just the thing for the occasion, the place, and the audience. You made a good point in noting that animal experimentation in England is no longer practised by physicians and surgeons, much to the detriment of the science as well as the art. I am very proud of you and the success you have had."

Welch himself did not attend the Congress, having gone to Europe to take the cure at Carlsbad. "It seemed rather absurd," he said, "after crossing the ocean for a Cure, to break all the traditions and take to rioting and feasting at once." From Carlsbad he had gone to the Lido, whence he sent this startled comment: "Unless you have seen it, you cannot imagine such a spectacle as the bathing beach on the Lido in July and August. It must be unparalleled. Men wear only swimming tights, and women not much more, and all bathe together from the beach."

Early in 1914 Cushing went to Philadelphia where he had been invited to give the Weir Mitchell Lecture. In it he reported the latest figures in regard to his patients with pituitary disorders. He had described something over fifty operations in his pituitary monograph in 1911—he now had performed 125 operations on 114 patients with only 10 fatalities, or a mortality of approximately 8 per cent. These were exciting figures, and the world began to look toward the Brigham as a center for research and surgery of the nervous system. Then war was declared in Europe in August of 1914, and Cushing began to spend considerable time on plans for the organization of a voluntary unit from Harvard to be sent to France early in 1915.

"*THE MARROW OF TRAGEDY*"

Chapter XVIII

IN A NATIONWIDE BROADCAST ON November 21, 1948, Edward A. Weeks, the distinguished editor of the *Atlantic Monthly*, told the story behind a book he had helped to publish early in his career. His comment on some reminders of the war—tin helmets pierced by bullets and half of a pair of field glasses—when in Dr. Cushing's office at the Brigham in 1928 led to the discovery that Cushing had kept a journal throughout his war duty. Weeks immediately visualized an arresting story, but Dr. Cushing put him off, saying it would have to wait until after his death. Regularly, on the anniversary of this meeting, Weeks called to enquire after his health, reminding Cushing cheerfully that he had been promised a book. After several years of this, Cushing was finally persuaded into selecting excerpts from the nine fat typewritten volumes that were his war diary. The result was a handsomely printed book of 534 pages with 35 illustrations.

"The marrow of the tragedy is concentrated in the hospitals," Walt Whitman had written in the Civil War, and Cushing used these words on one of the front leaves of the book. In the pages that followed, one fact was abundantly clear—that the changes wrought in most men by the unnatural tensions of war found little place in Harvey Cushing. Although war changed the complexion of his days, it did little to alter his habits. When the wounded came pouring in, he would not allow himself to be stampeded into forsaking the slow, painstaking methods which were the keystone of his success in the surgery of the brain. Each time he operated it was a personal matter between that patient and himself—the exigencies of war were to him no excuse for abandoning the things he had fought for so consistently throughout his professional career.

And when the end of the day came, even if this was in the early hours of the morning, he set down, as was his habit when away from home—as faithfully as he wrote the operative note after an operation—what the day had brought forth. He often wrote on a scrap of paper or the back of a temperature chart— sometimes by lantern light in a tent or bumping along the road in an ambulance. He augmented the written record with newspaper maps and photographs taken with a forbidden camera. Criticism and court martial threatened to penalize him for this divine disregard for regimentation, but posterity has a rare record of surgeon and soldiers facing up to the grim business of war.

The first entry is dated March 18, 1915, when on a cold, windy night Cushing and the other members of the volunteer unit from Harvard began their journey to Paris. They were headed for the Ambulance Américaine, the five- to six-hundred-bed hospital in the Lycée Pasteur, a school which the French Government had put at the disposal of a group of Americans in Paris. Under the leadership of Ambassador Robert Bacon and his successor, Myron T. Herrick, a military hospital and ambulance service had been organized in connection with the permanent American Hospital at Neuilly-sur-Seine. Financed through voluntary subscriptions, with a rotating professional staff largely recruited from the College of Physicians in New York, the Ambulance had asked American universities to supply for periods of three months sufficient professional personnel to staff certain wards of the hospital. The first of these units, financed by patriotic American citizens, had gone from Western Reserve University under the leadership of Cushing's friend, Dr. George W. Crile. During the early months of 1915 frequent letters were exchanged between Crile and Cushing about matters of personnel and equipment needed, with the result that the Harvard Unit, when it sailed, consisted of six surgeons, seven house officers, and four nurses.

On March 28 they landed in a heavy downpour at Algeciras and from there traveled to Madrid, where Cushing, ever on the trail of Vesalius, picked up "for a song" a copy of the rare first edition of the Spanish surgeon Valverde's Anatomia, published in Rome in 1556, in which many of the Vesalian plates were plagiarized. Passing through the Basque provinces on the way to Paris, Cushing wrote: "Cold and rainy—but early spring betrayed by fruit trees in blossom. Rugged, semi-mountainous country for we are in the foot-hills of the Cantabrian range of the Pyrenees. From Vitoria, founded in 581 by the King of the Visigoths, on to Irún-Hendaye."

Paris was not the gay city he remembered. Ominous-looking armored cars with machine guns, officers speeding by in motorcars, ambulances—gray except for their big red crosses, the splash of red of the old French uniforms, and the citizenry in black proclaimed a country at war. The Ambulance Américaine was a handsome building with its courtyard full of Ford motor ambulances manned for the most part by uniformed American youngsters. The 164 beds which Cushing's unit had charge of were at the moment largely empty.

But they soon had patients. "It is difficult to say just what are one's most vivid impressions," Cushing wrote, "the amazing patience of the seriously wounded, some of them hanging on for months; the dreadful deformities . . . the tedious healing of infected wounds . . . the risks under apparently favorable circumstances of attempting clean operations. . . ." He was not a little shocked at the fact that pressure was often brought to bear by the wounded for the removal of a bullet or other missile lodged in some harmless place so that they might exhibit it to impressionable friends—"souvenir surgery," Cushing called it, which often led to serious and needless complications.

Cases of frostbite and influenza-like colds were numerous. Many of the surgical cases involved buried missiles, "the vagaries of the foreign bodies being many." "The actual sur-

Dr. Villa the Italian Commissioner walked across
this morning to give us a greeting. He like the
<u>le Baldi</u>
Italian Dr.) is a *Sabglinguist* and comes from

northern Italy   naval Staff

Here he is reading Beatty's official report of
the sinking of the Blücher in the London Times
of war "the"   O'Ryan says why don't you come
in. He replies "give us Malta and we will"
"If it belongs to you" says O'Ryan "why don't
you take it away from us."

A page from Dr. Cushing's war diary, en route to France in
March, 1915.

gery itself, it would seem, is not very difficult," Cushing observed, "but the judgment of knowing what and how much to do, and the wheres and whens of intervention—these are the important things, only to be learned by experience. First, or last, most of the missiles apparently must come out."

His greatest test of ingenuity came one day when a man was referred to him with a shell fragment at the base of his brain. With the use of a big magnet he tried with different instruments and probes to extract the bit of steel, but with no success. Finally Walter Boothby, one of the surgeons with the unit, brought in a nail, the end of which he had rounded off. The nail was slipped down, 3½ inches, to the base of the brain, and the magnet swung into position. Slowly the nail was withdrawn, but there was nothing on it. Three times they tried it, carefully, slowly, but each time they failed to touch the fragment. In the meantime, a crowd had gathered in the corridors, and into the operating room itself had come Albert Kocher with a friend from Berne. The excitement and tension mounted, and Cushing was about ready to give up. He took his gloves off—and then decided to try once more. Again the magnet was swung into position, and this time when the nail was withdrawn, there was a small fragment of rough steel on its tip.

When there was a lull between battles, Cushing took the opportunity to visit other hospitals and installations. Alexis Carrel, now back in France, invited him to visit his Hôpital Complémentaire 21 and sent an official car to transport him to Compiègne. Evidences of spring throughout the countryside were a welcome contrast to the scenes in the hospital. "Nothing could be more peaceful and lovely than a well-groomed French forest in the early spring, its floor for miles on a stretch carpeted with flowers—lillies of the valley, anemones, and low-growing narcissus, the latter in such profusion as to give a yellow tone in among the trees as far as one could see—magnificent stands of beeches intersected by paths and formal *allées* of alluring kind. But our road lay *tout droit* through it all."

He also visited the Second Army in the Amiens sector, armed with his camera and two rolls of film. In his journal he recorded the number of men fighting on the Western Front, the kinds of guns, the number of beds in the Amiens Hospital (4,000), and other facts which could have caused him considerable embarrassment were it discovered that he had written them down. But he knew that this was history in the making and his interest in every aspect of the struggle made him seemingly oblivious to the fact that from a security standpoint he was treading on dangerous ground. He was close enough to the firing line on this trip to see some disconcertingly recent shell holes and to hear the frequent discharge of a cannon on the other side of the road.

Toward the end of April he visited the distributing station at La Chapelle—a 250-foot-long freight shed where the wounded were divided into three classes: those who could walk, those in wheel chairs, and the badly wounded on stretchers. Cushing described the scene thus:

The impressive thing about it is that it is all so quiet. People talk in low voices; there is no hurry, no shouting, no gesticulating, no giving of directions—nothing Latin about it whatsoever. And the line of wounded—tired, grimy, muddy, stolid, uncomplaining, bloody. It would make you weep. Through the opening in the curtain, beyond which one of the cars of the train could be seen, they slowly emerged one by one—cast a dull look around —saw where they were to go—and then doggedly went, one after the other each hanging on to his little bundle of possessions. Those with legs to walk on had heads or bodies or arms in bandages or slings, in the hurried applying of which, day before yesterday, uniforms and sleeves had been ruthlessly slit open.

The conditions in France among the wounded laid such a hold on Cushing's emotions that he somewhat highhandedly decided to leave the unit and return home to arouse people to the need for preparedness so that when America became involved in the conflict (and he looked on this as inevitable), our soldiers would be more adequately cared for.

Through the influence of Osler, who was heavily involved in war activities in London, he secured permission to visit

R.A.M.C. hospitals in Flanders en route to Britain. He left the Ambulance Américaine on May 1. "Eight months have passed since that eventful sunrise of the 6th of September when the German tide was checked in this very region north of Meaux, but it might almost have been yesterday. A battle leaves enduring scars. The dead still lie in shallow graves where they fell—the fields and roadsides are dotted with crosses; and every haymow of last autumn's harvest shows by the grim evidence about it how its futile protection had been sought against the scythe of another reaper."

He was soon closer to the front lines than he had yet been and saw the battle of Ypres from the Scherpenberg Hill. He visited No. 13 General Hospital at Boulogne, and a number of casualty clearing stations where he saw some of the first victims of gas attacks—"A terrible business—one man, blue as a sailor's serge . . . too busy fighting for air to bother much about anything else—a most horrible form of death for a strong man."

On May 6 he was in London, but immediately headed for Oxford where he got far from the war among Osler's books after a quiet family dinner with Sir William, Lady Osler, and her sister, Mrs. Henry Chapin of Boston.

In the morning there came news of the sinking of the *Lusitania*. At the Cunard office, when Cushing went to pick up his own passage, an anxious crowd was waiting with haggard, tearstained faces for more details. On the homeward voyage two days later they passed for an hour through debris, bodies, and overturned boats. The tragedy and the waste of it caused Cushing to land on home soil more grimly determined than ever to throw all his energies into preparing for America's entrance into the war.

He was, however, at first amazed and then incensed to discover that although people along the eastern seaboard were aroused over the sinking of the *Lusitania*, the United States for the most part viewed the conflict on the other side of the Atlantic with considerable indifference. General Leonard Wood, now Chief of Staff of the Army, and a few others were making herculean efforts to rouse the public to action, but many went along with President Wilson in believing that we should remain neutral. Cushing, filled with patriotism, accepted every opportunity offered him to speak on preparedness. In addition, he began actively to work for the Red Cross and presented to Mayor Curley of Boston the possibility of mobilizing three Red Cross hospitals on the Boston Common— to stimulate interest and to give needed experience to personnel. He also began the organization of a unit from the Brigham large enough to man an entire base hospital.

But he ran into obstacles on every side: added to lack of enthusiasm was the fact that disorganization in Washington resulted in orders and counter orders that frequently discouraged those who were interested in the beginning. And as for his plan for violating the sanctity of the Common!—he found even his good friends of the Saturday and Tavern Clubs unable to follow him in this flight of fancy. Fond as he had been of every corner of it in his medical school days, he saw no sacrilege in proposing that it now enter the service of the country. But Harvey Cushing was a Middlewesterner. In the Battle of Boston Common, as he called it, he fought a valiant fight, but he was doomed to defeat from the beginning. Henry Lee Higginson and his staunch friend, William T. Councilman (who had once said he was almost willing to die to get out of Back Bay), joined forces with him, but there were few others.

In the meantime, Dr. W. W. Keen, one of the senior advisers in surgery to the newly formed National Research Council, came to him for information that would help him write a report to the Council on "The New Discoveries and Their Application in the Treatment of Wounds in the Present War." The Council had been formed under the auspices of the National Academy of Sciences which had been granted a national charter at the time of the Civil War when Abraham Lincoln saw the necessity of enlisting the aid of the nation's scientists in the war effort. The need was now felt for an organization of younger men to organize the country's scientific talent for national defense and to make "such other applications of science as will promote the national security and welfare." It was the type of organization to which Cushing would give his fullest co-operation, and he promptly sent Dr. Keen a long and thoughtful reply.

Along with these extracurricular activities, Cushing was carrying a full schedule in his clinic. Miss Louise Eisenhardt, who had come to him as secretary in 1915,[1] was assisting him in the preparation of a book on *Tumors of the Nervus Acusticus and the Syndrome of the Cerebellopontile Angle*. Like the pituitary volume, it was to set a standard for the diagnosis and operative handling of this type of intracranial growth which affects one or both nerves from the ear, usually causing deafness. For the first time hope could be held out to patients suffering with these deep-lying tumors, so difficult to approach surgically, for Cushing had devised a method which reduced the operative mortality to approximately 10 per cent. Although some of these tumors recurred, the majority of the patients were relatively free of symptoms for considerable periods and could often return to former occupations.

In this monograph Cushing, according to Geoffrey Jefferson, the distinguished British neurosurgeon, "did for the first time very clearly what he was to do more and more as his experience grew—he came to recognize the fact that different tumors have a predilection for certain situations, a fact which general pathology tends too often to skim over. For it is a fact that new growths have strong preferences for certain organs and situations. . . . So it has proved to be within the cranium where different types, though theoretically they could appear anywhere, do so but rarely."

In 1915 Cushing published a paper "Concerning the Results of Operations for Brain Tumor" in which he reviewed the operative mortality statistics of the leading surgeons dealing with brain tumors. The mortality of Hermann Küttner of Breslau was 45 per cent; that of Fedor Krause of Berlin 50 per cent; Anton von Eiselsberg of Vienna reported 38 per cent;

---

[1] She later took her medical degree and worked with Dr. Cushing, until his death, as his brain tumor pathologist. She developed a remarkable facility for diagnosing tumors from fresh, unstained material while the operation was in progress, a practice which has now become more or less widely adopted.

although Horsley did not publish his figures, it was estimated that they were approximately the same (38 per cent). Cushing astounded his readers by submitting an average mortality of 8.4 per cent. It was higher with some types, lower with others. Furthermore, in the Vienna series of patients, 10.5 per cent of the patients were ultimately lost from meningitis occurring as a result of postoperative infection. In London, 11.7 per cent of Horsley's patients likewise succumbed from this cause. Cushing reported that he had lost but one patient and attributed the absence of sepsis to a careful method of closure of the galea as well as the skin, thus preventing the wounds from breaking down.

Cushing's family, now increased to five by the birth of Barbara, on July 15, 1915, saw little of him during these years, and on May 11, 1917, he was again on his way to Europe. The unit, which was to serve with the British Expeditionary Force as Base Hospital No. 5, consisted of 26 officers, 185 enlisted men, 81 nurses, 3 secretaries, and 1 dietitian. They landed in England, where many of the group were immediately invited by the Oslers to Oxford. "England in May! Some of us never here before; few if any of us at this most wonderful season. The roadsides abloom—hawthorns, yellow-tasseled laburnums, lilacs, red and white chestnuts—rock gardens with every imaginable flowering plant, iris, tulips, wallflowers, and flowering vines of all kinds. It takes a gray wall to show off wisteria properly."

On May 31 they were established at No. 11 General Hospital at Camiers—"a shockingly dirty, unkempt camp"—and received their first convoy of 200 wounded at 1 a.m. Cushing fell heir to the tent of the pathologist of the group they supplanted and to some straggling Scotch marigolds.

For the next year, especially during the winter of 1917-18, Cushing and his team operated sixteen and eighteen hours a day. Night bombings, which meant the extinguishing of lights, added to the hardships. Cushing also had to contend with criticism of his refusal to rush cases through, for while he was doing operations at his usual pace, some men died in his anteroom. But he felt that one job well done was worth two men only half alive.

By developing a careful technique for clearing away all the injured brain substance, Cushing had actually reduced the general mortality in serious wounds penetrating the brain from 50 to 28.8 per cent [2] in the series of cases he operated on in the forward clearing stations. Thierry de Martel, a pioneer French neurosurgeon, was the leading exponent of two other advances in dealing with cranial wounds—the use of novocain anesthesia and the sitting position in brain operations to lessen venous bleeding.

Bearing in mind the usefulness of records on the cases that passed through his hands—for the weapons of this war were creating a different type of wound than had been seen before—Cushing kept detailed histories of each patient. These excellent case records served later as the basis for a monograph which was one of his outstanding contributions resulting from the war. In 1940, a year after another world war had begun, there came to the Historical Library at Yale University an urgent cable from the officer in charge of neurosurgery for the R.A.M.C.—Hugh Cairns (later Brigadier Cairns), who had been Dr. Cushing's assistant at the Brigham Hospital in 1926-27 —asking for the names of the 119 men whose brain injuries Cushing had described. Since many of the records had been lost on their way back to the States in 1918, it seemed doubtful if the information could be supplied, but in Cushing's personal copy of his paper there appeared in the neat hand of his secretary, Miss Julia Shepley, who had been with the unit in France, the name, regiment, and home address of every patient living. These men were traced and examined for what they might contribute to the solving of the problems of a new war.

On the night of August 30, 1917, when Cushing had just turned in after a gruelling day, word was brought to him that Osler's son, Revere, was severely injured. He rushed in an ambulance to Casualty Clearing Station No. 47 where William

[2] In World War II the use of suction for this purpose, supplemented by the antibiotics, considerably lowered the mortality.

Darrach of New York operated at midnight on the bare chance of saving Revere's life. But there had been four shrapnel wounds and it was a hopeless fight. Cushing saw him buried the next morning beside a small oak grove where long rows of simple wooden crosses marked the graves of other young men, some who, like Revere, would have gone home a few days later on leave. "Surely this will take me home," he had said to Cushing when he had opened his eyes to find him at his bedside. The great-great-grandson of Paul Revere was thus laid to rest covered with the Union Jack, while six or eight American Army medical officers stood with bowed heads thinking of his father.

For Sir William and Lady Osler it was a cruel blow, their only solace in the loss of this beloved son being that Cushing had been with him when he died. To Mrs. Cushing, Lady Osler wrote: "Oh Kate, dear Kate, My darling fair baby has gone—just laid in that wet, cold Belgium, but thank God for two things—your Harvey was with him and he has gone to a peaceful spot. . . . My poor man is heartbroken. I feel very anxious for him. He puts up a bluff in the daytime but the nights—three nights—have been a torture—and I am watching near his door now in case he needs me."

In September, Base Hospital No. 5 was the target of a bombing raid. A lieutenant and three privates were killed, a nurse, three officers, and several enlisted personnel, and twenty-two of the patients were wounded. Not long after this disaster, Cushing heard of the death of John McCrae, the brother of his close friend "Tammas." Never strong, this young Canadian physician had burned himself out in the long second battle of Ypres, during which he had written the unforgettable "In Flanders' fields the poppies blow, Between the crosses, row on row."

February of 1918 found Cushing on a Paris leave to see General Leonard Wood who had had a close call when a Stokes mortar had blown up very near him, killing the French officer with whom he was talking. But except for a bad flesh wound, Wood showed no sign of having been through a harassing experience. "A long drive with him in the afternoon—quite lovely. In an unfrequented part of the Bois we passed a closed carriage out of which stepped a heavy, oldish-looking man in a dark blue military cloak, who then tenderly helped out a little old lady in black—Madame Joffre and her forgotten husband."

At the end of the month Cushing left for London to unburden himself of a collection of pathological specimens and clinical histories for the Harvard Medical School. The next day he dined at Brown's Hotel with his Yale professor, Russell Chittenden, and Graham Lusk, the professor of physiology at Yale (he having not yet secured his meat and bread card). "I expected an 8-gram roll such as 'Chitty' is supposed to live on, but instead had a very fine dinner with tongue, which they said the British do not call meat, and a bottle of cider which I strongly suspect was a bit fortified. They are over here in the interests of nutrition, and when their influence becomes felt I will see myself growing thin again. Lusk says the Germans claim to be winning the war by using the Hindenburg offensive and Chittenden defensive."

As usual he hurried to Oxford—"wintry cold, though things are growing and Prunus blossoms are out. Even the wall peaches in bud. The usual miscellaneous gathering at the 'Open Arms.' . . . Tea and many appear, including the Robert Chapins; then much over books in the library, where enter a strange pair—the enthusiastic Charles Singer, he of the *Studies in the History and Method of Science* which begins with the visions of St. Hildegarde—and the other an aged and shriveled university professor of Spanish with some rare medical incunabula under his arm."

On March 10 Cushing was again in France, traveling by back roads to Abbeville. "A wide expanse of fertile country being ploughed and planted by people dressed in fragments of old French uniforms—this fact, with the two huge aerodromes and anti-aircraft stations which we passed, alone indicating war. Off the direct road at Marquise and through Guînes near which was the Field of the Cloth of Gold, though there's now no trace of Henry VIII or Francis I unless the relic of the old earthen fortifications can be such." And the Bowmen of Agincourt had been supplanted by men with Luegers and Enfields and by Big Berthas.

At Abbeville he found the whole region surrounded by remains of Roman camps—"Caesar's defenses against invasions by the Belgians—the great Roman road from Lyon to Boulogne passed through the town, in whose local patois many Latin words are still used. Then in the fifth century came the Hun destroying as he went . . . and now in the whirligig of time the Hun tries to repeat the process."

In the spring came the offensive which attempted to divide the British and French armies and which carried the Germans to within seventy-five miles of Paris. On March 3 Cushing wrote: "This is the third day of what our local paper calls the *Gigantesque Bataille sur le Front Britannique*. There is a strange feeling of something critical impending. Yet it's a lovely spring day—warm—a little misty with no horizon. Windows are open and the sun streams in . . . We've had practically no wounded, which is ominous. Word has been sent to Wallace that Cutler and I will go up to Lillers immediately if needed. Meanwhile there is nothing to do but sit in the sun and stroll on the sands and wait. This is the hardest thing to do."

Tense days of inactivity were punctuated by periods of frantic operating when the wounded poured in. The Germans were definitely gaining ground. Everyone was on edge and impatient for the opportunity to do something when, on May 8, Cushing received orders to report at once to the Commanding General, Headquarters Service of Supply at Tours. He thought he was possibly being summoned for examinations for advanced rank and was deeply chagrined to discover that something he had enclosed in a letter home had put him into serious trouble. The paper, written by a colleague, had contained rather harsh criticism of a British surgeon. As far as Cushing was concerned, it was just part of his records—he was constantly sending Mrs. Cushing material that he asked her to save to go with the diary. But since he had already been called up once for quoting (which was strictly forbidden) an amusing bit from a British Tommy's letter that he had read as censor, this second offense brought the threat of court martial. There are several versions as to what actually occurred during the ten days while Cushing was kept in suspense. One is that the petition of many of the doctors in France persuaded Pershing to let him off. Another story claims that Cushing himself went to J. M. T. Finney, Director of Surgical Services, and although there had been no love lost between them at Baltimore when they were colleagues at the Hopkins, Finney, a fundamentally kind man, had interceded in Cushing's behalf, and his case was dismissed. To one of his pride, the incident was humiliating. He did not record the outcome in his diary— the only result appeared to be that he was transferred from British to American Headquarters.

After the proceedings had been dropped, he secured leave to go to Dublin, where he was made an Honorary Fellow of the Royal College of Surgeons in Ireland, joining the company of such bygone worthies as John Abernethy, John Hunter, Joseph Lister, and Herman von Helmholtz. The next morning his dinner partner of the night before, the Most Reverend Dr. Bernard, Archbishop of Dublin, took him to St. Patrick's.

The Archbishop loves the old place and when Dean became steeped in its lore. There was much to see in a short time. The huge monument to Richard Boyle of black marble and alabaster, with R. B. himself, Earl of Cork, in an upper berth, while some generations, down to an infant, the great Robert,[3] kneel and pray below; the interesting old brasses; the tombs with amusing inscriptions like that of Dame Mary Sent Leger, who, after disposing of four husbands, died in childbirth at 37 years of age, and "whose soule (noe doubt) resteth in all joyfull blessedness in ye heavens." His Grace dotes on the subtlety of the "noe doubt."

On June 17 he was transferred to the A.E.F., with medical headquarters at Neufchâteau, and shortly thereafter raised to the rank of lieutenant colonel, as Senior Consultant in Neurosurgery. When he wasn't operating with his own team in the

---

[3] The Honourable Robert Boyle, one of the most prolific and colorful scientists of the seventeenth century, carried on many experiments on the air which led to the discovery of oxygen a century later.

midst of battles, he was visiting other mobile units and casualty clearing stations to inspect and to offer assistance and direction. One of his duties was to attend monthly meetings in Paris of the joint British and American Medical Research Committee, where reports on present conditions and suggestions for future action were discussed.

The next month was one of the most strenuous he had yet lived through, although the Allies were at last beginning to hold their lines and slow down the German offensive. He moved about from one group to another frequently, often without food or sleep. One night he and a fellow officer took refuge in a boarded-up hotel during a six-hour bombardment, where they waited in the wine cave with the innkeeper's wife who wouldn't allow him to smoke for fear it would spoil the wine! On the 22nd he wrote in his journal:

Times and dates are difficult to figure out. This must be Monday. It's hot and quiet—the birds chirping—the hornets and flies troublesome. There's a smell of hay about as I lie on the grass in front of a square U. S. Army tent which is to be shared with Greenwood—two others were evidently here during the night shift.

We've been operating all night behind the 2nd Division in this newly pitched evacuation hospital which had never seen a battle casualty till forty-eight hours ago and found itself equipped with hospital supplies dating from before the Spanish War—no X-ray —no Dakin's fluid—no nurses, nor desire for any—not a prepared sterile dressing—no sterilizer suitable for field work—and little compressed bundles of ancient gauze and tabloid finger bandages with which to dress the stinking wounds of these poor lads.

On August 6 he reported that he had been in bed three days with an attack of some undiagnosed malady which was like flu or grippe. After two strenuous days around Château-Thierry, where Mobile Hospitals 1 and 6 were joining forces, he had returned to Neufchâteau one night, cold, wet, and supperless, so weak suddenly that he had to ask his driver to help him upstairs. The fever had come over him after he had stopped operating late one night on a case regarded as inoperable, and Elliott Cutler, one of his Brigham staff, had put him to bed in his cot. He was up on the 7th but feeble. Advised by Thayer to go to the Riviera for a rest, he got only as far as Paris, where he spent five days in a hotel tossing with fever. He returned to Neufchâteau on the 18th and managed to keep going for the rest of the month. On September 1 he casually mentioned that he had discovered the threatened blindness which had rushed on him in the last ten days was an accompaniment of the muscular enfeeblement of the grippe.

Through the Saint-Mihiel and Argonne battles he stayed on his feet, working steadily, but by October 8, when he went to Paris for the Research Committee meetings, he admitted that they had become so numb he could not feel the floor when he got out of bed. His friend Richard Strong kept him at his apartment for four days, after which, although his legs were numb to the knees and he could scarcely stand, he returned to his post. Three days later, when he had a bad time operating because of his double vision, and when his numbness and unsteadiness had increased, involving his hands, he finally gave up and went with another friend, Sidney I. Schwab, to the hospital he directed at Priez-la-Fauche.

During these weeks of increasing disability, nobody knew exactly what was wrong with him, least of all Cushing himself. It was now clear that it was something far more serious than grippe, but whether neuritis or what, nobody could definitely say. As a matter of fact, he had begun to notice some weakness in his legs as early as the preceding spring. He had been walking one Sunday with Gilbert Horrax, his devoted operative assistant (a Hopkins graduate who had been the Arthur Tracy Cabot Fellow in the Surgical Laboratory at Harvard in 1913-14), and when they were about four miles from camp, he said "Gil, I have to go back." Horrax, in surprise, asked why. "Something seems to be the matter with my legs. I am too tired to go on." No more was said. Both of them put it down to fatigue from the long hours of operating. Although Dr. Horrax remembered this incident later, it did not seem to help toward a diagnosis.

The necessity for hospitalization must have caused Cushing deep concern, but nothing of his discouragement was set down in his diary, and his increasingly alarming symptoms were noted briefly with the objectiveness of any medical report. He occupied himself with his fellow patients, with following the progress of the fighting, or with such things as cutting out clippings about birds that he thought might interest his son Bill. To Mrs. Cushing he wrote: "Please don't bother Popsy or any other M.D.'s about me. It's not the thing to be ill in the Army, and I'm keeping very low about my transient malady lest I have to go before a Board and get canned as a decrepit. Give me a week or two and I'll be quite fit again."

As the Allied armies pressed forward on an ever-shortening front, there was encouraging news of victories. Cushing had been following the receding German line on an official map with pins and a ball of yarn, but he was no longer able to hold and stick in the pins. However, he wrote cheerfully to Mrs. Cushing: "Your October 7th letter has just come with one from Mary, the dear . . . I'm glad you've got a fur coat for the Puss Cat [his pet name for Mrs. Cushing]. Hairy side out? or skinny side? May get one myself of the sheepskin kind just like Bryan O'Lynn's . . . Miss Shepley is here to-day doing some business for me—I still am keeping a little hold on my office affairs—pour passer le temps. She's been a perfect trump all through—please tell her mother so for me."

By November 5 he was getting slightly restless: "Isn't it rotten luck to be laid up at this time. Miss Shepley tells me the offices are deserted—everyone 'up front.' An interesting time—the period of getting into redeemed villages and seeing the joyous population—what are left of them." Six days later, when people all over the world were celebrating the Armistice, Cushing, wrapped in a blue-gray dressing gown, watched the autumn leaves hurrying past his hospital window and imagined that even they were expressing joy in their zooming and whirling. By November 16 he was well enough to return to headquarters at Neufchâteau. Here he found his colleagues "too squalid, and uncomfortable to talk to one another, we scarcely need to do so while familiar shibboleths resound in our ears—that this was to be a war to end all wars, and that the world from now on will be made safe for democracy. We wonder. We shall at least see what democracy can make of it."

ADMINISTRATOR

Chapter XIX

CUSHING RETURNED FROM FRANCE in February of 1919 full of enthusiasm for the establishment of a national institute of neurology for study of the vast amount of neurological material resulting from the war—not only for the purpose of helping those suffering from war neuroses, but for the advancement of medicine. During the spring he spent a great deal of energy and time stirring up interest both among individuals and among the foundations—the Carnegie Foundation for the Advancement of Teaching and the General Education Board of the Rockefeller Foundation. But his efforts came to nothing. The foundations felt unable to provide the ten-million endowment needed for the project, and although the Surgeon General attempted to carry it forward in Washington, some of his superiors in the War Department, and the determined economy of a reactionary Congress, presented insurmountable difficulties. The wealth of material was lost in the files of the Veterans Bureau, and there was little follow-up on the cases from which so much might have been learned toward returning men to a useful existence and toward saving lives in the next war. To Cushing it was more than a personal disappointment, it was a public tragedy.

In June, two honorary degrees—a Doctor of Laws from Western Reserve and a Doctor of Science from Yale—were added to the recognition of Cushing's war service already taken by the British government when it conferred on him the order of the Companion of the Bath, and by General Pershing, who had cited him "For exceptionally meritorious and conspicuous services as Director of Base Hospital No. 5."

September brought the disquieting news that Sir William Osler had one of his heavy colds—brought on from a trip in an open motor, necessitated by a railway strike in Britain. The cold progressed into a fever and finally into pneumonia. He told Mrs. Osler on October 13 how it would end, but he continued to fill each day as full as they would let him with reading, writing, and sending cheerful notes to the wide circle of those whom his affection had warmed and cheered for so many years. "I make pleasant excursions from one side of the bed to the other & am enjoying life immensely," he told one friend. His last letter to Cushing in his own hand was dated November 14. A physician to the last, Sir William made notes on the progress of his illness. The end came on the afternoon of December 29. Although he had a definite physical ailment, he really died of a broken heart. The loss of Revere had been more than he could bear.

Osler's death touched Cushing deeply. He had lived close within the circle of Sir William's influence for more than twenty years, and no one had been so near to the inner reaches of his mind and heart. In the early days Osler had not hesitated to speak a good-natured word of caution when it seemed indicated, and his pride in Cushing's successes was a father's pride. Osler in every way had offered Cushing an ideal—in his keenness as a physician, his popularity as a teacher, his integrity as a scholar; in his abundant enthusiasms, his vitality and hearty enjoyment of life, his amazing productivity, his fascinating and endless knowledge of the historical backgrounds of medicine, his daily acts of thoughtfulness and generosity.

To give vent to his emotion, Cushing immediately set down an appreciation. Although he stated at the beginning that "in the first shock of grief at the news of Sir William Osler's death, it is difficult for anyone who felt close to him to say what is in his heart," nevertheless, in the warmth and simplicity of the brief story of Osler's life which followed, he revealed more than he knew. He chose some lines from Isaiah as the final expression of what Osler had been to those who loved him:

And a man shall be as an hiding place from the wind, and a covert from the tempest; as rivers of water in a dry place, as the shadow of a great rock in a weary land.

This tribute, entitled "William Osler, the Man," was published anonymously in the Boston *Evening Transcript* of January 3. Immediately Lady Osler had read it she asked Cushing (she had first thought of William Thayer) to write the official biography of Sir William—"I am convinced that there is no one else who understands as you do." Although he had many misgivings as to his capabilities, Cushing told her that whatever she wanted or thought Sir William would have liked, he would try to do.

He spent a month in Oxford that summer collecting material and daily questioning Lady Osler about details until she sometimes protested good-naturedly. The year he had estimated for the task lengthened into five—he spent much of the first two in a painstaking search for material, since Osler had saved little in the way of letters. Miss Madeline E. Stanton, a young Smith graduate, was added to the staff so that Miss Shepley might spend her entire time on the biography.

The loss of Osler, following upon his own illness and disappointment as a result of his failure to implement the idea of the National Institute of Neurology, made Cushing's readjustment to the routine of the clinic difficult. During the war, David Cheever had managed the surgical service [1] with the assistance of Conrad Jacobson as resident, but Jacobson left shortly after Cushing's return, and Elliott Cutler took his place. In order to make a place for Gilbert Horrax, who had been with him all during the war, Cushing appointed him to the staff as Associate in Surgery. From April 1919 until just before Cushing retired, Horrax shared the operative burden, later handling all the trigeminal neuralgia cases and doing

---

[1] Although John Homans did not go over with the group from the Brigham, he eventually was sent overseas. William C. Quinby, urological surgeon, joined the staff in 1916.

many of the time-consuming openings and closures so that Cushing would not have to be so long on his feet. Although Dr. Cushing had at first feared that the clumsiness of his hands and feet resulting from his illness would cut short his operative career, his dexterity soon returned, but he now wore glasses to operate and began to sit whenever possible during the longer procedures.

After his conversation with Horrax in France, the subject of his legs was never mentioned between them, but in a quiet, unobtrusive way Dr. Horrax did what he could to save him. He brought loyalty and understanding in an unusual degree to his selfless devotion to his Chief, and it is widely stated that he mastered Cushing's meticulous surgical technique more thoroughly than did any of his other men. "If you have seen Gil operate, you won't want to see me," Cushing would say. But his fondness for Horrax guaranteed no immunity from his brusque criticism. Although a saint in disposition and as slow to anger as his Chief was quick, Horrax sometimes resented this treatment momentarily, but he would remind himself that this was Cushing's method of teaching medicine and would hold his peace.

Percival Bailey, a brilliant young graduate of the Medical School at Northwestern University, came to the Brigham at this time as Arthur Tracy Cabot Fellow for 1920-21. After a subsequent year abroad, he returned to begin a histological study of the brain tumor material Cushing had amassed. He remained with Cushing nearly ten years. "He was not an easy man to work with," Bailey said. "We disagreed often, sometimes vigorously. When the tension became too great I went away for a while. But I always came back. My debt to him was incalculable."

During 1920, the first of a series of voluntary graduate assistants, largely from foreign countries, were attracted to the Brigham. Charles P. Symonds of London and Frédéric Bremer of Brussels were the initial incumbents. Patients also were coming from long distances, referred by physicians all over the country. Sometimes they came unheralded, as once did a member of the Chamber of Deputies of Peru who arrived with many official attendants, far too ill himself to explain that he was there because a Peruvian physician knew of Dr. Cushing's reputation and felt his only hope was to go to Boston for an operation.

With the increasing burden of work, Cushing's office staff was busy from eight-thirty in the morning, when he arrived, until after normal closing hours. His daily routine varied little—breakfast before eight, then off with the children—Gus leaving him at the hospital before taking the children to school. Unless he had been called back during the night, he invariably looked fresh and full of energy upon arrival. His hair had begun to show gray during the war, but he was still thin and wiry, always impeccably dressed, and conservatively—except for his neckties, which once prompted a former resident to perpetrate a parody entitled "The Tie that Blinds." His hat was set at a slight angle and, like the twinkle that appeared in his eye at unexpected times, always gave him an air of youthful jauntiness.

He started with the morning mail and an hour or more of dictation. Operations were usually scheduled for ten o'clock and might last from four to six hours, after which he dictated a detailed operative note, sometimes drawing a sketch to accompany it. While dictating, he was accustomed to having toast and tea—it might then be three or even four o'clock and he would not have eaten since breakfast. In fact, about the only time he ever ate lunch was on those days when he joined the Saturday Club.

There followed dressings and visits to patients awaiting operation, and when he finally returned to his office, both patients and secretaries greeted his coming with relief. In between he might have had conferences with his house staff, looked in at the Surgical Laboratory in the Medical School, or, more often, stopped at his own hospital laboratory to look over brain specimens and indicate what sections he wanted prepared for microscopical study. His day rarely ended before seven.

During his years at the Brigham, Cushing was able to spend less time than formerly in the laboratory. However, he kept closely in touch with what was going on there—suggesting problems, advising, and, when the experiments were completed, going over the written results with great care. He sometimes resembled Kronecker in trying to impose his own unique style and was as surprised as Kronecker had been to meet with resistance, but he was finally convinced that his assistants liked to write up their results in their own way.

As an administrator, Cushing was conscientious but he preferred other aspects of his work. The controversy over the full-time plan and the interruptions of the war had prevented until now the full expression of his capacities. He had long since discovered that the free spirit of the Hopkins did not exist at Harvard, and, face to face with the solid structure of long-standing university policy at Harvard, he missed the elasticity of attitude to which he was accustomed. Whenever he enthusiastically put forth ideas for change or reform, he invariably ran into a paralyzing and disheartening lack of interest and cooperation in the places from which such changes had to emanate. This, of course, aroused in him a brisk irritation that he often took no pains to conceal—a fact which doubtless nullified his efforts on occasion.

Where the lines of administration crossed those of medical education, Cushing was consistently practical, periodically asking the question, Is the student being adequately prepared to give good medical care to the patient? This might result in a letter to the Dean suggesting a re-evaluation of the third- and fourth-year curriculum, or a shake-up in the out-patient teaching because he felt the students were giving more service to the hospital than they were getting out of it in the way of education.

He tried also to prevent his service from becoming static by refusing to set up rules and regulations. Although his own habits and idiosyncrasies might impose just as rigid a discipline as written regulations, nevertheless he encouraged his men in original thinking and supported them wholeheartedly in their projects. Regimentation in any form annoyed him, and since the Dean often seemed the personification of all retarding and exasperating influences, they had many brushes. One of his early battles was to get the Arthur Tracy Cabot Fellow relieved of responsibility for supervision of the animal farm that supplied the laboratory with experimental material, and he brought the subject to the attention of the Dean with the same persistence with which he had written his father about rugs for his room at Yale.

Another thing that was a source of continuing annoyance was the Dean's method of calling faculty meetings. He invariably sent out the notices so that they were received the day before the meeting. This resulted in poor attendance because of previous engagements, and the administration was able to pass measures which might not have been passed had a larger group been present. Cushing was regular in his protests.

The thing for which Cushing agitated the longest was better salaries for his surgical staff. Every year one or more letters went to the Dean, but despite persistent efforts, he never succeeded in materially improving the situation. The attitude that stood in his way seemed part and parcel of the narrow policy which prompted the Dean to question the necessity for the Laboratory for Surgical Research in the Medical School when there was a similar laboratory in the Hospital. In Cushing's reply, which ran to three pages, he said that a hospital was not a suitable place for experimentation with large animals; and he then set forth in a calm and objective manner his ideas about the importance of research, both in securing positions and in growing professionally thereafter. Underlining this forceful statement of his philosophy was something of his disappointment that the prize so long coveted, a professorship at Harvard, fell short of his expectations. But he possessed an indomitable optimism—he always hoped that if things didn't improve, perhaps he could do something to improve them.

By 1919 the number of neurosurgeons in the country had grown to the point where it was felt the formation of a society would be valuable for the discussion of mutual problems. This group of eighteen men [2] became known as the Society of Neu-

---

[2] Alfred W. Adson (Rochester, Minn.), Edward Archibald (Montreal), Charles Bagley (Baltimore), Claude C. Coleman (Richmond), Harvey Cushing (Boston), Charles E. Dowman (Atlanta), Charles A. Elsberg (New York), Charles H. Frazier (Philadelphia), Samuel C. Harvey (New Haven), George J. Heuer (Cincinnati), Gilbert Horrax (Boston), Allen B. Kanavel (Chicago), W. Jason Mixter (Boston), Howard C.

rological Surgeons. Dr. Cushing was elected president, and the
first official meeting was held in the autumn of 1920 at the Brigham Hospital. The early meetings were largely occupied with
discussion of technical problems, many of which have long
since been solved. At the 1921 meeting in Philadelphia, there
was much talk, pro and con, of the then new procedure of ventriculography,[3] which Dr. Horrax has called one of the most
epoch-making contributions to intracranial surgery ever announced. Writing in 1942, Horrax said: "The importance of
this diagnostic method, not only for the localization of hereto-
fore unlocalized brain tumors, but also for the more accurate
localization of many growths whose situation could not be
ascertained with absolute exactness, can hardly be over-
emphasized. It brought immediately into the operable field at
least one third more brain tumors than could be diagnosed and
localized previously by the most refined neurological methods." In 1921, however, it appeared to be a radical procedure
and some of the older surgeons adopted it slowly.

It might have been expected that Cushing, although he was
conservative, would have at once visualized the possibilities of
this new diagnostic aid. But it had been introduced by his old
assistant at the Hunterian, Walter E. Dandy, and there were
reasons beneath the surface which probably explain some of
Cushing's reluctance to adopt ventriculography immediately.
During their association at the Hopkins, Dandy and Cushing
had not seen eye to eye on some research Dandy was carrying
on in the Laboratory. From this time on, each seemed to bring
to the forefront the combative nature of the other, and when
Cushing was picking men to go with him to the Brigham, he
did not invite Dandy to join the group. Dr. Dandy remained at
the Hopkins and became known for his daring in attempting
far more radical surgery than Cushing advocated. So distinguished an authority as Geoffrey Jefferson felt that he eventually surpassed his preceptor in technical steps and innovations

Naffziger (San Francisco), Ernest Sachs (St. Louis), Alfred W. Taylor
(New York). Walter E. Dandy of Baltimore was asked to join but
refused the invitation.
[3] Injection of air into the cerebral ventricles. If the X-ray shows displace-
ment of the ventricles, operative intervention is indicated.

in surgical procedure. Be that as it may, although Cushing was sincere in his distrust of the new method (since accidents had occurred in injecting the air and since he felt it might lead surgeons away from doing careful neurological examinations), it is possible that the events of the past may have colored his opinion without his being aware of it. It was some time before he adopted ventriculography as a routine measure in his own cases.

One of the 1923 meetings of the Society of Neurological Surgeons (there were usually two a year) was held in Boston. Before the annual dinner on the first evening, Dr. Jason Mixter gave a cocktail party which was such a success that they were late arriving at the Harvard Club. When they were barely finished with the soup, Dr. Cushing jumped up and said: "It's time to go now. I have arranged a clinic for you at eight o'clock, and the patients are all lined up." This filled everyone with consternation. Nobody wanted to stop at the beginning of a good dinner and attend a clinic arranged without their knowledge. Dr. Ernest Sachs as secretary took Cushing aside and remonstrated with him. "All right," said Cushing angrily, "if you're going to make this an eating club, I'm going to get out." Some of the men reluctantly attended the clinic, but most did not. The next day, when the group convened at the Brigham, Cushing was serenely affable—as if he had done nothing to spoil a pleasant dinner for his associates the evening before.

Cushing firmly believed in the value of medical gatherings for the interchange of ideas and for keeping abreast of the work in other centers. He therefore attended the meetings of all the local and national organizations of which he was a member. From his experience at the Hopkins, he also knew the value of a local medical society, and his enthusiasm was a large factor in making the Harvard Medical Society a vital influence in the School. He made free use of his many contacts outside Boston and outside medicine to arrange meetings of interest to students. And he encouraged young physicians interested in the history of medicine, as is evident from the following letter from Chauncey Leake, then at the University of Wisconsin (now Dean of the Medical School at the University of Texas at Galveston):

I thought when you were kind enough in your last letter to me to suggest that I come to Boston to talk to you about Percival's Code of Ethics that you were just making a nice gesture to a youngster out in the sticks. I find, however, to my great delight, that you are one of those rare persons who means exactly what he says.

Cushing also asked men from other hospitals to participate when out-of-town guests were to speak on subjects in their field, and often sent the next day a thoughtful letter such as this to Dr. Francis Benedict, Director of the Carnegie Nutrition Laboratory in Boston:

Dear Benedict: Just a line in the cool of the morning to express again my appreciation for all the trouble you took to give that demonstration here last evening. I know that those things are not done without preparation—even by such as you. It was a friendly and neighborly act, and I only regret that the entire student body had not been there, ten deep, to hear you. Medicine, alas, now-a-days is a circus of many rings and the students may be captured by a trapeze act while something really important is going on in another tent.

Not only did he write innumerable letters to speakers and students, but he also paid the bills, as one secretary discovered to his surprise when he submitted an account for printing and stenographic services during the year. He promptly received reimbursement for $85.40. "I am sending you a check to cover your expenses as has long been my custom," Cushing wrote him.

Cushing never lost his interest in sports. Despite the fact that he suffered frequently from the poor circulation in his legs, he played a devastating game of tennis, as anyone who had the temerity to oppose him soon discovered. Baseball and football took him regularly to Yale, and there was much reminiscing about "the good old days" when Walter Camp, long the football coach at Yale, stayed with the Cushings while in Boston in December attending a dinner in his honor.

Medical school affairs also called him to New Haven on occasion. In April, 1921, he was invited to arrange a program and act as toastmaster at a farewell dinner in honor of Joseph Marshall Flint, the retiring professor of surgery. Dr. James Rowland Angell had taken President Hadley's place at the helm of the University, and Milton C. Winternitz, who several years earlier had come up from the Hopkins full of vigor and new ideas, had been appointed dean. Francis G. Blake, of the Rockefeller Institute, and Samuel C. Harvey had been secured for the chairs of medicine and surgery, and the plans Cushing had long cherished for the Yale University School of Medicine seemed about to materialize. He planned the dinner with great care, inviting Dr. Welch, Simon Flexner, Ross G. Harrison, William H. Carmalt, and others to attend.

In May, H. C. had joined with his friends Malcolm Storer and Edward C. Streeter (who had just been appointed lecturer in the history of medicine at Harvard) in calling a meeting of physicians in New England who were interested in the "historical and cultural aspects of medicine." The enthusiasm which launched this, the Boston Medical History Club, has been rekindled through the years, and the Club is still in existence.

In the autumn of 1921, on the occasion of the seventy-fifth anniversary of the introduction of ether anesthesia at the Massachusetts General Hospital, Cushing was asked to give a twenty-minute address. He did not choose to discuss the discovery of ether or to pay customary tribute to the illustrious names associated with the hospital since its inception. Instead he spoke for forty-five minutes (instead of the allotted twenty) on "The Personality of a Hospital," extolling the virtues of those faithful employees—night orderlies, apothecary clerks, waitresses, laundresses—who in giving a lifetime of loyal service were no less responsible than the surgeons for the "particular flavor, tone, and color of the hospital."

Many letters of congratulation came to him as a result of this address, one from Dr. Halsted pleasing him as much as any of them.

Dear Cushing: I am so pleased to receive a copy of your Ether Day Address, which I had missed. . . . Can it be a sign of "progeria" that I enjoy so greatly reminiscences, particularly of those who can see, interpret and appraise? The M.G.H., born aristocrat, has been the breeder of fine Brahmans and I can well understand the pull it has on the cockles of the "pups."

I happened to be in London when Bigelow described his lithotrite and evacuator. Samuel D. Gross also I saw only once and this was at a lecture by Sir James Paget on plant pathology. It was on this occasion that old Darling, asleep in the front row of the gallery, dropped his cotton umbrella on the head of a spectator below, much to the amusement of everyone except Paget. I regret so much having missed the opportunity to see Oliver Wendell Holmes. I loved John Homans, as everyone did, and Arthur Cabot. For Jack Elliot I have always had a very high and warm regard, and wish that you would remember me to him. Graves told me the other day that Elliot is still riding to hounds. . . .

To return to "The Personality of a Hospital"—such a happy theme—I read it twice and shall read it again some day.

Heuer departed yesterday for Cincinnati. . . . Weed is doing finely; you judged him aright.

I am promising myself the pleasure of seeing you and Mrs. Cushing and the children before all are married. With love to the family, I am, Ever yours, W. S. Halsted.

In June of 1922 Cushing sailed for Europe, accompanied by Mrs. Cushing. He had several responsibilities, the first a lecture at the IIIᵉ Réunion Neurologique Internationale. He chose to speak on the diseases of the pituitary, and the lecture was translated into French for him by Paul Martin, a young Belgian neurosurgeon who had been working in the clinic as a Rockefeller Fellow. Percival Bailey, who had been studying that year with the French neurologist Pierre Marie, read the paper for him at the meeting, after which there was a large banquet that brought together an impressive number of the world's greatest students of the nervous system.

A few days later, in London, Cushing was made a "Perpetual Student" of St. Bartholomew's Hospital as he took over the surgical service for two weeks. *The Lancet* commented: "Although recognized as the leading neurological surgeon in the world, Professor Cushing did not operate while he was in this country but spent his time in observing methods of instruction, talking to students, and teaching in the outpatient and casualty departments of the hospital."

On June 7 he gave a second paper, this time the Cavendish Lecture at the West London Medico-Chirurgical Society, after a dinner in his honor. At the suggestion of Lady Osler, with whom he and Mrs. Cushing were staying, they were accompanied to London by a young Rhodes Scholar from Minnesota, John Fulton, who was studying with Sir Charles Sherrington. Cushing discovered that this young man, thirty years his junior, was as enthusiastic about Osler's books as Osler himself had been and already possessed a wide knowledge of them—it was natural that they would find much of common interest. For Fulton it was a momentous occasion, and his deep devotion to Dr. Cushing dated from this memorable evening.

The lecture, Cushing's first formal presentation on the tumors he had named meningiomas, was superbly prepared down to the last slide, and the large audience, unusually responsive to the force of his personality, cheered him heartily at its conclusion. After a few more days at Oxford, he and Mrs. Cushing returned to Boston, where he spent the rest of the summer on the Osler biography. In August there was a pleasant interruption when the French government honored him by making him a *Chevalier* of the Légion d'Honneur. President Lowell presided at the brief ceremony, and General Gouraud presented the award, pinning the ribbon on his coat with a safety pin procured at the last moment from an aide who, having taken it from a vital place, had in turn to ask Mrs. Cushing for one to replace it—a situation which afforded Cushing considerable amusement.

During these years when he was occupied with the book and could go less frequently to Little Boar's Head, he occasionally had the care of the children, particularly Bill, who was now old enough to have a summer job or affairs of his own that kept him in Brookline. This closer contact gave Cushing a new view of his children. It was brought home to him forcibly that they were growing up and developing individualities of their own, and, in approaching adulthood, they made demands on him as a parent which he could no longer ignore.

A FAMILY OF
INDIVIDUALISTS

Chapter XX

Harvey cushing was adored by his children but, having dedicated himself to medicine, he often sacrificed his family to his profession. He was almost a guest in his house—a delightful and familiar guest who enjoyed and contributed much to its hospitality, who could exercise the privilege of an intimate of the household by chiding or disciplining its members but, after stirring things up, could make a graceful exit and return to the main business of his life.

It was Katharine Cushing who, like Betsey Maria Cushing before her, carried the real burden of parenthood and understood its heartaches and its satisfactions. Until the children reached their 'teens, she arranged for their schooling, had their full care during the summer from June to September, and was ever their counsellor and confidante. In their home she displayed her feeling for color and love of antiques, and the combination of her appreciation of fine materials with a nice sense of utility and function always resulted in an attractive and gracious setting. In every room there were photographs and objects of art and sentiment which expressed the personality of the occupants and made the house look hospitable and "lived in."

But Kate Cushing did more for her family than provide pleasant surroundings and "creature comforts." She worked hard and untiringly to create a spiritual atmosphere in which her brilliant husband and her more-than-usually gifted chil-

dren might grow and develop. Harvey Cushing was no ordinary parent, and often the children, when small, did not
understand his preoccupation with other things. Unques-
tionably she herself would have been happy to claim more
of his attention for their personal interests, but outwardly she
gave no sign. Only intimates of the household, such as Lewis
Weed, when helping her put the children to bed, or Gilbert
Horrax, walking with her on a summer's evening in Little
Boar's Head when Dr. Cushing had stayed in Boston, guessed
what was in her heart.

The atmosphere of the Cushing household was not always
placid, for Mrs. Cushing had a strong nature and a quick
temper that matched her husband's, but this perhaps was the
salvation of their marriage—this and a love for one another
that was long-standing and deep-running and strong enough
to withstand the impact of two highly motivated individuals
working out a life together. An understanding commentary
on their relationship has been made by Mrs. Albert Bigelow,
a warm friend and close neighbor in Brookline:

It is not possible to write about Harvey and not write of
Kate also. She not only forestalled all his needs, but was in every
way the perfect companion for him, for not only did she have
a mind and character but she carried herself well and had a
beauty of face and expression that well matched his distinguished
appearance when they went about together. . . .

I think another way in which Kate helped Harvey was by being
just as decided as he was. I don't believe she put up with irritable moods and probably discouraged them by not being over
sympathetic, but helped instead all she could by providing cheer
and comforts. I suppose it *was* a fault that he was so absorbed by
his work, that although he loved his children he had little time to
take responsibility for them, and I believe he leant on Kate far more
than she did on him. This is all speculation, yet in painting a
portrait, it is what the artist has to go by to bring out the character of his subject. . . . It is probably far from easy to live
with a tense, sensitive, brilliant being such as Harvey was, but I
know Kate superbly achieved her role in guarding his strength
to enrich the world and in helping him to fulfill his destiny.

Because Cushing like any father had high hopes, perhaps undefined, for his first-born, he seemed to be particularly critical of all that William did. Bill was a most attractive and popular lad with a beguiling smile, and in a happy mood was charming and lovable. But his nature was very like his father's, and the battle of wills that was sometimes waged between them was the counterpart of that between Cushing and his father many years before. Bill was fond of people and action and sports, to the detriment of his studies, and this was a constant worry to his father. From France during the war Cushing had written: "We must not expect our children to be phenomena. Bill will get really interested in something one of these days and find himself. I'm sorry for his lack of ambition and application, but then it's not so rare at his time." In 1920 it was Mrs. Cushing who was taking Bill's part. Writing from the HF Bar Ranch in Buffalo, Wyoming, where she had taken Bill and Mary, she said: "He is liked and admired by young and old. He never loafs or hangs around, is full of business—riding, fishing, rounding up cattle—if he would only work as hard at his studies as he works at this life! But he's full of promise if we only handle him right. Mary is just the way you would know she would be—so dear and thoughtful of me—rides like a trooper and is happy all the time. She has her happiness safe inside."

The discord between father and son went deeper than the matter of application to schoolbooks—it seemed as if the more Cushing loved the boy, the more determined he became to bend him to his will. William, on the other hand, to whose inner self his father was a stranger—his father having been too busy to fish with him, to take him on trips, to grow up with him—bitterly resented such highhanded interference with his affairs. Something of this can be glimpsed in the letters Dr. Cushing wrote to Mrs. Cushing during the summers he and Bill spent together in Brookline:

Bill blew in last night an hour late for dinner with that defiant look of his. I told him in some heat what I thought of it, and subsequently apologized, but he is still sulking this morning and got up an hour late. . . .

This is the 2nd blow up in two weeks—perhaps not so bad after all, and we may grow to understand each other. He has engaged to play ball Saturdays and Sundays so we'll not be coming down. For I think I'd better stay here if he does.

The baseball team Bill joined was the Brookline All Stars. When they played the "House of David Bearded Giants," whom Gus called Mormons, Cushing and Gus attended. "Bill says they are nice fellows—polite on the bases despite their whiskers." Bill's late hours and a girl who called three or four times a day and tied up the telephone for long stretches goaded his father to another expression of irritation: "I just told Bill if he didn't take his lasso and sombrero off my table—they've been here since Wednesday—I'd hang myself with it. O House of David!! Oh, Osler's Biography!! The cat's the only thing around here in a family way. Damned if I am anyhow. Hope you are enjoying your summer. We probably won't be down Sunday. Play the Mormons again and Gus wouldn't miss it."

Then came a letter which said "Bill and I are making progress."

Quite an extraordinary episode last night. We were going to dine at 7:30 with Mr. Sargent. We had been playing tennis till seven and came in to dress. At seven thirty I began to howl for Bill—no sign of him. Suddenly he blew in hot, sweating, *in his baseball clothes*! He had stepped off for half an hour to play ball. My, I was mad. Can't you imagine? Well, I went alone—somewhat late—wondering what would happen when I got home. What do you suppose? Instead of a sullen boy or no boy—here was Bill studying! Very contrite—very apologetic. I could have cried. He's in here now reading me an extract from the Spectator —your old copy—and giving me tips about Addison and Steele.

All this may have something to do with the fact that he is going somewhere to spend the week end with a girl—from St. Louis, I believe.

Remembering the letters that went back and forth between Cushing and his father about "sophomore," junior, and senior societies, it is amusing to find a similar exchange in the next generation. Bill was writing from Andover, where he was preparing for Yale, having transferred from Milton Academy because his father thought it would be good for him to be among boys who might later be his companions in college.

Dear Va, You know that I got into that Frat a few weeks ago. I didn't know that I had to pay anything outside of what I spent on the week that I was running. I went down to the house the other day and saw that I had some other fees. Golly, at first I didn't believe that it was right, but I found out that I owed the Frat $88.30. . . . That seems pretty steep to me but perhaps I don't know much about that kind of thing. I ran up a couple of bills last month and I'm pretty low just now when it comes to raking up a sum like that so I wonder if you could help me out.

Cushing replied:

It is quite a sum, as you say, and I think that perhaps they should have warned you beforehand. Perhaps some day when you become a pundit yourself in the Society, you may be able to hint to the others that it is a good thing to warn candidates for membership about the expenses, so that they can ask their parents.

However, I am glad you made the election, and I hope you are going to find they are a fine lot of fellows in the Society, and that you will get some satisfaction out of it.

There were other letters from father to son:

How are things going? I wrote you a sassy note about your marks which were shocking. I hope you will buck up on them this month. . . .

I wish that I might run up to see the game Saturday, but I have promised to go down to New Haven to preside at a dinner for Flint who is leaving the Medical School and to whom we are trying to give a proper send-off. I hope you will take a fall out of the Exeter people; but winning the game is not the whole thing. . . . It is a great art to be a good loser, and shows perhaps more sportsmanship than to be a good winner. . . .

I am so glad to have had your note and your itemized account. It's quite all right for you to set up the other boys for an occasional treat, but to take thirty-six at a time is quite an item. I don't want you to be stingy with the other boys, and I am sure you will never be. At the same time, I want you to get in the habit of reasonably conserving your resources and of coming to me without any hesitation when you are hard up.

The memory of his own reluctance to approach his father for money prompted Cushing to give Bill, and later Henry, a generous allowance when they were at Yale.

I think it will be more satisfactory for you to have a definite sum each month, so that you will know where you stand. But you had better let me see your month's expenses, or perhaps we can go over the matter together when we come down for the Princeton game.

I am delighted to hear of your good marks. 'It's dogged as does it.' I am sure you are liking the mathematics and hope that the history and English will not come too hard.

You will be amused to hear that Hen was arrested by a policeman Hallowe'en night in what I take to be the annual performance of ringing the church bell. Poor lamb, he must have been scared out of his wits; and it never occurred to him to run away.

By the end of his first year at Yale, Bill and his father were on easier terms. "Well, Va," Bill wrote him, "the year is almost over. I know I didn't by any means cover myself with glory as far as the Freshman year was concerned, but I hope to do better next year. The next thing to think of is this summer. I think it might be a good plan for me to write to Mr. Bursch of the General Electric and ask him what kind of a job he would give me or could give me if I came up for a couple of months this summer. [Bill had worked for General Electric before, getting up at four in the morning to get to Lynn on time for his job.] I would sort of like to go out west and have a good time but somehow it doesn't appeal to me as much as it might have a few summers ago. I think I would rather stay in Brookline or go up to Little Boars Head with the family than go out there."

In another letter Bill came to his father for advice as to whether he should continue in the academic course or transfer to Sheffield, as some of his friends were doing. In this letter there was a paragraph that again had a familiar ring: "Yesterday was tap day. One of the most moving sights that I ever saw or hope to see in connection with college. Barney and Johnny Bordley went Elihu and Hank Baldwin went Wolf's Head. Two fellows fainted during the half hour. One when he was tapped and another when the boy next to him was tapped." His father's reply was a long one—it revealed the new relationship between father and son and much of Harvey Cushing himself:

May 17, 1924

Dear Bill:

Thanks for your letter. I don't really believe I can advise you. I sympathize with you a lot, however, in the matter, for I know how hard it is to make decisions in life. However, you'll have to begin to make them for yourself. The important thing is, having made a decision, stick to it without misgivings. I really have no choice to express. All that you say about a liberal education is true, but as you know, many a man gets an education without ever going to college at all. It depends a lot more upon the man than it does upon the institution. Between 'Sheff' and academic, therefore, there need be no choice if a man goes at his work hard and gets the most out of his friends and his tasks before him. Your Uncle Ben was a 'Sheff' man for example.

On the other hand, I have always thought the academic men were a little more stable and got more out of college and college life than the men in the Scientific School, but here my impressions are coloured by the impressions in my own time, when the 'Sheff' men were only in New Haven for three years and when, I think, the society system was at its worst. Things may be different now, but I suppose something of the old order must continue.

It's foolish for a parent to expect his son to follow in his own footsteps. Much better to let him map out his own career.

Of course it would please me some day to pat you on the back in the hall on College Street; but then, after all, if you should make good and your friends were going the other way, you might choose Bones, or Wolf's Head, or, for the matter of that, might not make a senior society at all. . . . The primary motive of the societies is partly a reward of apparent merit, and in addition to the good-fellowship the societies foster a source of inspiration.

I say "a reward of apparent merit" because many a good man, as you of course realize, never makes a senior society, and there are many heart-burnings over it; but it was true of my class, as of many others, that time shows the best men have been overlooked and some of the poorer ones chosen. As a matter of fact this you will find happens through life. . . .

This letter brought the following response from Bill on May 19, 1924:

Dear Va, Thanks for your letter. Va, I have something more that I want to say to you. I think that I am just beginning to realize just how weak and selfish I have always been. You have often told me that I was selfish and didn't think of anything but my own personal pleasure. I always meekly agreed and then went upstairs and stormed around bemoaning my fate in having a parent who wasn't so lenient as some others. I am just beginning to realize that you have always done the right thing. I only wish you had taken me across your knee and spanked me. I don't know what started me thinking. Perhaps I have come to the turning point. . . .

There was another letter from Bill:

It was awfully nice to see you. I'm glad that you could get away and have supper with us last night. It does us both a world of good. I can't quite explain what I mean except to say that it makes me feel toward you more as friend to friend than father to son. Perhaps it ought not to make any difference but somehow it does.

Two years later, on June 12, Bill was killed in an early morning motor crash near Guilford, Connecticut. The word came to Cushing just as he was leaving to perform an operation on a woman who had gone blind the day before. He shut his study door for a time, made some calls, and then went through with the operation, not one of his team knowing until afterward what a strain he was under. Bill's death was a blow from which he did not recover for a long time. He was filled with remorse for not having given the boy more companionship and attention, and the only thing that brought him comfort was the fact that he and Bill had come to an understanding.

Cushing's relationship with his other children was somewhat less tempestuous, although he was equally strict. He and Henry had periods of not seeing eye to eye and sometimes they were as much at odds as he and Bill had been, but he often took Henry's side. One summer, as Henry was setting off to camp, he wrote Mrs. Cushing at Little Boar's Head: "Hen is quite justified in wanting to change his bathing suit: it's neither

male nor female and buttons on the shoulder! Impossible!!"
As with Bill, there eventually came the time when father and
son began to understand one another.

The girls aroused his fatherly (and his Victorian) instincts
when they grew up to the point of wanting to smoke or to
entertain in the drawing room beyond ten o'clock, which was
about the time he was well settled down to writing in the adjoining study. He felt that any self-respecting young man
should go home at that hour—a belief dictated perhaps more
by his own convenience than by other considerations. Cock-
tails, as well as cigarettes, they were forced to consume *sub
rosa*, he not becoming reconciled to the family partaking publicly until after they had left Boston.

With Mary, his second child, he had much in common—she
had his keenness of mind, his sense of humor. After attending
Miss May's School in Boston, she went to Westover at Middle-
bury, Connecticut, whence he had this letter from her:

Dearest Va—I loved your letter. I wish I could write such original ones as you.

I am so proud of you—that you are made a Chevalier of the
Légion d'Honneur. I know it's a great honor and you deserve it.

This is Sunday afternoon. One of my roommates is reading, and
the other, in whose head genius is burning, is writing a story for
the school magazine "The Lantern."

This morning we all went to church in a couple of dreadfully
seasicky trolley cars, and in our civilized clothes. After trying
awfully hard to sit up straight, I only got "fair" in posture, and
after running around the hockey field to get long winded, they
put me in as goal guard. I am feeling rather squelched; but "If at
first you don't succeed, etc." and I shall keep right on trying. Loads
of love—Sis Cow.

Much later, when one summer the whole family, with the
exception of Dr. Cushing, went to Europe together, she wrote
him from the *Samaria:*

Beloved Phad—So clear and beauteous is the day—so uncompli-
cated the existence of even such a "family of individualists," as
Mum calls us, on board this pleasant boat, that I think you would

thoroughly enjoy us. It's nearly perfect, but the utter complete-
ness of all of us being together is lacking without you.

Hen is trying to be extremely nonchalant—as though he had frequently sailed the shining seas—but he was up very early this morning and doesn't want to miss a trick. . . .

Barbara is wildly excited and everywhere at once. She seems
to grow more beautiful every day.

Later

All is well except that Babe succumbed to the rough weather
and has spent the last two days in the cabin. The rest of us go gaily
on. I'm a winner at deck tennis if I do say it. What do you say
we get a net and tie it up between two trees in our back yard—it's
a slick game . . .

Dearest love—we all miss you like the devil and keep wishing
you were here—Sis Cow.

A neighbor who saw a great deal of the Cushing children
in Brookline (again Mrs. Bigelow) described Betsey as being
more like her father than any of them: "Although fair like
Kate, her sensitive, eager features and her affectionate way of
coming forward to greet me wherever and whenever we meet
reminds me of him. She also goes straight for anything she
wants to do and nothing can stand in her way once she has
made up her mind. She is most understanding and wants always
to help others."

Mrs. Bigelow also described a jaunt on which she and her
daughter Gwladys joined forces with Dr. Cushing, Betsey,
and Henry for a trip south—she to Summerville, the Cushings
to Thomasville, Georgia, to visit Perry Harvey. Upon arriving in New York, the children wanted more than anything
to have tea at the Waldorf, and although Cushing was eager
to take a look at the first proofs of the Osler biography which
were at the Oxford Press, he did not disappoint them. On the
way, when he stopped to ask a question of a policeman in the
middle of the street, the man became so interested that he left
his post and followed along for half a block talking with him.
At tea, Cushing ordered all the toast, jam, and cakes the children could eat and they then went to the station to board a
southbound train. Betsey's every thought was for her father,

and she asked the porter for an extra blanket (since he was just getting over the grippe) and hoped he would sleep late because she knew he would read his book (*Arrowsmith*) far into the night. After a visit to the Azalea Gardens at Charleston (which Cushing was all for omitting when he discovered it cost two dollars each), the party went their separate ways. When Betsey had returned to school (she was now at Westover), she wrote:

Dearest Fa—I meant to write to you as soon as I got back here. I've never had such fun in my life as we had in Thomasville and it was sweet of you to take me. I really feel so well, because I had such a lot of exercise etc. and I hope that you feel all well, too, now. Didn't we have fun in New York? I wish we had had more time to look at the picture in the Grand Central. . . . Please write me soon, Faddie dear, All my love, Bet.

On another occasion when he had temporary charge of Betsey and Henry, H. C. wrote Mrs. Cushing:

I let Bet and Hen go to the carnival at the C. C. for skating under the promise they would come home at 9:30 prompt and be in bed at 10. They were—but they skated an hour in the rain which began at 8:30 and came home sopping. Can you beat 'em? But they seem all right today and Bet has gone in to spend the p.m. with her beloved and Hen is now making a date with the Grays. Does this have a familiar sound? I'm glad you are away from it for a while, as yours is quite a job.

Cushing set aside the established custom that a surgeon never operates on a member of his own family and did appendectomies on both Betsey and Henry. In 1930 he performed a much more serious and extremely delicate operation on Barbara when he removed a growth from her neck lying dangerously near the jugular vein, facial nerves, and much else. The operation was successful and the incision healed without a scar. Many wondered how Cushing could undertake an operation of such delicacy on his own child, but he did so not only because he thought he had as steady a hand as most, but because he was very reluctant to put the heavy burden on any of his colleagues.

Eventually Barbara, too, reached Westover. This time it seems to have been her father's side of the correspondence that was preserved. Although sometimes containing fatherly advice, his letters usually were lighthearted and whimsical— such as this which began: "The beautiful darling! Such a summer and I scarcely saw her except when she was mumpish or dentiferous. Now that you've lost all your four wisdoms, I suppose your whole character will have changed for better or for worse, in the words of the wedding ceremony. . . . I hope you are getting broken to harness. Good fun when you do finally all get the color of your uniforms and settle down to get some fun and some work out of each day. I expect you'll be president of your class or whatever it is you most want. With your grace and smile (which I suppose constitutes charm) and your good mind, you can beat them all."

This "family of individualists" was thus bound together with unusually strong bonds of affection. Although the children realized their father could never belong entirely to them, they sometimes had a wistful feeling which was perhaps best expressed by Barbara when at about the age of eight she wrote him in a round, childish hand:

Dear papa stay home with me. and Dont go earning money. We'll just do Something funny. I'll give you my Pennies. and I'll give you my shiny Buckle. I'll arrange all for you.

"THE SEVERE ASCENT OF HIGH PARNASSUS"

Chapter XXI

LATE IN AUGUST OF 1922 THERE came news from Baltimore that Halsted was seriously ill—he died on September 7. In the appreciation which Cushing immediately wrote for *Science*, the warm friendship that had developed between Halsted and his former resident was clearly reflected. Cushing carefully recorded all of Halsted's many important contributions to medicine and surgery and concluded his tribute with an admission of his own tardiness in recognizing him for what he was.

His loss to the Johns Hopkins Hospital which he served so faithfully and long, and to which he bequeathed his property, will be irreparable. It will be equally so to his many and devoted pupils. One of his long series of resident-surgeons—who, as others have done, came to know him better after leaving his service, just as many sons learn to know their fathers not until after they have grown up—has in all respect and affection written this inadequate note of appreciation: "Who knows whether the best of men be known, or whether there be not more remarkable persons forgot, than any that stand remembered in the known account of time?"

Late in October, at the meetings of the American College of Surgeons, Cushing had the responsibility both of a presidential address and of a technical paper; also he had the pleasure of presenting the Bigelow Medal to his old friend, Dr. W. W.

Keen (now in his eighty-fifth year), on behalf of the Boston Surgical Society. The medal (established by the son of Henry J. Bigelow), designed to honor outstanding surgeons, had been given for the first time the preceding year—to William J. Mayo.[1]

Although devoting all of his "spare" time to the Osler biography, Cushing did not neglect local affairs. He planned a special meeting of the Harvard Medical Society in January to celebrate the centenary of the birth of Louis Pasteur—which had fallen on December 27, 1922. He also saw to it that the students had opportunities to meet informally the distinguished surgeons who came each year to act as Surgeon-in-Chief pro tem for a period of approximately two weeks. Dr. Christian had begun this custom on the medical service, and Cushing took it up with enthusiasm. Although some of the surgeons were from this country, many came from abroad and offered the students a refreshing insight into the medical activities of other nations. This year the visitor [2] was Sir Harold Stiles of Edinburgh, who occupied the chair once held by Lister. The influence which Edinburgh had exerted through the early fathers of the Harvard Medical School was thus once again felt in Boston.

---

[1] Subsequent recipients: Rudolph Matas of New Orleans (1926); Chevalier Jackson, Philadelphia (1928); George Grey Turner of England (1931); J. M. T. Finney, Baltimore (1932); and Cushing (1933).

[2] Others were Dr. Dean D. Lewis, Rush Medical College, Chicago, 1920; Mr. G. E. Gask, St. Bartholomew's Hospital, London, 1921; Sir Cuthbert Wallace, St. Thomas's Hospital, London, 1923; Dr. Charles F. Hoover, Lakeside Hospital, Cleveland, 1924; Sir D'Arcy Power, St. Bartholomew's Hospital, 1924; Dr. Evarts A. Graham, Barnes Hospital, St. Louis, 1925; Dr. Clarence L. Starr, Toronto General Hospital, 1926; Dr. Emmet Rixford, Stanford University, California, 1927; Sir Charles Ballance, St. Thomas's Hospital, 1928; Prof. René Leriche, University of Lyons, France, June, 1929; Prof. D. P. D. Wilkie, Royal Infirmary, Edinburgh, October, 1929; Prof. Gunnar Nyström, University of Upsala, Sweden, May, 1930; Prof. Otfrid Foerster, University of Breslau, Germany, October, 1930; Prof. Vittorio Putti, University of Bologna, Italy, 1932; Dr. George J. Heuer, New York Hospital, July, 1932.

In May, Cushing addressed the American Neurological Association on the subject of "Neurological Surgeons: With the Report of One Case." He was not unconscious of the changed order of things which permitted him, a neurosurgeon, to become president of an association long devoted exclusively to neurology. "That surgeons should have been admitted into this intimate guild now nearing its half-century of existence speaks well for the open-mindedness of its members. . . . The fusion will be of benefit if for no other reason than that the balance sheets of surgery should periodically be audited by those not actually engaged in its practice."

A third invitation to accept the chair of surgery at Western Reserve came during the summer when it became known that Dr. George W. Crile was relinquishing the post. But he declined for the same reason given the preceding year to Dr. Weed, Director of the Johns Hopkins Medical School, when Weed pressed him to become Halsted's successor—at fifty-four he was set in his ways and didn't believe he could stand another transplantation.

When the Distinguished Service Cross was presented to him somewhat belatedly in 1923 (the award is actually dated 1926), he had a prompt letter from General Leonard Wood, then Governor General of the Philippines: "Sincere congratulations on the award of the D.S.M. I have not heard of any award for some time which pleased me more than this." In 1920, when Wood was being proposed as the Republican nominee for President (for the second time; he had been defeated by Charles Evans Hughes in 1916), Cushing had taken as active a part as he ever did in anything political. Among other things, he signed, with several other Boston physicians, a letter in the *Boston Transcript:* "On Why the Medical Profession Wants General Wood," reprints of which were used as campaign material. But their efforts were in vain. Although public opinion was strongly in favor of General Wood, whose work during the war had increased his popularity, the Republican convention nominated Warren G. Harding.

In June of 1924, at a meeting of the American Neurological Association, Cushing and Percival Bailey presented a paper describing a type of cerebellar tumor which they had named "medulloblastoma." Through Bailey's microscopic studies of the tumors in Cushing's collection, he had discovered that this type of tumor was pathologically different from the type that formed slow-growing cysts. The medulloblastomas are prone to occur in children and to recur, sometimes many times, and Cushing, although he knew the outlook was unfavorable, would operate again and again on the same child in an attempt to give it a few more months or years of life. There was always the hope, too, that some day he might find a way safely to remove that part of the brain where the cells originated.

The Osler biography, on which he had spent evenings, Sundays, and every summer since 1920, had grown far beyond his expectations both in length and in time required for completion. However, by May of 1924, he was able to send the manuscript, via Miss Shepley, to Oxford where the University Press was to print the volume. He too went to Oxford at the end of June to make final arrangements and to read the early galleys as they came from the press. In his first letter to Mrs. Cushing, written from the *Scythia*, he told her of his send-off at the boat: "Elliott and Carol [Cutler] came down and a flock of about 15 house officers in their white suits led by the genial Sosman. I was overcome." From Oxford he wrote again (on Wednesday, July 2):

I am on what they call an *up* train—*viz.* not one going *down* to London. [He had it reversed.] . . . Have seen the Press and made promises regarding the amount of MS. they were to get each day —which has meant working till 2 a.m. the last two nights. . . .

Chapman at the Press wants me to cut out another 500 pages. Golly! It would mean another six months. Meanwhile Bill [Francis] has been the greatest help—he's read the Canadian Period picking out innumerable small errors and points I would never have seen. You can have no idea how complicated it is. You mustn't say "next fall" but autumn. "Headmaster" means a master of heads not a school master which should be Head Master with capitals whereas head-prefect is with capitals and hyphenated, &c. . . . Julia [Shepley], thank Heaven, has become already saturated with

all this and calls on Bill when in doubt so I'm pretty safe. Lady O.
very nice about it though she insists on my taking her out of the
tub in the plumber's shop and such descriptions.

Dr. Francis was engaged in the monumental task of com-
pleting the catalogue of Sir William's library, barely begun at
the time of his death although he had written an introduction
and done annotations for many of the books in his own original
way. When Dr. Francis had completed the volume (he had
the assistance of Archibald Malloch, whose father had been a
close friend of Osler's in Canada, and of Reginald H. Hill of
the Bodleian Library), the books, according to Sir William's
will, were to go to McGill University, his alma mater. The
catalogue, like the biography, was more of a task than was
estimated,[3] so Cushing well understood Dr. Francis' problems. "Poor Bill. My sympathies go out to him. A gentle,
learned, modest, hardworking, lovable cus. He leads a hard
life with his job."

No. 13 Norham Gardens was thus a beehive with the biography and the catalogue going on at the same time. In addition, the house was constantly full of friends who sought out
Lady Osler as eagerly and faithfully as they had always come
when Sir William was alive. "Popsy and a Dr. and Mrs.
Freeman (he of Hopkins Med. 1905) here all day. . . . [Also]
Prof. Sherrington in A.M., Mrs. Chapman, wife of Secy to
Press in P.M. At 4.30 Myra Tutt with 2 young, very sweet,
soon a Noah's ark disgorging Barkers—a herd of them, then
several local people—Carr and Margaret Sherrington who have
left Cornell for a fine post in London, John Fulton and his
Lucia for tennis.[4] That's all I can recall at the moment, but
it was a lot, especially the Barkers."

As to the progress of the book, it seemed to him that it went

---

[3] When published in 1929, the *Bibliotheca Osleriana* contained 7,785
entries and ran to 785 pages.

[4] John Fulton was still at Oxford and was in and out of the Osler library
practically every day, occasionally helping Dr. Francis. Several letters
had passed between him and Dr. Cushing in the two years intervening
since their first meeting—in 1923, just before Dr. Fulton's marriage to
Lucia Pickering Wheatland of Topsfield, Massachusetts, Dr. Cushing

slowly. "Apparently it's a question of metal, as they say, at least 'Scroogs the Mono' says so. Scroogs the Mono! Did you ever hear the beat? Mr. Scroogs runs the monotype machine. These people are the greatest for abbreviations. Our American slang is nothing to it." Although the book was far from complete, he felt he could not stay longer and had taken return passage for August 9. "Julia will have to stay and finish Vol. II and do the index. She's quite capable of it and by that time it ought to be smooth running." At the end of the letter he added, "Sorry about the bronchitis but glad to know Hen went to camp o.k. He'll be the better for it in the fall. Gracious, I mustn't say fall—*autumn!*

> "There was a young person named Ball
> Who fell in the spring in the fall
> Love to all, Va."

During his final week he worked feverishly, hardly leaving the house except to play tennis occasionally with Bill Francis or John Fulton. It was discouraging that everyone who read proof discovered more errors—he constantly found his punctuation changed and all his "forebears" turned into "ancestors." And then there was the Bishop of Ripon! The Bishop was a "Delegate" of the Press, a distinguished authority who often read manuscripts for them. He had discovered on Galley 7 that Cushing's description of the Parker Society contained a grievous error—for the Society dealt merely with the Reformation and not with the Early Fathers as he had stated! "How in thunder was I to know?" he demanded in a letter home. "I never heard of the Parker Society and never met our Early Fathers. And it's now in pageproof. But the Bishop is one of the delegates and something must be done. It's too funny."

The outgoing secretary of the Medical Research Council,

---

had written: "Such exciting news about you. A first in physiology; a first in matrimony; first in the hearts of his countrymen. But I am sure from what I know and have seen of you, that you are still keeping your feet on the ground. What are your plans, and when are you coming home to take a Chair in Physiology?"

Sir Walter Morley Fletcher, who had been close to Osler, arrived for the week end, and Cushing immediately set him to helping with the proofs. Sir Walter, however, lured him away from duty to call on his friend John Masefield in the hope that together they could persuade Masefield to write a poem on science and surgery.[5]

The *Life of Sir William Osler* was finally published in two volumes in 1925. It began thus:

William Osler, the youngest son in a family of nine, was born July 12, 1849, in a parsonage at Bond Head, Tecumseth County, near the edge of the wilderness in what was Upper Canada. How this came about, as to place, time, and circumstance, needs telling from the very beginning.

It ended with the oft-quoted and beautiful passage:

So they—the living—left him overnight; alone in the Lady Chapel beside the famous 'watching-chamber' which overlooks the shrine of the Saint, and with the quaint effigy of his beloved Robert Burton near by—lying in the scarlet gown of Oxford, his bier covered with a plain velvet pall on which lay a single sheaf of lilies and his favourite copy of the 'Religio,' *comes viae vitaeque.*

And perhaps that New Year night saw, led by Revere, another procession pass by the 'watching-chamber'—the spirits of many, old and young—of former and modern times—of Linacre, Harvey, and Sydenham; of John Locke, Gesner, and Louis, of Bartlett, Beaumont, and Bassett; of Johnson, Bovell, and Howard; of Mitchell, Leidy, and Stillé; of Gilman, Billings, and Trudeau; of Hutchinson, Horsley, and Payne; of the younger men his pupils who had gone before—Jack Hewetson, MacCallum, and McCrae; and in still greater number those youths bearing scars of wounds who more recently had known and felt the affection and warmth of the 'Open Arms'—doubly dead in that they died so young.

Between these two passages there is unfolded the crowded life of a man whose activities and friends covered two continents. It was a straightforward day-by-day account, told in minute detail and with warm admiration and affection.

---

[5] Masefield later, when visiting in the United States, came to watch Dr. Cushing do a brain operation.

Through the inclusion of much of Osler's own writing—both formal and informal—his physical radiance and zest for life stand out from the pages alongside his accomplishments. There was little attempt at critical evaluation, reflective pondering on Osler's inner life and motivations, or assessment of his impact on his century. These were left for the reader to infer from the wealth of material presented. Absent, too, were all indications of the long and close relationship between the biographer and his subject—a relationship which could not have failed to leave its mark on the older man as it had on the younger. But in the style of the book and its arrangement, in the finished quality of its prose, and especially in its omissions, the discerning will find the biographer clearly revealed.

The *Life* received immediate and wide recognition and was handsomely praised not only by friends, but in the public press as the greatest medical biography that had ever been written. Cushing was particularly pleased with the many letters from physicians and students who had not known Osler personally. He was also proud of a letter from a literary critic—Stuart P. Sherman of the *New York Herald Tribune*, who had praised the book enthusiastically in his columns:

Dear Dr. Cushing: I am very fond of valorous people who do difficult things; far more than is *possible;* and I rate the writing of that "Life," even in four *vacations*, as among these things. It is a pleasure to hear that you thought it not unintelligently reviewed; but that pleasure was nothing to the satisfaction I had in reading the book, and so in feeling the encouragement of those two strenuous souls, Osler and his biographer.

The following year (1926) the biography was accorded the Pulitzer Prize in Letters by Columbia University. William Osler, who had always brought out the best in Harvey Cushing, had once again called forth the full measure of his talents and devotion. As Dr. Francis has said: "No one but Osler himself has done so much for Osler's immortality."

For Cushing, writing had now become the medium of expression for his artistic talents as sketching had been in his youth. From the first he had had the knack of presenting his clinical papers in a fresh, vigorous style, and his skill increased with experience. There were some who thought he over-dramatized in his technical papers, thus threatening the impartiality expected of a scientist, but there is no doubt that they made interesting reading. Even his Annual Reports had a refreshing vitality rarely found in this traditionally dull type of writing.

But it was in his essays that he displayed his greatest skill as a writer. These fall into three categories: his writings on medical education and the medical ideal, his biographical appreciations of his contemporaries, and his historical essays. Among the first are such titles as "The Physician and the Surgeon," "The Clinical Teacher and the Medical Curriculum," "Experimentum periculosum; Judicium difficile," "Realignments in Greater Medicine," "The Medical Career," and "Medicine at the Crossroads."

In many of his biographical pieces there was a serene, affectionate tone that make them documents of great warmth and understanding. In his tribute to his cousin Perry Harvey, the inseparable friend of his childhood and college days, he outlined the happy hours of youth and the more tenuous, but none the less loyal, relationship of later years. His tribute to "The Mayo Brothers and Their Clinic," although less personal, was no less warm.

There was nothing mysterious or supernatural about this twentieth-century Lourdes at whose doors incredible numbers of the lame, halt, and blind have for years been daily delivered from the ends of the earth. Nothing supernatural—unless possibly the flawless, lifelong devotion of two brothers for one another be so regarded. . . . Their father, the senior Dr. Mayo, pioneer and Indian fighter, was still alive when I first came to know the clinic in its early simplicity. There were then but two operating tables, at one of which "Dr. Will" officiated, at the other in an adjoining room "Dr. Charlie." They were thus affectionately differentiated by everyone—staff, patients, employees, and fellow townspeople—not to mention the countless visiting doctors who even then were wearing a path to their door.

To quote more would be to detract from the pleasure of reading the whole,[6] a pleasure that may be repeated in "The Doctors Welch of Norfolk," "William Beaumont's Rendezvous with Fame," and in his appreciations of Halsted, James Ford Rhodes, William T. Councilman, and others.

Something of the same intimate, informal style lends great charm to his historical essays. The problems of the day fell away from him when he entered his study after supper, and he was soon in imagination walking the streets of pastoral Gloucestershire with a country doctor named Edward Jenner who, a century and a half before, had noticed that although almost every other person was badly pock-marked, the dairymaids seemed immune to the scarring disease. With Jenner he shared the thrill of discovery that the cowpox which they frequently caught had made them immune to smallpox.

Or he was in Vermont when Nathan Smith, the founder of the Dartmouth School of Medicine and later the bright star of the first faculty of the Yale School of Medicine, was introduced to the healing art.

A hundred and fifty years ago a young Harvard undergraduate named Josiah Goodhue because of a swollen knee was obliged to leave college, and in due course became the pupil-apprentice of the doctor in whose care he had recovered and in whose activities he became interested. He started practice in Putney, Vermont, became the pioneer surgeon of these parts, and ere long was summoned to Chester to amputate the leg of a man who had been severely injured. He had never before performed a major amputation, and, needing help, asked the bystanders if someone would volunteer to hold the leg. A farmer boy who happened to be teaching in the district school at Chester stepped forward and accepted the trying task without flinching.

Or, on a journey entitled "From Tallow Dip to Television," Cushing was in Boston in the days when its population consisted of but 12,000 persons and the dwellers of Beacon Hill were legally entitled to "pasture and exercise multiples of two

---

[6] The sketches here mentioned, together with several essays on medicine, were published after Dr. Cushing's death by Little, Brown and Company (1940) in a volume entitled *The Medical Career*.

legs on Boston Common: two legs, a goose—four legs, a cow—six legs, a cow or a pig and a goose." He brought old Dr. Edward Holyoke from his Salem home where he had trained thirty-five apprentices to ask some embarrassing questions of the present-day scientists and educators at Harvard, and sent him back again in his one-horse gig, "scorning that modern impediment to progress, the red light," as he disappeared in the direction of Salem.

Despite the fact that the stimulation and diversion offered by these wanderings in the past seemed to make his essays write themselves, Cushing worked many hours over them, writing and rewriting. Wide reading, of course, preceded the stage of pen and yellow pad. Stories of his own Western Reserve perhaps came easiest to him and "The Western Reserve and its Medical Traditions" and "The Doctor and His Books" (the latter given at the opening of the Allen Memorial Medical Library in Cleveland) are among his best essays. Early in the first one we find a passage on traditions that gives us the key to several of his own inner doors:

Tradition, indeed, is the most powerful binding influence the world knows. It lies deep in most of us, and pride in tradition supplies the glue which holds people and groups of people in cohesion. Pride in family and friends, in Alma Mater and profession, in race and birthplace, in state and nation. The controlling subconsciousness of one's stock and upbringing is something from which time and distance can never wholly wean us.

A year or so after he wrote this essay, Mrs. Cushing drew his attention to an *Atlantic Monthly* article in the same vein—"Olympians in Homespun" by Lucien Price. The spell of the Western Reserve was on this native son also, and in his vivid description of the vigorous environment created by the early settlers, Cushing recognized a kindred spirit. "Hardscrabble Hellas," the story of the boys' school that antedated the Western Reserve Academy, later the University, was also a source of delight to Cushing, and he and Lucien Price became warm friends.

Cushing's writing brought him other friends outside his pro-

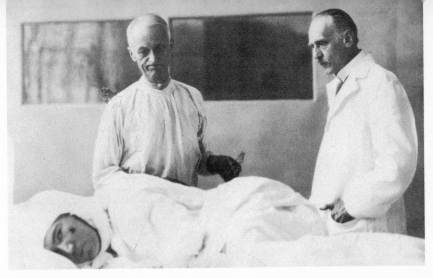

DR. CUSHING AND DR. OTFRID FOERSTER IN A MOMENT OF PERPLEXITY, 1930

SURGICAL STAFF OF PETER BENT BRIGHAM HOSPITAL, 1929

front row: Richard U. Light, Donald E. Dial, Richard W. Farnsworth, Thomas I. Hoen, Louise Eisenhardt, William deG. Mahoney, John E. Scarff
middle: Harlan F. Newton, Gilbert Horrax, John Homans, Gunnar Nyström (Surgeon-in-chief pro tem), H.C., David Cheever, Francis C. Newton, John H. Powers
top: Kenneth W. Thompson, two students, John H. Lawrence, Arthur T. Hertig, Bronson S. Ray, William T. Green, Eric Oldberg, George Armitage, William R. Henderson, Richard H. Meagher, Edward B. Castle.
Courtesy of Walter W. Boyd

PLATE 9

ARNOLD KLEBS, WILLIAM WELCH, DR. CUSHING, AND SIR CHARLES SHERRINGTON
BERNE, 1932

AT VOLENDAM EN ROUTE TO INTER-
NATIONAL OPHTHALMOLOGICAL
CONGRESS, 1929
Photograph by Dr. Klebs

H.C. AND GUSTAVE ROUSSY, DEAN OF
THE FACULTY OF MEDICINE, PARIS,
1933

PLATE 10

fession, for the time and painstaking effort he expended on it resulted in craftsmanship of such quality that he was widely read outside of medical circles. His pen thus became a powerful adjunct to his scalpel in spreading the broad concepts of medicine to which he had dedicated himself. "Few indeed have been the disciples of Aesculapius who have climbed 'the severe ascent of high Parnassus' and at the same time been successful in their vocation. For the laity has ever been shy of the physician who allows his mind to soar above the level of most practical and mundane things; and a genius so inclined has, in reciprocation, not uncommonly failed in his profession from an equal shyness of the public." Such a fate was not meted out to Dr. Samuel Garth, Cushing pointed out in "The Kit-Kat Poet." No more was it meted out to Cushing himself, and Gay's lines about Garth might likewise have been penned about him (if "prose" be substituted for "poetry"):

> Whenever Garth shall raise his sprightly song,
> Sense flows in easie numbers from his tongue;
> Great Phoebus in his learned son we see
> Alike in Physic as in Poetry.

Chapter XXII

Cushing and bailey, following their paper on medulloblastomas in 1924, continued their work on the classification of the different types of tumor by publishing jointly a volume on tumors of the glioma group in 1926. There were three principal categories of brain tumors: those growing from the brain covering (meningiomas); those arising from glands within the head (pituitary and pineal); and those of the glial cells found in the brain and spinal cord. The glioma group of tumors formed approximately 40 per cent of all intracranial new growths, and their appearance under the microscope differed widely; but Bailey after careful study came to the conclusion that all of these tumors had a common cellular ancestor and he made up a family tree showing their origin and interrelationship.

As the authors pointed out, this could have been done only with a large series of cases available, and then only if these cases had been followed throughout their span of life. Cushing had the detailed records and an unrivaled collection of brain tumors, and Bailey had gone to Madrid to learn the methods for their study devised by Ramón y Cajal, del Río Hortega, and the other members of Cajal's school. The result, entitled *A Classification of the Tumors of the Glioma Group on a Histogenetic Basis with a Correlated Study of Prognosis*, was received with enthusiasm all over the world. It was dedicated to "Professor S. Ramón y Cajal and to the disciples of his distinguished school of Spanish neurohistologists."

The study had been largely financed by the Philip H. Gray Fund, established in 1923 by the widow of a patient who had died of a malignant glioma. It gave Cushing $10,000 a year for ten years for study of tumors of the glioma type. Mr. Chester C. Bolton of Cleveland supplemented this fund several years later in gratitude for Cushing's care of his son Charles after injury from a diving accident. Such generosity helped materially toward accumulation of the approximately $30,000 that Dr. Cushing had to provide each year to pay the running expenses of the laboratory, the salaries of Dr. Bailey, Dr. Eisenhardt, a photographer, artist, technician, and so forth. Additional income came occasionally from large fees charged wealthy patients with the understanding that these would be turned over immediately to the laboratory. The balance Cushing made up out of his own pocket.[1]

During the summer of 1925, Cushing was engaged in a last editing of the glioma monograph and in the preparation of the Cameron Lectures which he was scheduled to give in Edinburgh in October. This lectureship, established by Dr. Andrew R. Cameron of New South Wales in 1878, had previously been graced by such distinguished physicians as Pasteur, Lister, Ferrier, Horsley, and Macewen, the only American having been Simon Flexner. Three lectures were required (honorarium £200), and Cushing chose as the title for the first lecture, "The Third Circulation and its Channels." He summarized the papers published by him and his pupils since 1901, most notably those on the origin of the cerebrospinal fluid which Lewis H. Weed had begun at the Hunterian in 1912. The second was on "The Pituitary Gland as Now Known"; again he summarized the work of his laboratories ever since his interest had been stimulated by Edward Sharpey-Schaefer in 1908; including developments in the field since the publication of his monograph in 1912.

The third lecture, on "Intracranial Tumors and the Sur-

---

[1] Dr. Cushing also provided supplementary support for the Surgical Laboratory in the Medical School to augment an inadequate budget. Out of the $5,000 which was his salary during his entire service at Harvard, he also had to pay his secretary.

geon," covered the historical background of the subject, tumor classification, and gave data on his own cases, which now numbered 1,146. The three lectures were subsequently published under the title, *Studies in Intracranial Physiology and Surgery*. His audiences had come to expect something superior from Cushing and they were not disappointed. "His distinction is—and it is a distinction which places him for all time in the front rank of scientific investigators— . . . that he has regarded and studied his specialty from every conceivable angle."

Early the following year (1926) Cushing went to Baltimore to be present at the unveiling ceremony of a portrait of Revere Osler in the new Tudor and Stuart Club where Revere's books, given by the Oslers to Johns Hopkins University (together with a gift of money), were to be placed. At the same time Cushing attended a dinner to honor Dr. Dean Lewis of Chicago, who was to take Halsted's chair of surgery.

It was not long before Cushing's attention again turned to the Hopkins when Dr. Weed consulted him about a library that they were planning in honor of Dr. Welch. After the architect had come to Boston to show him the preliminary plans, he wrote Dr. Weed most enthusiastically. "What a monument to Popsy this library will be! It ought to become the most important in the country next to the Surgeon General's." He had only two suggestions for improvements on the plans—one in respect to the stacks and the other on a point he considered basic in a library, that it be on the ground floor without a single step which might act as a deterrent to students using it.

In June he gave the Commencement address at the Jefferson Medical College in Philadelphia, where Thomas McCrae occupied the chair of medicine. During the exercises he received an honorary Litt. D. His address, "Consecratio Medici," offered him an opportunity to expound a favorite theme—the doctor-patient relationship. This theme was part and parcel of his deep-rooted convictions about medical education. A clinical teacher himself, he was inclined to believe that a student learned more medicine at the bedside than during his preclinical indoctrination in the "pure" sciences. He had elaborated upon this in a

paper entitled "Experimentum periculosum; Judicium difficile," presented at New Haven (1925) when he and Dr. Welch
were invited to help dedicate the new Sterling Hall of Medicine.

Even when the relation [of preclinical subjects to ultimate goal]
is obvious, it would seem to be a needlessly long and uninteresting
process. The anatomist describes the form and situation of the
pancreas; the embryologist shows how it buds off from the gut;
the histologist in turn points out the acini and the islets; the physiologist presents the accepted theories of the manifold functions of
the normal organ; the biochemist discloses the complicated ways
of detecting and of quantitating the various sugars; the pharma-
cologist perhaps demonstrates the action of the newly discovered
insulin and explains how it is prepared; the pathologist, getting
down to more solid ground, shows in turn the diseased organ; and
finally, after two years of this, the student first sees a patient with
symptomatic evidences of pancreatic disease, possibly brought to
light by a carbuncle or a gangrenous toe.

 How much simpler to have shown the patient first, to have
briefly explained how diabetes came to be recognized and what
its complications may be, how step by step the mysteries of car-
bohydrate metabolism have partly been unraveled and the principles of our present-day treatment established—in short, the solid
facts of the matter in the order in which they were discovered.
Is not this the logical method of presenting our increasingly complex subject? . . . Could science be prevailed upon to concede to
the clinic from the beginning of the course a single hour a day,
if necessary from eight to nine in the morning . . . the average
run of students would certainly face their subsequent laboratory
hours not only with greater interest but with a clearer appreciation
of why it is necessary to get the best possible scientific grounding
for their future career.

 It was a challenging theme for an address at the opening of a
building to house preclinical laboratories. And his stand, of
course, brought him into conflict with his preclinical colleagues, for they believed that the student was unprepared to
appreciate the disease conditions encountered in the clinic before he had had a broad background in the biological sciences.
Undoubtedly many resented the fact that Cushing thought a

busy practitioner could better teach students the basic scientific principles of medicine than physiologists, anatomists, and pathologists whose main concern was teaching and research. But this did not keep him silent. He even went so far as to say that "there is much that a present-day medical student might envy in the opportunities offered to a young man of a century ago, apprenticed to such a person, let us say, as Nathan Smith, with the chance to get at the outset an intimate knowledge of people and of people's maladies; to discuss the problems of the sick room with the master while driving him in his gig as he went on his distant house-to-house rounds; to have his collateral reading directed; and subsequently to take a short course somewhere in the so-called fundamentals and get his degree." And again: "I do not believe that students can begin to think in terms of the patient too early in their course, nor too early begin to interpret and record what they can see, hear, and touch— perhaps even smell and taste—at the bedside."

This gospel of observation and deduction grew up alongside another tenet that had its roots in the same soil. "No one can be a good physician who has no idea of surgical operations, and a surgeon is nothing if ignorant of medicine." This was a theme on which Cushing ruminated throughout his professional life— and he practised it.[2] At a time when the tendency to specialize was growing, he preached vigorously the principles of "the good old days" when the family doctor was physician, surgeon, technician, psychiatrist, and physiotherapist all in one. He believed that the modern physician in relying on all the aids which science had placed at his hand to assist in diagnosis and treatment—X-rays, laboratory tests of all kinds, etc.—tended to lose sight of the value of examination, observation, and common sense. "It would be an admirable thing," he thought, "if every student, before his graduation, be required, under the control and supervision of his teachers or the district physician of the community, to engage in an actual house-to-house practice,

---

[2] In 1939 Dr. Cushing was made an Honorary Fellow of the Royal College of Physicians of London. He was the only surgeon ever to receive this honor, and in the two centuries and half of its existence, the College had appointed only six Honorary Fellows.

armed perhaps with nothing more than a clinical thermometer, a stethoscope, his fingers, and wits, supplemented perhaps by a microscope and a few simple dyes. In this way he might learn something at least of the living conditions which modify the health of the people he now only meets in the dispensary, surrounded by all of the paraphernalia and instruments of precision supposed to be necessary for a diagnosis."

This was oversimplification of course, but it made his point —that specialists can become too specialized—and it emphasized a fact of growing importance, namely, that to consider the mind and body of a patient is not enough, a knowledge of his environment is essential in order to remove the causes which brought him to illness.

When it came to teaching, Cushing's ideas were equally "practical." Because he was not an easy lecturer, he had, from the first days at the Hopkins, done most of his teaching in the operating room or by clinical demonstrations rather than in the formal lecture. He believed even more firmly that students learn by doing and was supported in this conviction by the popularity and success of his operative course on dogs at the Hopkins, described in a lecture to the Yale Medical Alumni Association back in 1906. "It will make of the students better and more trustworthy assistants when, later in the curriculum, they are privileged to take part in the more responsible operations on man—occasions when slips in technique must not occur." He had concluded with this statement—a belief that was not modified or shaken by the years—

Emphasis is laid .... upon the fact that the operation is not the beginning and end of surgery, but a therapeutic measure alone; and that those employing this manner of treatment must have the same knowledge of disease, the same ability to make examinations, the same instincts to follow pathological material to the laboratory and to investigate there the causes and symptoms of disease, as should characterize any other well-trained members of the body medical.

Mr. Geoffrey Jefferson has called this paper one of the most fascinating in surgical literature, "since it illustrates an approach to surgery bearing the hall-mark of what one might call the University mind at its highest level applied to humanitarian purposes."

In Boston, Cushing offered an elective clinic on Saturday mornings for first- and second-year students. In addition he had a regular Wednesday noon clinic for third-year men, in preparing for which he spent the entire morning each week, much as if the subject to be considered were completely new to him. Despite this careful preliminary planning, the clinics were always informal, and on one occasion an opinionated student remarked that he wished Dr. Cushing would sometime prepare for his clinics!

Cushing also had staunch convictions about the value of postgraduate study and research, especially abroad. The memory of his year in Europe was always close to him and he appreciated the broadening influence of an opportunity to observe and work in foreign hospitals and clinics. It led him in 1925 to write to Dr. Weed that he and Mrs. Cushing wished to make $25,000 available for a graduate fellowship at the Hunterian Laboratory. Dr. Weed not only expressed gratitude to Cushing, but thoughtfully wrote to Mrs. Cushing also: "All I can say is that this gift of yours and Dr. Cushing's is just like you both. Both of you have always been so wonderfully good to the young people around you: you have so markedly broadened the viewpoint, the horizon of so many of us. And now this personal influence is going to be continued permanently."

A similar fellowship was established (by outright gift of $25,000) in the Department of Surgery at Yale named in memory of their son William. And at the Brigham, Cushing began in 1921 to turn over to the Trustees a portion of his fees from patients for the establishment of a "Surgeon-in-Chief Fund" created to send men from his staff abroad for study (or, if deemed wise, to some American institution). On his retirement, in 1932, the Trustees designated the fund, then grown to nearly $35,000, the Harvey Cushing Fellowship Fund. The Treasurer of the Trustees, Mr. E. D. Codman, called the fund a representation of "the finest spirit of loyalty to the Hospital, the staff and its future beyond any gift the Hospital has received."

It was this June (1926) that William had been killed. After a brief time at Little Boar's Head with the family, Cushing returned to Boston and endeavored to bury his grief in hard work. His legs had grown increasingly worse. The incessant smoking he had done while writing the Osler biography had aggravated his circulatory difficulties, for the arteries in both legs were already permanently affected by an ascending thrombosis. He made no mention of his discomfort, however, but his staff were not unaware of the reason why he would stop two or three times while going down a long corridor on the pretext of discussing a case or to make comment on what might be going on outside a window. Nevertheless, he did little to slacken his general pace, in fact he seemed to increase it— occasionally scheduling two operations a day instead of one. And he would appear completely oblivious to the annoyance he caused everyone when he so often scheduled these "double-headers" on Saturdays.

Several improvements had come about in the control of hemorrhage since the days when Cushing had invented his tourniquet. This had long since been replaced by injecting the skin with the blood-constrictor, adrenalin, and by the use of the silver clips he had devised in 1910. Blood transfusion was now used during operations, but blood coagulants had not yet been developed. The problem continued to be a serious one, and there were many types of tumor still unapproachable because of their profuse bleeding.

In the autumn of 1926, Cushing used for the first time an electric cautery apparatus in a brain operation. In general surgery and in genito-urinary surgery, high-frequency currents had been used for some time in dealing with both benign and malignant growths, but it was Cushing who established their value in neurological surgery. With the co-operation of Dr. W. T. Bovie, a physicist with the Harvard Cancer Commission who had previously developed apparatus for dealing with cancerous growths, he experimented with currents and equipment until they had one current that would cut tissue without attendant bleeding and another that would coagulate a vessel which might have to be cut during the course of an operative procedure.

The first occasion was not without its drama. The New England Surgical Association was having a meeting in Boston and many members attended, and a member of the visiting staff brought five French guests to witness the event. The homemade apparatus was wheeled down the street from the Huntington Hospital, where Dr. Bovie had his laboratory, and had to be carefully adjusted after the rough journey. Such was the excitement and confusion in the operating room and the suspense as to whether the apparatus would work that the student who was to act as blood donor, should one be needed, fainted and fell off his chair. And the first assistant, a resident who had arrived from England about three days previously, found the whole procedure more than he could cope with and Dr. Horrax had to be found and called in. But the result was most gratifying, and Cushing was so encouraged that he immediately began to call back all the patients on whom he had not dared to operate before he had this electrosurgical device. The Liebel Flarsheim Company became interested in the project and later Mr. Liebel presented Dr. Cushing with the first unit constructed commercially.

Cushing's mortality figures began to climb somewhat because he was attempting to remove what had been considered inoperable tumors. Nevertheless, his success on the whole was phenomenal. Writing and almost everything else were forsaken while he spent more and more time in the operating room. Had Dr. Horrax not assumed a large portion of the burden, Cushing's health would doubtless have suffered. The new assistant resident, Mr. Hugh Cairns, said the Battle of the Marne was nothing compared to the stress and strain of being Dr. Cushing's assistant that year.

Recognition of the work of his clinic came from several different directions during the following year. He sailed for England on June 4, accompanied by Betsey (now eighteen) with Miss Stanton as her companion—and incidentally a useful helper in connection with his three papers, yet unfinished.

His first responsibility was a lecture on acromegaly from a surgical standpoint before the Medical Society of London. He was amazed and delighted to have that great student of the nervous system, Sir David Ferrier, now eighty-four, come from virtual retirement to hear the lecture. His subsequent travels resembled a triumphal tour—at Glasgow he inaugurated a lectureship to honor Sir William Macewen, who had died in 1924, and received an LL.D. from the University. His paper was a milestone in neurosurgical history since it described for the first time the use of electrocautery in the removal of brain tumors. He next attended a meeting of the Society of British Neurological Surgeons at Manchester, where he visited the John Rylands Library and had opportunity to meet again his warm friends, Mr. and Mrs. Geoffrey Jefferson.

In Dublin on June 28 Cushing received, in an elaborate and colorful ceremony, the degree of Honorary Master of Chirurgery from Trinity College. He was also made an Honorary Fellow of the Royal Academy of Medicine of Ireland. After a week in Paris he went to Edinburgh to give an address at the Lister Centenary celebration. The inspiration for his paper had come to him the preceding spring when standing in front of the Lincoln Memorial in Washington. Stirred almost to tears by its beauty, it came to him that this man who had freed men from slavery could be compared to the man who had freed mankind from sepsis, and his address, "Emancipators," is one of the most moving of all his essays. A third honorary degree, an LL.D. from Edinburgh, was later followed by election to honorary fellowship in the Royal Society of Medicine and honorary membership in the Society of British Neurological Surgeons.

But his pleasure in these honors was soon overshadowed. He returned home immediately his lectures were over because he was faced with another operation on General Leonard Wood. He found General Wood eager to have the ordeal over, and although reluctant to undertake so important a procedure after being absent from the operating room for over a month, he acceded to the General's wish. He found a massive recurrence of the meningioma which presented problems taxing all his skill and ingenuity. Four transfusions were necessary during the seven-hour operation, and when at last the General was resting quietly in his room, untoward symptoms appeared which necessitated re-elevating the flap. Once again he hoped that all was well, but General Wood's condition became rapidly worse and he died in the early evening. The loss of any of his patients always had a profound effect on Cushing, but this courageous man who had been a valued friend for so many years was a double loss. In severe self-criticism and unconsolable dejection, Cushing wrote: "He was a great man. I've never lost a patient after operation that so upset me. It was *so* near success. . . . If I had used better judgment he would certainly have been saved."

A GOOD DOCTOR

Chapter XXIII

THERE IS NOTHING MORE SINCERE nor more heart-stirring than the gratitude of a sick person to the physician who has helped him regain the precious gift of health. Harvey Cushing's files are crowded with letters from his patients—and letters to his patients, because he followed for years the lives of those his skill had helped. He followed them for two reasons, his own personal interest in their welfare and for what a record of their subsequent history would contribute to the progress of medicine.

Although he was a specialist in a large medical center, Cushing's relationship with his patients was much like that of a country doctor; indeed the country doctor was the prototype of what he thought a physician should be—what he aspired to when he said that he wanted above all to be "a good doctor." In reading the letters he encouraged his patients to write each year on the anniversary of their operation one fact will be apparent over and over again—that while few of his patients were unaware that in the eyes of the world he was a great man, the feeling that he was their friend was uppermost in the minds of all of them. They sent him birthday and Christmas cards and remembrances, told him of their marriages, babies, and other events important in their lives, and asked his advice about many things. And his replies assured them of his interest in all their concerns.

Of the thousands who loved and admired him, a few, chosen

at random, will illustrate the warm friendliness and interest that existed on both sides. Just as Cushing made each operation a personal issue between him and the forces threatening his patients' lives, so throughout their days he stood between them and any recurrence of the same misfortune. For many, of course, one operation sufficed, but there were others who, because of the nature of their tumors, had to return again and again.

Dr. Fulton wrote during the year he was one of Cushing's neurological assistants:[1]

In going over the histories one is continually impressed with the Chief's perseverance in dealing with the more malignant group [of cerebellar tumors in children]—the medulloblastomas. Though these children return time after time, often after a period of six or seven months, with recurrence of symptoms, the Chief always goes in again with the hope that this time he may be able to remove the tumor in its entirety. He fights for the life of these unfortunate children with the ardor of a religious missionary and seems never willing to admit that it is a losing game. His attitude is much that of Dr. Joslin in his struggle with diabetic children. Dr. Cushing had one patient with a medulloblastoma who had lived four years (the usual survival period being about fourteen months after the onset of symptoms). He was so elated over the fact that he reported the case, and then had his hopes shattered six months later when the child returned with an enormous recurrence and died several months later. Now that the new electrosurgical technique has been developed, he attempts radical extirpation of the tumors with renewed hope that now at last he has found something which will enable him to deal with the cases effectively, but alas! one of the cases done only last November came back a few days ago. The Chief's only comment was, "I didn't do it as well as I should have."

But no matter what the nature of his patients' illness, Dr. Cushing kept in touch with their subsequent progress with in-

---

[1] Cushing persuaded John Fulton that he should have a medical degree in addition to his doctorate in physiology. He accordingly entered the Harvard Medical School and received his M.D. in 1927.

terest and sympathy. There was twelve-year-old John D., a very bright, lively boy who, because of pituitary malfunction, was undersize for a boy of his age. In 1922 Dr. Cushing removed a supracellar cyst. After the operation he kept in close touch with John's progress and after three years suggested that he return to the hospital to try some injections of pituitary extract in the hope that his growth would be stimulated. John's father wrote in March of 1925, "John is overjoyed at the prospect of entering the Hospital and seeing you again." Two weeks later Cushing reported:

This is just a line to let you know that John has been behaving splendidly, making friends with everyone, "taking his medicine" like a little man, and with no complaints. Inasmuch as it means pricking him with a needle and making him a little sick to his stomach once every forty-eight hours, it shows how co-operative he is. He is the pet of the hospital and is allowed many privileges. So I think you may feel at ease.

But the experiment was unsuccessful and Cushing reluctantly admitted defeat, writing John's father on May 15:

I think you are quite right about John. We do not seem to be making any great progress just now and I think the hospitalization may have been carried on as long as justifiable. I may say, however, that he is just as cheerful and loveable as he can be. I brought my small boy down here the other night with a broken arm and went into the ward to dress him. It was nine o'clock and the ward was dark and they should all have been asleep, but John was entertaining the patients with a bed-time story over which they were in a gale of laughter. We shall miss him greatly when he leaves.

While the family were in Little Boar's Head in the summer of 1929, Cushing once again called in some of his patients suffering from pituitary dwarfism, taking a few of them into his house to save them the expense of the long hospitalization. But the growth hormones which Tracy Putnam had found effective in animals in his experiments at the Surgical Laboratory did not accomplish the results in humans that Cushing had hoped and again he had to send John home without the desired gain. "He's been a perfect angel—patience on a monument."

There was a prominent naval captain who came to Dr. Cushing with a meningioma like General Leonard Wood's which threatened to cut short a brilliant career. He was descended from a long line of naval men, his father having been an admiral, and a great uncle a former Secretary of the Navy who founded the United States Naval Academy at Annapolis in 1845.

In less than two months after the first operation, a second was made necessary by postoperative complications, but after that, the patient made a good recovery, received a promotion to Rear Admiral in due course, and returned to duty. In 1937 he wrote Dr. Cushing: "Beside yourself, Cairns, and some of the hospital staff, few can know of the great battle you fought to save my life, and how unsparingly you gave of your time and unequalled skill and knowledge to pull me through and restore me to useful service. . . . I am able to run this Naval District . . . without undue strain or fatigue."

There was Milton W. Ferguson, who first came to Cushing at the Hopkins in 1907 when he was eight, almost blind from a cerebellar tumor. The last of five operations was done in 1925, and when Milton sent his annual report in 1936, Dr. Cushing wrote him:

Dear Milton: Thanks for your letter with its Easter greetings. I am always so happy to hear from you, particularly when, as now, you say that your head is feeling better and that you feel like a new person.

You say that it was April 11th, 1925 that I last operated on you, but it must have been nearly twenty-five years since a small boy in knickerbockers who was unsteady in his gait turned up at the Johns Hopkins Hospital and was subjected to an operation, then supposed to be very dangerous and which amounted to nothing more than opening a cyst. If we could only have known in those days that there was a little nodule of tumor in the wall of the cyst which could be removed, you would not have had all this trouble from loss of vision. But there is no use crying over spilt milk, and you fortunately were a born optimist. So that's that, and I am sure you have got more out of life than a lot of people do who have a good pair of eyes.

Please give my regards to your father, and believe me, Always affectionately yours.

Milton Ferguson wrote many letters to Cushing over the years, and Dr. Cushing never failed to answer. They discussed Braille, George Gershwin, laxatives, Dr. Cushing's having met his sister at a Grenfell lecture, or Milton's having seen a picture of the three Cushing girls in the Boston *Post*—"I think my sight is improving," he wrote. Their last exchange was after Dr. Cushing's seventieth birthday: "First of all may I send you my heartiest congratulations upon your birthday anniversary. The news came over the radio tonight and was I thrilled!"

Six months later another letter came from Milton Ferguson, written in the simple dignity of deep grief:

My dear Mrs. Cushing and family: It was a great shock to me this morning when I heard over the radio that Dr. Cushing had passed away. I hardly know what to say.

My associations with Dr. Cushing were perhaps unique as he saved my life five times. . . . I looked forward every year to April 11 to make my report to him on my condition and always got a prompt and cheery reply. It is like losing a very dear friend, as you must realize that a blind person has few friends to whom he can go for advice when in trouble. . . .

. . . I will close by saying I share with you the very great loss to us all in his passing.

But although Milton Ferguson had to have five operations, there were others for whom Dr. Cushing had to fight even harder, aware often, as with the recurrent medulloblastomas, that it was a losing battle. He knew, for example, that Timothy Donovan, who inherited the charm but not the luck of the Irish, could live only a few years at best. He removed four tumors in seven years, and the difficulty he had with the fourth caused him to say: "After this desperate procedure the unanimous feeling was 'never again.' But Tim was not so easily discouraged. To the surprise of all he walked into the hospital eight months later, January 20, 1927, with a gleam in his eye as much as to say 'I told you so.' "

A year later he was back again for the sixth time, and on this occasion a junior staff member wrote on his record that another operation seemed hopeless. "Euthanasia appears to me the only indication." Cushing, in writing up Timothy Donovan's case in his monograph on the meningiomas several years later, was led by this comment to write:

Both patient and surgeon may philosophically decide that life is no longer worth living; yet each will instinctively rebel at bringing it to a close, though this would be so painless and easy during an operation by exsanguination or an overdose of the anaesthetic.

No fine distinction can be drawn between courage and cowardliness. All of us know plenty of people, leading useful lives, who once went under an anaesthetic in the hope of not waking up, leaving the surgeon, whatever his misgivings, to go about the legitimate business of doing that for which he was trained. His hardihood depends greatly on the state of his digestion, the soundness of his sleep, and freedom from extraneous worries. He may shrink today from an operation that he approaches with confidence tomorrow. So, when after a few days, poor Tim aroused sufficiently from his stupor to indicate that he was ready, that was enough.

Even this was not the end. Tim Donovan returned twice more, but died six months after the last operation—mercifully, since with each recurrence the period of mental deterioration grew longer.

But there was a case more heart-stirring than this because it did not at first appear so hopeless and because the patient was able to live a normal and extraordinarily rich life in between the recurrences of her tumor. This patient was Dorothy May Russell of Salem, Massachusetts—a talented pianist who came from a family of musicians. In 1919, shortly after leaving the Graduate School of Fine Arts at Syracuse University, she was admitted to the Brigham Hospital with a suspected tumor since for six months she had been gradually losing the use of her right arm. Her convalescence was slow after the removal of the growth, but when she returned home, she seemed happily on the mend. She wrote Dr. Cushing immediately:

My dear Dr. Cushing: It seems strange not to be able to see you any more. I used to watch for you in the afternoon and was always so glad when you came. Now I cannot watch for you but I think of you. . . .

For the past five years I have gone to Syracuse University this month [September] and it seems strange not to be going back now. . . . I have made all sorts of plans for the future, that glorious time when I shall have two good arms, hands and fingers. Then you can pity the neighbors when I practice again. My hand is gaining all the time which gives me all kinds of courage. . . . Most gratefully and respectfully, Dorothy Russell.

Within three months she was back, and again in four, and during the next four years had to return about twice every twelve months. Realizing that a concert career was now impossible, she began to give music lessons (at twenty-five cents a lesson) and to study the violin. Once she wrote: "I have thought of you many times . . . and hoped to write you that I was feeling 'bully' and had entered the Conservatory as a violin major. Now I cannot tell you either. . . . I am sorry I have to write about my losing consciousness, but I am *not* complaining. You must think I am one of your 'worstest' patients and I would desire to be one of your 'bestest.' However, I have some good news to tell you. I can practice three hours a day on the violin and my arm is growing stronger all the time."

In 1923 Cushing wrote her family physician: "Dorothy Russell has been back again with, I am glad to say, only a small nodule of tumor in the scalp. So far as I can make out there is no intracranial recurrence. She is a good girl and has been very cooperative and I shall stick to her, if necessary, to the end, but hope that this may prove to be the end." But it was far from that. On her tenth admission, Dr. William Van Wagenen's comment in the case record was: "A thin, undernourished young woman with one of the most unusual personalities I have ever had occasion to meet. It was astonishing to find any human being who could maintain mental equilibrium so well, and have a sense of values so completely undisturbed as has this woman after her long siege of difficulties."

At one point her mother wrote Dr. Cushing: "Dorothy is so distressed that we have been unable to pay you for your many operations, and great kindness. Yesterday she sent for me to come to the hospital. She said 'Mother, I just can't lie here and take Dr. Cushing's time and owe him so much. Won't you put me in the open ward and pay him the difference?' I think our great obligation to you, and our inability to meet it has been one cause of her anxiety to succeed." [2] To this Cushing replied: "If I were not interested in Dorothy and her trouble and not eager to see her make a perfect recovery from her baffling malady, I would have sent her to the public ward and turned her over to someone else long before this. . . . If she gets well, as I am sure she is going to do, that will be quite sufficient payment for me."

After three years of struggle with the violin, Dorothy Russell had to give it up too. Her mother described to Dr. Cushing the day she finally admitted defeat:

One day after trying to practice she put the violin in the case and put the case away and also the music saying, "It is hopeless, no need to try longer," with such a look of despair on her face, but turning to me and adding "Don't mind so much, Mother, see I am not crying." I could not keep the tears back, but she met it bravely. She never touched the violin to play after that.

With splendid courage she next turned to harmony and was successful in selling a few of her songs. She was then partially supporting her family with her music lessons, but these were interrupted periodically by her visits, now yearly, to the hospital. In 1927 Dr. Cushing wrote to the Boston Music Company without her knowledge, telling something of her story. This resulted in their buying two of her manuscripts, for her work had real merit. One, for the organ, she asked for permission

---

[2] Dr. Cushing always made a point of inquiring about a patient's financial status when the history was being taken. His charges were always moderate (his usual fee for a craniotomy being $250 to $500), but if he discovered that the patient had limited means, he sent no bill at all or a very small one. If the patient came from a distance, he never thoughtlessly asked him to return to the hospital for a routine check-up, but made arrangements if possible for him to see someone near at hand.

to dedicate to Dr. Cushing: "The 'Twilight Reverie' is an unpretentious bit. I would wish it better than anything Beethoven has ever done to dedicate it to you, but it is the best I have done up to the present time. While the composition is small, the spirit and affection that accompanies my wishing to dedicate it to you is very big. I hope you will understand." His reply was: "Do as you like, but not having any music in my soul, to my everlasting regret, I am afraid that to dedicate a piece of music to me would be enough to spoil it."

After each operation there came the joyful feeling of well-being, and the ability to accomplish more work. "I am going to try so hard to make good, to be of some use in the world so that you may not feel that your skill and kindness have been wasted." This indomitable spirit kept her at her teaching until ten days before what proved to be her last hospital admission, in December of 1932. Many of her pupils won scholarships and other honors in music. "Every pupil seemed to feel a greater incentive to be something and do better work by being with her," her mother wrote.

During 1932 she had had two operations, the second bringing the total to seventeen. When she returned to the hospital on December 17 (her twenty-first hospital admission) she was in a state of semi-stupor. If she heard the carolers in the ward on Christmas morning, she gave no sign. There was nothing more Dr. Cushing could do, and she died in the late afternoon.

Her brain was set aside at autopsy for further study. Ten years passed before he had the courage to examine it. In his meningioma monograph, he wrote: "In the postmortem protocol it is stated that no description [of the brain] had been received and the opinion is expressed that one might never be. But even a pathologist surely might make allowances should a surgeon fail to show great enthusiasm over a lifeless brain he has handled a dozen or more times when pulsating and alive; learning meanwhile, both at and between sessions, things about its quondam possessor no microscope could ever disclose. One does not get the whole story from the autopsy."

FOUNDER OF A "SCHOOL"

Chapter XXIV

As the special techniques which had made possible the development of brain surgery came into wide use through the men Cushing had trained, he began to be called the founder of a "school." And because he taught not only techniques but a broad approach to medicine, he will stand in history as a leader of men long after his technical contributions have been replaced by new advances.

Men were attracted to Cushing not alone because he was known as the world's most eminent neurosurgeon but because of his compelling personal magnetism. Through it he inspired a rare degree of loyalty in those who worked with him although many of them ruefully admit that he could make them more angry than anyone they had ever encountered. But although he did not always have the warmth, Cushing possessed something of the physical radiance that was Osler's and he could quickly win again those he had antagonized. It was to this charm that he owed his many loyal friends in college and medical school and when he made use of it, it was difficult to resist him.

The atmosphere of his clinic was largely created by his colorful personality. His own energy, his ranging enthusiasms, his high standards of performance kept things moving at a rapid tempo. Because many of his patients came with desperate or out-of-the-ordinary conditions, there was an unusual air of suspense surrounding his activities, intensified by the fact that he had a way of investing any situation with drama. The distinguished visitors from foreign shores, and the honors from home and abroad that were constantly coming to Dr. Cushing, also added interest. But work was carried on under military discipline, and Cushing as commander-in-chief was unpredictable. He might spend hours helping a junior assistant with a paper but have no patience at all if the man left something undone in the clinic. On such occasions he had a way of correcting that was hard to forget. Dr. Carl W. Rand of Los Angeles remembers one such occasion vividly.

At lunch one day Cushing told Rand that he would like that afternoon to do a dressing on a certain patient who had been operated on the previous week for a cerebellar tumor. Preceding Dr. Cushing in order to have everything in readiness, Dr. Rand split the tremendous crinoline dressing that extended from the top of the head to the waistline in the form of a cast so that it could be more easily removed. "Never was Cain more severely castigated for his misdoing!" Rand wrote later. "I do not recall exactly what was said after his first look of astonishment, and toss of the head, but I can never forget that succeeding hour. I was given a lesson in the technique of dressing a wound which was indelibly impressed on my memory, and then left in gloomy silence to ponder on it for the next several days." Thereafter he seemed unable to do anything right and when he had almost reached the point of desperation, Dr. Cushing asked him to come to Sunday dinner the following day. Dinner, however, was a matter of embarrassment to Rand despite the efforts of Mrs. Cushing, who did her best as an understanding and gracious hostess. The rest of the evening is best described in his own words:

Doubtless he too was aware of my uneasiness, and after coffee had been served he excused us from the family circle and led the way into his library. . . . As I sat and watched he began to look over his stacks of books until his hand fell upon a large thin folio, which showed signs of age although it had evidently been rebound. He drew up beside me and laid it open upon the table. It proved to be a first edition of Sir Charles Bell's "Illustrations of the Capital Operations of Surgery," Part I, Trephine, published in 1820. He went over it carefully, as only a book lover can, paying especial attention to the part that dealt with "dressing after trepanning." . . . To my utter surprise when I left he handed the book to me as a gift. To make it even more precious, I discovered upon later examination, that it had been given to him by William Osler. Surely a *coup de grâce* in wound dressing never to be forgotten.

This experience could probably be duplicated with variations by almost any man who ever worked under Cushing. But despite uncomfortable incidents (some of which were not resolved as agreeably as this one), the general atmosphere in the clinic was a healthy one of give and take, enthusiasm and co-operation. It was well described in an entry in the diary of John Fulton at the time of the fifteenth anniversary celebration at the Brigham in April of 1928:

He talked to us as though he were speaking to members of his own family, and one somehow carried away the feeling of being in a happy family group. This, I think, is the secret of the delightful spirit of co-operation which pervades all departments of the Brigham Hospital, and I somehow feel that when the Chief's accomplishments come eventually to be enumerated, the spirit of co-operation and friendship which he has inculcated in the Brigham group will be looked upon as one of his great achievements.

His assistants saw many sides of him and each was attracted by a different aspect of his complex character. J. Paterson Ross, who was a junior associate for six months during 1923, has a vivid recollection of a visit to the Ugly Lady in the circus who had come to Dr. Cushing's attention because of her acromegalic headaches. Cushing's work on the pituitary had made him particularly aware and sympathetic with the abnormal conditions which so often found their way to the circus, and he had a lifelong interest in the problems of these people. At one time he wrote indignantly to *Time* magazine about a woman whose picture they had published under the caption of "Uglies." He explained that, previously a vigorous and good-looking woman, she had become the victim of the disease acromegaly and had accepted the offer of Mr. Ringling's agents to pose as "the ugliest woman in the world" in order to support her four fatherless children, but "she suffers from intolerable headaches, has become nearly blind, and permits herself to be laughed at and heckled by an unfeeling people. . . . Beauty is but skin deep. Being a physician, I do not like to feel that *Time* can be frivolous over the tragedies of disease."

Dr. Leo Davidoff, a well-known neurosurgeon in New York, remembers that one time in 1924, when he was assistant resident, Dr. Cushing had been in a particularly disagreeable mood, finding fault with everyone and especially with him. "As you know," Davidoff said, "it was never his policy to apologize for this kind of behavior. The next morning, however, he felt better again, greeted me most cordially, and we started on rounds. The first room we entered on the private pavilion was that of a new female patient. He asked her what she complained of and she declared a change in her disposition had occurred which made her disagreeable to all her friends. The Chief looked at me with a twinkle in his eye and said 'That's no sign of a brain tumor, is it, Davidoff?' "

Dr. Cushing's rare skill in drawing people out reminded Dr. William K. Livingston, professor of neurosurgery at the University of Oregon, of an incident which occurred during his medical school days. During an informal conversation with Dr. Cushing, Livingston ventured to ask him to what he ascribed his eminent position. Cushing immediately seized upon a slang word which Livingston had just used. "By being cagey," he told him with a twinkle. He went on to explain that during his early years he was constantly aware that his co-workers often had a wider grasp of certain subjects than did he. In such cases, he made a habit of drawing them out, learning directly all he could of the subject. He would then supplement this information with reading until he felt he knew as much if not more than the man he had been drawing out. As a result, he frequently had something in reserve—some special bit of knowledge—that singled him out from his fellows. "Sometimes," he told Livingston smiling, "that difference was very, very slight, but it gave me the reputation for being cagey, and I've always tried to maintain that reputation."

Nearly all of his men were struck by his constant desire to check on himself by keeping some kind of tally or score. He made a habit of reviewing his material constantly and often used the term "batting average" in the evaluation of his work. It was an example in avoiding complacency that many of his men found worth while to follow.

Dr. Thomas A. C. Rennie of the New York Hospital had an experience that revealed yet a different facet of Dr. Cushing's character. One evening, when Rennie was an intern in medicine, he was sitting in the residents' quarters about 11:30 p.m. playing the piano. He was tired and, completely absorbed in the music, did not turn around to see who had entered the room. He knew only that someone stood behind him with his hand on his shoulder and after some five or ten minutes moved away. As the person left the room, Rennie looked up and realized that it was Dr. Cushing—realized, too, that he must have climbed the long flight of stairs, since the elevator did not run so late at night. He felt chagrined and remiss in courtesy.

Several days passed, but though he saw Dr. Cushing several times in the hospital corridor, there was no opportunity to speak to him. One afternoon, however, when he was working in the laboratory, a nurse came in in some excitement and said Dr. Cushing wanted to speak with him.

He was phoning [Rennie writes] to ask my advice about his maid, Nellie, who was sick at home with a sore throat, and to know whether I would come out in consultation that evening to see her. He said he wanted a consultation with a good medical diagnostician, and phrased his request in so gracious a manner that I, a mere pup on the service, could hardly fail to be flattered. I agreed to meet him in his office within a half hour and drive home to dinner with him. I stuffed my pockets with swabs, test tubes, and media, and joined him promptly.

With more diligence than skill I examined Nellie, and took innumerable throat cultures. After dinner Dr. Cushing asked me if I would be good enough to play for him. I did my best with what limited Brahms and Beethoven I knew, and he listened quietly for almost an hour. He then asked me if I would play for him his favorite piece of music. My heart sank, for I was sure he was going to ask for Stravinsky or Shostakovitch. At least I would find out what a great man liked in music. My anxiety was unnecessary, for I *could* play his favorite piece. It was "Old Man River." The next morning he left at the front desk with a note John Hunter's *A Treatise on the Blood, Inflammation and Gun-shot Wounds.*

One summer Dr. Cushing returned from a trip abroad to discover that in his absence the library had been moved upstairs in the Medical School and its former quarters taken over by the Dean for administrative offices. This was too much. Not only did the men have to climb stairs to get to the library, but it was for the convenience of, of all persons—the Dean! Dr. Reginald Fitz, Associate Professor of Medicine at the Medical School and Chairman of the Committee on the Library, received an immediate call from Cushing and the full blast of his wrath. After he had delivered himself forcibly of his sentiments about libraries, about deans (that they should all be in the cellar and the more prisonlike the quarters, the better), and several other things, he stamped out, leaving Dr. Fitz feeling as if he had been at the center of a cyclone. The next day two notes of apology to him with roses for Mrs. Fitz arrived at his house.

Despite the fact that Dr. Cushing could loose a verbal barrage without much warning, he almost never was heard to swear. Paul Martin of Brussels, the first man from abroad to serve as his resident, remembers one rare occasion when he and Dr. Cushing were walking down the corridor and Cushing suddenly threw open a door and stepped into the room. He discovered to his chagrin that painters were in the process of painting the floor and with his foot squarely in the wet paint, Dr. Cushing said "Dam" and then added somewhat shamefacedly "nation."

In the autumn of 1927 Sir Charles and Lady Sherrington arrived in Boston to spend a week with the Cushings while Sir Charles gave the Dunham Lectures. Their visit was followed by one from the eminent French brain surgeon, Thierry de Martel, and the equally distinguished neurologist, Clovis Vincent. Their purpose was not only to observe in Dr. Cushing's clinic but to make him an *Officier* of the Légion d'Honneur,[1] the highest honor France bestows on a foreign civilian. The decoration was bestowed on him at tea time at 305 Walnut Street, with Dr. Cushing standing under a picture of the Rheims Cathedral and with those friends present who happened to drop in on that afternoon.

Mr. M. A. DeWolfe Howe, then Editor of the *Atlantic Monthly* and one of his Saturday Club friends, persuaded Cushing during this year to let the Atlantic Monthly Press publish a volume of his essays. He accordingly collected fourteen of them under the title *Consecratio Medici*. He also committed to press another technical monograph on tumors—this time on tumors of the blood vessels. In addition, he published eighteen papers, among them an essay on "The Medical Career" which received warm praise when he gave it at Dartmouth College in November; also a technical paper on visual disturbances resulting from meningiomatous tumors at the base of the brain (presented to the American Medical Association), which won him the award of the Herman Knapp Prize in Ophthalmology the following year. A provocative essay on "Who Put the Fox in Foxglove?" was read to the Club of Odd Volumes but never published.

While he was at Little Boar's Head with the family during the summer, the sad news came of the death of Lady Osler. When he wrote a few days later to Edith Gittings Reid, a close friend of the Oslers whom he had known well in the Baltimore days, he said, "Let us imagine the three of them happily reunited—Muz, Dad and Isaac [2]—in as good a world as they helped this one to be. Heaven could hardly be better."

Affectionate whimsy of this sort was his refuge when he had to speak of things that touched his heart. Earlier in the year when Mr. Goodwillie died, he had written Mrs. Goodwillie: "When it comes my time to go to a better place, he will be one of the first people I shall look for. We will kick our right legs in the air [their special gesture of greeting] and be happy to be together again."

---

[1] He had been made *Chevalier* in 1922.

[2] Revere, because of his fondness for fishing, had been nicknamed Isaac Walton.

Harvey Cushing was not a conventionally religious man, although in his life of service to his fellow men can be found the very essence of Christian teaching. He lived so vitally in the present that the question of the hereafter seemed something very remote. He rarely spoke of death, although he once wrote his good friend Alan Gregg of a mutual acquaintance: "I am glad he went off suddenly and without a lingering illness. It's the way doctors would like to go and ought to be privileged to go." In a letter he wrote near the end of his life to his old colleague Howard A. Kelly is to be found a rare mention of religion: "No, I don't think anyone would talk religion to George. I do not pretend to understand the psychology of it; but a good many of us, I imagine, had a peculiar kind of Calvinism drilled into us in our youth that has left us inarticulate and quite unable to talk simply and sensibly about the 'supreme question.' Nor do we necessarily regard it as the supreme question, believing that to lead clean and useful lives while we are here is more important than cogitating over the hereafter."

On April 8, 1929, Cushing reached his sixtieth birthday. Two years earlier, Elliott Cutler, who had gone with him to France and had been at the Brigham until he went to the Western Reserve, had asked all of Cushing's older pupils to contribute papers to a birthday volume. It was published as a special issue of the *Archives of Surgery* (of the American Medical Association) through the interest and co-operation of Morris Fishbein. The birthday party at which the volume was presented to Cushing was held on Saturday afternoon, April 6, with nearly a hundred present, including the Cushing family. When Cushing began his speech of gratitude he was almost incoherent with emotion, but he gradually found words to express himself. Comic relief followed in the presentation of a flamboyant necktie and the reading of the poem once before mentioned, called "The Tie That Blinds," by Kenneth McKenzie, a former assistant resident who had come down from Toronto for the party. Within a week thereafter Cushing wrote by hand to all of the eighty-two contributors to the birthday volume.

Later in April, Betsey's engagement to James Roosevelt was announced at a tea at the Cushing house. Governor and Mrs. Roosevelt, Franklin, Jr., and John came over from Albany, New York, for the occasion and were photographed with the Cushing family and their close friend, Jonas Lie, the artist, and his daughter. But Dr. Cushing managed to escape when he saw photographers approaching, so he is conspicuously absent from the picture.

On May 29, Cushing, as representative of the Osler Club of London, attended the dedication of the Osler Library at McGill. A room had been especially constructed in the Medical School building to receive the books, and Cushing commented that while the alcoves, oak wainscoting, rugs, etc., were most attractive, the books themselves "would furnish any, even a poor room." Osler's former assistant, William Thayer, gave the principal address. "Thayer was simply inspired—the best thing I have ever heard him give. It included a perfect tribute to Bill Francis which was timely and what I particularly went up to hear."

Late in the summer Cushing was heavily involved in the 13th International Physiological Congress, which brought to Boston physiologists from all over the world. Dr. and Mrs. Edwin Cohn, assisted by an able committee, had arranged the affair with such thought that it proved to be a marvelous success. Cushing had as his guests Sir Walter Morley Fletcher, Professor and Mrs. Leon Asher from Berne, Professor Bottazzi from Naples, and a former assistant, Dr. Frédéric Bremer from Brussels. Dr. Asher, when going through the customs upon his arrival in Boston, was surprised to have the official ask him his destination and even more surprised to have him, when he found he was to visit Dr. Cushing, wave him on without investigating his luggage. Later, at a formal tea given by one of the leaders of Boston society, the hostess tried to draw Dr. Asher out about what sort of man Dr. Cushing had been when he was studying in Berne. Asher, with a twinkle in his eye, admitted that he was a "lady killer," and was startled when his questioner responded quickly: "He still is!"

One of the leading figures at the Congress was, of course,

the great physiologist, Professor I. P. Pavlov of Russia, who was within a month of his eightieth birthday. He was eager to watch Dr. Cushing operate, and Cushing accordingly scheduled an operation which went off very successfully despite the fact that Pavlov in his intense interest repeatedly came dangerously near the operative field with his whiskers.

After the Congress, Cushing sailed for Sweden, where he was to give a lecture on cerebellar medulloblastomas on September 4. The invitation had come through a young pathologist, Arvid Lindau who two years previously had described a new disease which Cushing had called "Lindau's disease"—a condition involving tumors of the blood vessels of the retina and central nervous system and sometimes causing degeneration of internal organs such as pancreas and kidney. This trip to Sweden brought him the opportunity to visit Dr. Erik Waller, a scholar-physician who possessed one of the finest private collections of early medical books in all of Europe. With Dr. Waller, a busy country surgeon, Cushing found much in common, and this visit was the beginning of an enthusiastic friendship.

Cushing was also entertained by the well-known Swedish explorer, Sven Hedin, who had visited his clinic as a patient the year before with his sister Alma. As a token of gratitude and admiration, Hedin presented Dr. Cushing with a beautifully illuminated parchment scroll, seventeen feet long, copied from an important early surgical manuscript of the fourteenth-century surgeon, John of Arderne. Cushing had been particularly interested in the manuscript when in the Royal Library in Stockholm, and the copy became one of his most choice possessions.

He made his presentation to the King of Sweden the subject of a delightful fantasy for the entertainment of his children when he returned home. Shortly after this state occasion, he bade farewell to his hospitable Swedish hosts and flew to Amsterdam, where he was met by Ignaz Oljenick, who had shortly before completed two years as a voluntary graduate assistant at the Brigham, and by his friend Arnold Klebs. He had first met Dr. Klebs in Baltimore when Klebs was practising in this country, and despite the fact that the two men were completely opposite in personality and tastes, a warm friendship had developed between them. Klebs was a man of great erudition and sophistication, with a hedonistic philosophy of life that recognized none of the Puritan restraints which had been Cushing's heritage, yet in their love of books and the history of medicine they had a strong bond in common. After Lady Osler's death, it was to Les Terrasses, Klebs' villa at Nyon overlooking Lake Geneva (to which he had retired in 1912), that Cushing went instead of to Oxford.

On this occasion they proceeded from Amsterdam to Scheveningen—to the 13th International Ophthalmological Congress where Cushing was to read a paper on blindness caused by brain tumors impinging on the optic nerve. His official responsibilities over, they motored to Nyon to rest for a day before starting for Milan to attend a book auction where Cushing acquired some particularly fine early works, several of which were incunabula. At Bologna they visited another avid collector, Vittorio Putti, the eminent orthopedic surgeon who lived at San Michele where Cushing had found so much to interest him when he first visited there in 1901. Stopping at Zurich to have luncheon with Felix R. Nager, the Swiss otolaryngologist, Cushing acquired an incunable—the Hartmann Schedel copy of Pietro d'Abano's *Conciliator* printed at Mantua in 1472—which became the oldest and one of the most treasured items in his now extensive library.

On his return Cushing had the happy duty of giving the principal address at the dedication of the Welch Library. The gathering was reminiscent of the lively meetings of the Johns Hopkins Hospital Historical Club, and "Popsy's" boyish pleasure and enthusiasm seemed no less at seventy-nine than in the days when Cushing had sat with him on the front row and discovered those truths which he now expressed so cogently.

But there is a spirit world of books, and the ideas they contain wander forth to haunt and torment those whose grasp they can elude, to solace or stimulate those who have learned the secret of their capture. . . . From the spirit that hovers over some obscure volume, of parentage and birthplace unknown, times forgotten

upper left PROFESSOR CHITTENDEN, DR. CUSHING, AND GOVERNOR WILBUR CROSS
At dedication of Beaumont Memorial Highway, 1935
upper right ON AN ULCER DIET
lower left WATCHING A CROQUET GAME AT 691 WHITNEY AVENUE
Mrs. Cushing, David Wheatland, Mrs. Fulton, Mrs. Wheatland, and John Fulton
lower right DR. CUSHING AND ANOTHER GUEST OF THE HARVEY CUSHING SOCIETY
MAY 1935
Courtesy of Robert H. Crowell, Jr. (upper right) and Richard U. Light

PLATE II

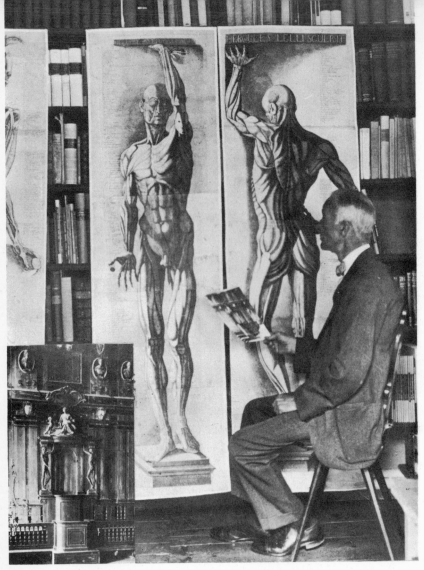

STUDYING CATTANI'S COPPER ENGRAVINGS OF THE ERCOLE LELLI FIGURES
*The insert (a copy of which Dr. Cushing holds in his hand) shows the écorchés
in the anatomical theater at Bologna*
Photograph by Dr. Klebs

PLATE 12

may be reconstructed, the sequence of discovery unraveled, the tendencies of thought traced, the relation of yesterday and tomorrow better understood.

This, then, is the true function of the library, to quicken the dormant book so that it may speak again; and with those who treat it lovingly and compassionately its spirit enters eagerly into communion. To these a library becomes a laboratory for the crystallization of ideas perhaps long expressed, out of which process new ideas have their birth.

Books—and men—it was on these that Cushing depended for the furtherance of those traditions to which he had dedicated his own energies and genius for what was now many years. During the preceding summer, Arnold Klebs, who was an excellent photographer, had caught Cushing in an unusual pose, leaning on a stone parapet of the Axenstrasse overlooking Lake Lucerne. He was resting on his elbows, his square hands clasped loosely before him, the familiar cigarette between his fingers. In his eyes was a reflective, far-away look, as if he were "hearing oftentimes the still, sad music of humanity." It might have been the likeness of an ascetic or a philosopher. Harvey Cushing had always worn his years lightly, but this picture, snapped when he was unaware, recorded undeniably the fact that he was no longer young.

ADDING UP THE SCORE

Chapter XXV

Iν 1930, AT THE AGE OF SIXTY-ONE, Cushing reluctantly faced the thought that he and Henry Christian had placed the retiring age at the Brigham at sixty-three. That the time was uncomfortably close was brought home to him by the fact that he was already being offered other chairs—Dr. Welch was trying to persuade him to return to the Hopkins and take his place as professor of the history of medicine, and President Angell and Dean Winternitz of Yale had invited him there (where the retiring age in the Medical School is sixty-seven). Although in the full swing of his busy clinic he found it difficult to think of retirement, his friends were not discouraged. Dr. Welch broached the matter a second time when he arrived in Boston in February of 1930 to stay with Cushing and to speak at a fund-raising meeting of the Boston Medical Library. In April, Cushing went to Washington to join in the gala functions arranged to honor Dr. Welch on his eightieth birthday. A luncheon sponsored by President Hoover was followed by a dinner in the evening, and at this, to Cushing's embarrassment, Dr. Welch announced that he was to be his successor.

Accounts of such occasions went regularly to John Fulton, who had returned to Oxford as a Fellow at Magdalen College and was teaching physiology. Cushing kept in touch with all of his former assistants, but Fulton was singled out for special attention because of his enthusiastic interest in books—"I have been doing but little with books lately, though it is an evil day if something doesn't turn up. However, I ordered some Leonardos the other day from Berlin and I am horrified to see that they take up more room than the Murray's Oxford Dictionary. Luckily Kate is in the South fattening up Barbara and Betsey. I think I shall have to build a cupboard under the dining room table where they won't especially be noticed and where we can pull them out at dull dinners. No, I have no copy of Raynaud's original thesis [1] and would be delighted to have one."

Fulton in turn kept Cushing in touch with events in England in which he had a particular interest. Dr. Cushing occasionally gave him bookish commissions and in one instance he asked that he take a copy of Robert Bridges' poems to him at Boar's Hill and enquire "if he will do me the supreme favour of writing his name in it. You may tell him that I collect poetry written by doctors, even if they happen to be poet laureates." The Poet Laureate died before Dr. Fulton was able to see him, but the commission had stirred him to do some research on Bridges, the result of which he sent to Dr. Cushing. In thanking him, Cushing enclosed a letter "from my friend, Lefty Lewis. . . . I wanted you to read his characterization of Streeter and his sad and gentle enthusiasm about you. This will be enough to let you know that Lefty is a man of humor and one after your own heart." This was Fulton's introduction to the man who was to exert a considerable influence in future affairs of concern both to Dr. Cushing and to him. He replied: "I have just had your letter of May 27th in which you enclose the amusing communication from your friend 'Lefty' Lewis. I assume from his name that he must at some time have occupied with distinction the centre of a baseball diamond. . . . I am returning Mr. Lewis's letter with this; I suppose he is 'Mr.' for you do not mention that he is a physician—in fact, I am just a little vague as to what he does do, but I can assure

---

[1] Maurice Raynaud was a nineteenth-century neurologist whose paper on symmetrical gangrene, published in 1862, has become a classic. The condition he described is known as Raynaud's disease.

you that I am eager to make the acquaintance of anyone who writes such a letter."

Dr. Cushing enjoyed this sort of lighthearted exchange, and when writing to someone of whom he was especially fond, he slipped even more easily into a whimsical vein—as in this letter to Mrs. Fulton, written in May of 1930, which gave hint of approaching events:

Dear Lucia: I am simply delighted to have your letter written in John's absence. I wish he would go away oftener and leave you home so I could hear from you directly. . . . Of course I shall expect to spend 99.5% of my visit next July with you. And you can reserve a seat for me in *your* car, thank you.

Jimmy and Betsey will also be browsing around England at the same time on their honeymoon, and they will probably be using John's car. If he is good, therefore, we can take him with us in the rumble. If D'Irsay and Winternitz and H. M. Evans and Sudhoff have not already gotten ahead of me by booking their rooms for the summer, you will please tell them that everything's let for July.

Betsey and James Roosevelt were married on June 4, 1930, at St. Paul's Episcopal Church in Brookline, and although Cushing had complained of prematrimonial neurasthenia, "nowadays purely a parental disease," and had told Betsey that Gus would probably have to give her away, he nevertheless was on hand in correct morning attire with topper, morning coat, and spats despite the 90° heat. He reported to Klebs: "Our front yard looks like a circus and I feel like Mr. Ringling —the wedding ringling."

When the excitement caused by the wedding had died away, H.C. began working on the Lister Memorial Lecture which would take him to England in July. For the first time in twenty years he had become convinced that disturbances in which the pituitary were involved were due not entirely to dysfunction of the gland but to impairment of nerve centers adjacent to it. He had paid little attention to the work of Bailey and Bremer in his laboratory, but when John Beattie (then teaching anatomy at Montreal) spoke before a meeting of the Harvard Medical Society on the excitability of the hypothalamic area at the base of the brain and the work he had been doing with G. R. Brow and C. N. H. Long, Cushing became interested. He commenced studies which confirmed in human beings what Beattie, Brow, and Long had discovered in animals, namely, that centers in the hypothalamus control visceral processes such as sweat glands, activity of the stomach and intestines, and so forth. Since these reactions can also be brought about in moments of extreme emotion, it explained why tumors impinging on the hypothalamic area had resulted in emotional disturbances in his patients. It was these observations which formed the basis for his Lister Lecture in London on "Neurohypophysial Mechanisms from a Clinical Standpoint." In the huge and enthusiastic audience were Arnold Klebs, Jean Morelle, who had traveled from Louvain, Ignaz Oljenick from Amsterdam, and other former assistants from all parts of Britain.

Lord Moynihan, as president of the College of Surgeons, then presented Cushing with the Lister Medal "for distinguished contributions to surgical science." In the evening he was the guest of honor at a dinner in the House of Lords given by Lord Moynihan for the Council of the College. This state occasion was followed the next evening by a simple dinner which gave him equal pleasure because it was attended by a large number of former members of the Brigham group and such good friends as Klebs and Geoffrey Jefferson. Jefferson, in proposing a toast, pointed to his devoted following of pupils and acclaimed him as the founder of a school.

The promised visit to the Fultons in Oxford afforded opportunity to rest up for his Oslerian Oration—also for spending his lecture honorarium on books and for pursuing Vesalius in the Bodleian Library. The meeting of the Osler Club on July 12 (Osler's birthday) was held at the house of Alfred W. Franklin, one of the group of student members who offered a contrast in years to Sir D'Arcy Power, then seventy-five. Young and old enjoyed Cushing's informal talk about the preparation of the Osler biography, for he included many incidents he had omitted from the book.

He saw many old friends on this visit—Sir Charles Sherrington, Sir Henry and Lady Head, Sir Arthur Keith, and Mr. G. Buckston Browne—with whom he visited Down, Darwin's birthplace (which Mr. Browne had purchased and presented to the nation), Sir Walter Morley Fletcher, and Geoffrey Keynes, about whom he had earlier written to John Fulton: "Gracious, how delighted I would have been to have heard Keynes talk to the Osler Club! He is a most energetic fellow, as you say, and though he is a good surgeon, he is becoming so distinguished a bibliographer that this is likely to overshadow his vocational contributions which have always been good."

Shortly after Cushing's return home in August, he welcomed Otfrid Foerster from Breslau, one of the leading neurologists in Europe, as the Surgeon-in-Chief pro tem. The whole staff soon discovered that the energy of their Chief, home from a European vacation, was as nothing compared to that of Foerster, who kept them up talking until three in the morning and then was in the operating room ready for a brisk day's work at seven.

During Foerster's visit Cushing gave the Arthur Dean Bevan Lecture in Chicago and there met Dr. Welch, who was full of enthusiasm for the Huntington Library which he had just visited, early Spanish medical publications, and Cushing becoming his successor—to which he continually made public allusions, much to H.C.'s embarrassment. He saw Dr. Welch again in Cleveland late in December at the meetings of the American Association for the Advancement of Science and described something of what went on to John Fulton, who was now the professor of physiology at Yale. "I am just back from Cleveland. We had a thrilling time—I clung to the trail of Popsy and Klebs, though it nearly finished me. Klebs and I left Cleveland Wednesday night with our tongues hanging out. Popsy was just preparing to see the New Year in with a group of young folks under Pat's [Ned's son, Edward Cushing] leadership. I am sure he was the liveliest one of the party."

The year 1931 was a high point in Cushing's career—he reached the two thousandth verified tumor and he found an answer to a disease condition that had been baffling him for over twenty years. But before the year was far advanced he was laid low by the circulatory difficulties in his legs and feet. The pain and discomfort from which he was rarely free had increased to the point that he was irritable and short of patience and was less able to stand long hours at the operating table. On February 16 he went into the hospital with gangrene threatening both extremities. Six weeks without tobacco and a course of physiotherapy healed the gangrenous patches and reduced the pain, and the strict regime enforced by one of his devoted junior house officers, Richard Meagher, whose Irish wit made him more than a match for his Chief, helped him back on his feet.

During his uneasy convalescence, he and John Fulton carried on an entertaining correspondence about the religious preferences of chimpanzees—which Dr. Cushing concluded would probably be Congregationalism. H.C. started it by a reference to some chimps he had heard of on his visit to Cleveland; it was furthered by Fulton's receiving an unexpected shipment of eighty-five monkeys from a friend on the Gold Coast. "I have one running around without its left hemisphere who absorbs pituitrin like a sponge!" he told Dr. Cushing. To this Cushing replied:

Dear John—As W. O. used to say about books—it's a sad day when something from you doesn't come in. Bartels redivivus! For thirty, perhaps forty, years Bartels, who was an old *diener* of Ludwig's, was actually in charge of the Physiological Laboratory in Bern though Professor Kronecker was unaware of it. Even in those days he was good at monkeys. I haven't heard from him for years. But I am glad that you and he have gone into business together and that you have representatives on the Gold Coast. Why don't you enter the eighty-five in the next freshman class? I judge from what you say that they are just as good without their left hemispheres as with them, and that this is true also of many coonskin-wearing freshmen.

But in the midst of this light banter, he couldn't help asking: "But where do you put the pituitrin in the ape without a hemisphere? The ventricle, of course, must be open and the space formerly occupied by the brain full of fluid. Perhaps that accounts for the absence of reaction, just as in our hydrocephalic cases."

Cushing took advantage of his confinement to prepare the Balfour Lecture which he was scheduled to give in Toronto on April 8. In it he pursued further the subject which had formed the background of his Lister Lecture—the relation of the hypothalamus to visceral function. He turned to his records and studied instances in which acute gastric complications had followed cerebral operations. It was disclosed that only those in which the base of the brain had been encroached upon were followed by gastric complications. Cushing's contributions as a "pure" scientist have sometimes been challenged and some of the bold deductions that a surgeon is frequently called upon to make Cushing stubbornly held to, but in this instance his conclusions were later vindicated in the experimental laboratory.

Shortly after his return from Toronto, a special ceremony was arranged at the Brigham. Dr. Eisenhardt, who had carefully kept Dr. Cushing's operative statistics, had previously warned him that he was approaching his two thousandth case of verified brain tumor, and on April 15 he had sufficiently recovered from his illness to be able to perform the operation assisted by Dr. Horrax. His assistant, Richard U. Light, and Walter W. Boyd, house officer in surgery—both amateur photographers of professional skill—recorded the occasion for posterity. While Dr. Cushing was still in his operating gown, the staff gathered to hear Dr. Eisenhardt review some of the figures and to hear Dr. Homans' presentation of their gift, a silver cigarette box. It was a "family" gathering but it marked an event of importance to medicine as a whole, for the careful and complete records of this unique tumor series offered a gathering of clinical data of inestimable value not only to contemporary surgeons of the brain, but to future surgeons interested in the life history of brain tumors.

Ten days after this occasion Cushing wrote to Dr. Fulton: "I am just back from attending Popsy's belated 81st birthday dinner at the Maryland Club in Baltimore—a pleasant and amusing occasion. Baltimore is much changed during these past twenty years, but the Maryland Club goes on unaltered, the same paper on the walls, the same old father terrapin in the cellar, the same old Baltimoreans wearing imperials standing in the window. It is just like a visit to Madame Tussaud's."

At the end of April, Cushing gave the William H. Welch Lecture at the Mount Sinai Hospital in New York, but after that he canceled speaking engagements outside Boston and tried to follow an easier schedule, for he had ahead of him a strenuous trip to Europe, where he was to speak at the first International Neurological Congress at Berne in September. In June, however, he attended three commencements, one at the University of Rochester, where he received a D.Sc., the Harvard Commencement, at which he also received a D.Sc. (he referred to it as his "honorary P.D.Q."), and the Yale commencement where, at his fortieth reunion, he and Perry Harvey roomed together and "renewed their youth."

When Cushing sailed for Europe late in August he was accompanied by John Fulton and as soon as they reached Cherbourg they were joined by Hugh Cairns and later by Georges Schaltenbrand. Arnold Klebs awaited them in Berne, where he had arranged for a large suite at the Hotel Bellevue overlooking the Bernese Oberland. The Congress opened on Monday, August 31, in the Municipal Casino with the greatest students of the nervous system in attendance—Sherrington, Pavlov, de Martel, Foerster, and Cushing—and with eighty-one-year-old Dr. Welch presiding benignly over all. For Cushing the occasion had special meaning. It was here in Berne that he had received his strongest impetus to embark on a career in neurosurgery and now after thirty years he had returned to give an account of himself. At the first session he and Sherrington were given honorary degrees. That they were to be awarded was a complete secret, and Dr. Fulton, charged with the responsibility of seeing that the recipients attended the session, had not a little difficulty. Sir Charles, when called early, meekly agreed to be on hand, but Dr. Cushing, who wanted to spend the morning on his paper, was not pleased to be awakened and could not see why he should go. He grumbled further at being urged to sit down front, but the reason for it all was soon apparent, and both Sir Charles and Dr. Cushing were so moved that it was fortunate they did not have to reply to the extravagant words of praise of Professor Asher, Cushing's old friend, who was now rector of the University.

Cushing's own paper was presented in the afternoon. More of his pupils had arrived from various parts of Europe until there were twenty-five in the audience when he began, somewhat haltingly, to give a résumé of his lifework. There was complete silence in the hall as he spoke of his early experiences in Berne and then began to outline the factors which, in the years that followed, had enabled him to achieve his spectacular reduction in mortality rate in cerebral operations. "Younger men picking up where I leave off can reduce the mortality still further," he said. He paused a minute and then added: "Gentlemen, this will be the last report on the statistical results of brain tumors as a whole that I shall ever publish." Stunned silence greeted this statement before the applause burst forth. Dr. Fulton wrote: "His paper was brilliant but there was a tragic air of finality about it, which everyone felt even though unexpressed. Old animosities were put aside and he was hailed by everyone as the supreme master of a great specialty."

Arnold Klebs gave a brilliant dinner for forty that evening in honor of Dr. Cushing and Dr. Welch, and the following night Cushing invited his pupils to meet *his* masters. Seated around the table were Sir Charles Sherrington, Dr. Welch, and Dr. Klebs, Wilder Penfield of Montreal, Otfrid Foerster of Breslau, Geoffrey Jefferson of Manchester, Gaston de Coppet of Berne, George Armitage of Leeds, Ignaz Oljenick of Amsterdam, Hugh Cairns of London, Herbert Olivecrona of Stockholm, Dimitri Bagdazar of Bucharest, Thierry de Martel of Paris, Paul Martin of Brussels, Daniel Petit-Dutaillis of Paris, Jean Morelle of Louvain, Norman Dott of Edinburgh, Frédéric Bremer of Brussels, Frederic Schreiber of Detroit, Percival Bailey of Chicago, John Fulton of New Haven, and Franc Ingraham, Richard Light, Tracy Putnam, Richard Meagher, and Frank Fremont-Smith of Boston.

In a letter to Mrs. Cushing, H.C. described some of the details:

. . . Popsy and Klebs have been wonderful. Their rooms are just below ours and command a marvellous view of the Alpen Ketten. They gave me and Sherrington a surprise doctorate of Berne at the opening session Monday—nice but embarrassing.

I enclose the seating for a dinner given Tuesday for the Brighamites who are here. Imagine my surprise when Meagher and Light turned up!!

This noon the same crowd are going out to put wreaths on Kocher's and Kronecker's graves and on that of Klebs' father as well for he was Prof. of Pathology [2] here.

Cushing next wrote from Les Terrasses at Nyon:

We motored here from Berne on Saturday—John, Popsy, A.K. and I. Stopped at Fribourg for lunch at the Aigle Noir and filled ourselves full of two or three kinds of Welch "Rabbit" after a course of blue trout and reached here in time for tea. Sunday Sherrington and Graham Brown joined us—also Franc Ingraham and the Oljenicks. It's a lively place. Yesterday we had luncheon at an old patrician chateau belonging to the de Saussures since *circa* 1600. . . . Popsy leaves Thursday and I will join him for a few days in Paris before he sails.

Everyone asks for you. I often wish you and Sis—one or both— were here. The Klebs constantly lament your absence. They are *very* nice and simply perfect hosts. As much like the Open Arms as anything could possibly be.

During the days in Paris, Dr. Welch persuaded Cushing to take his place as an official delegate at the centenary celebration for Michael Farraday, which was to be held at the Royal Institution in London. Immediately after he sailed for home. He found that Welch had arrived and already arranged a luncheon in New York so that he and several others might meet Dr. Henry E. Sigerist, a distinguished European scholar who was Director of the Institute of Medical History at Leipzig and who was to give lectures on the history of medicine in Baltimore. These lectures aroused such enthusiasm that a few

---

[2] It was he who first described acromegaly and with Löffler the diphtheria bacillus.

days before Dr. Sigerist came to Boston in the autumn to speak at the Brigham, Dr. Cushing formally declined the chair at Baltimore and urged Welch to make an effort to secure Sigerist. He would have been proud to occupy the professorship, he said, but until they had chosen his successor he could not concentrate on his own plans for the future.

After Sigerist's visit he wrote more urgently, saying that Sigerist had captivated everyone by his learning, enthusiasm, and personal charm. "I cannot imagine a more suitable person for the post or one more certain to develop it in the way you would desire." Sigerist was offered the chair several weeks later and ultimately accepted.[3]

Early in January the matter of Cushing's successor was settled, and President Lowell notified him that it would be the man of his own choice, Elliott C. Cutler. Mr. Lowell added that there was some awkwardness in announcing the appointment since Dr. Cushing had not yet resigned. This Cushing immediately did with the blunt explanation that since his term of service automatically ended that year, it had not occurred to him that it was necessary to resign from a position he was not entitled to hold. It was not until after this that President Lowell offered Cushing a professorship in the history of medicine. Only those who knew him well guessed that he was deeply hurt because Harvard was the last to offer him a place.

A few months later, President Robert E. Vinson of the Western Reserve asked him to become Cutler's successor at the Lakeside Hospital. This fourth call to the Western Reserve strongly tempted him and the idea of changing places with one of his pupils was somewhat intriguing. He thought of taking his Brigham staff—"they were a fine group, Meagher, Glenn, Ray, Bishop, Mahoney, and Kendall, and would have made things easy for me"—but in the end he decided that to take

---

[3] During the sixteen years from this time until the spring of 1947 when Dr. Sigerist resigned to devote his full energies to the preparation of an eight-volume history of medicine, he more than fulfilled Dr. Cushing's prophecy. His place has been taken by Dr. Richard H. Shryock, formerly Chairman of the Department of History at the University of Pennsylvania, who assumed his duties on October 1, 1949.

over an active service in a new setting at his time of life was
foolish.

In the meantime there was a steady barrage of letters from
New Haven. Dr. Fulton had written the previous year: "There
is nothing in Baltimore like this—here we have youth, enthusiasm and above all co-operation—qualities which you have always engendered and could stimulate further. The proposal
made last December stands and we all want you to think about
it." This was shortly followed by a handwritten note from
Mr. Angell who said that although not unmindful of their
promise not to annoy him, his flexible conscience nevertheless
allowed him to say that they often thought of him. After a
visit to New Haven in November, H.C. had written (also by
hand): "We had a delightful time in New Haven and enjoyed
particularly the privaledge of staying with you." As to the
proffered chair—"This is largely a matter of legs—mine and the
chair's. I'm much better than I was a year ago but I still tire
with disconcerting ease and I consequently hesitate to inflict
myself on anyone who may expect more of me than I can
give." A reference to his grandfather brought from Mr. Angell: "With every respect for your excellent grandfather, I
trust you will not feel that you must adopt at sixty . . . the
regimen he found appropriate at ninety." Then in a more serious vein: "You have made the most brilliant contributions to
your profession and to mankind. . . . You have many years
of fine work before you and all we ask is a chance to furnish
the conditions in which you can carry on to your own satisfaction."

Dr. Fulton also tried to lure him with lively descriptions of
the activities of the Beaumont Club, the Elizabethan Club, and
other groups in which he knew Dr. Cushing would be interested. "I saw Herbert Thoms last night at the meeting of the
Beaumont Club, and he was immensely pleased by your letter
about his excellent etching of Paré. I believe he is sending you
a copy of his engraving of Beaumont's birthplace. Mr. Hen-
drickson, the Professor of Classics, read a remarkably interesting and erudite paper on Fracastoro's poem [*Syphilis*]. He is
translating it and has unearthed all manner of interesting in-

formation concerning the derivation of the word syphilis."
And again: "John Donley is coming down from Providence
today to talk to our medical history group on Greek medicine.
He is a very learned and charming fellow." But although
Cushing in his replies revealed his interest in all of these things,
he still could not bring himself to a decision.

Early in the year he had given a paper at the New York
Neurological Society in which for the first time he put forth
his conviction that certain baffling symptoms, long classified
under the vague term of "polyglandular syndrome," were in
fact due to an increase in the basophilic cells of the pituitary.
He gave the name pituitary basophilism to this syndrome
which subsequently became known as "Cushing's disease." He
had first become curious about these symptoms when an un-
married Russian girl, referred to him by a New York physician, had been admitted to the Hopkins suffering from painful
adiposity of the face, neck, and trunk. Although many of her
complaints were similar to those caused by tumor, her sight
was not affected and an operation therefore did not seem indicated. Three years later she appeared at the Brigham Hospital
in Boston, but again, after two months' observation, no answer
was found to explain or relieve her condition. Dr. Cushing began to watch the literature for reports of other cases and over
a period of twenty years carefully studied six examples of
similar disorders which came to the Brigham. But although
these patients were extremely uncomfortable, they rarely succumbed to their disease; and when autopsies were occasionally
reported on such patients, it was usually stated that the
pituitary body showed no apparent abnormality. However, in
two or three of the later cases, a small tumor was recognized
although the pituitary was scarcely enlarged.

In preparing for his Lister Lecture, Dr. Cushing came across
an autopsy report of a case of this nature by Dr. William Raab
of Prague. Although a basophil adenoma was disclosed, neither
Dr. Raab, nor Professor E. J. Kraus who later studied the
postmortem findings, related its presence to the clinical manifestations of the polyglandular syndrome. But the patient's
symptoms and appearance were so like those of a patient Cush-

ing had under observation that he jumped immediately to the conclusion that his patient, too, had a basophilic adenoma. He was then determined to secure autopsy reports on any patients who succumbed, and when Dr. Harold Teel, one of his junior co-workers, discovered an unmistakable basophilic adenoma in a case of polyglandular syndrome, he felt sufficiently sure of his conclusions to announce them. The recognition of this new disease entity stands as one of Cushing's most original contributions to clinical medicine. Imagination had never been lacking in his investigations, but his major achievements had more often been accomplished through hard work than through sudden flashes of genius. This disclosure proved that although he might have reached the age of retirement, there were still closed doors that he could open.

On May 6, 1932, some thirty-five enthusiastic young neurosurgeons and neurologists met at the Peter Bent Brigham to form an association to be known as the Harvey Cushing Society, and William Van Wagenen and Glen Spurling, the chief organizers, were elected the first president and vice-president. After watching the operation scheduled for the occasion, one of his former assistants commented: "I have never seen the Chief operate with greater ease and sureness. It seems to me that his technique has progressed even during the last year." Cushing's pleasure in this honor was expressed to Tracy Putnam, Secretary of the Society, to whom he wrote when the meetings were over: "I am very proud of you all and that I should have been immortalized by having you use my name is a source of pride and gratification."

Shortly after this, John Fulton (with A. D. Keller) published a neurological monograph entitled *The Sign of Babinski* which was dedicated to Dr. Cushing. Cushing's reply contained a sketch of a monkey perched on a tavern sign on which he had drawn the typical "upgoing" toe and called it the "Sign of Babinski." He said: "A great book *multum in parvo*! I shall expect to put up at the above whenever I come to town. The very expectation of it gives me up-going toes which indicates, I take it, the loss of my cortical dominance, long appreciated. Best love to you both. Affy, H.C."

In July the Boston *Evening American* carried a paragraph headed in large type "Dr. Cushing Should Stay." It continued:

When Dr. Harvey Cushing reached the terrible old age of 63 years last April, announcement was made that he must retire as surgeon-in-chief of the Peter Bent Brigham Hospital this fall because of the age limit. The Boston Evening American then said and now repeats that this silly requirement should be abandoned in favor of this eminent brain surgeon and specialist. . . . Harvey Cushing is at the pinnacle of his career. He is still a young man and will be a young man for many years to come, we hope and expect. The world . . . recognizes his extraordinary ability and we of Boston should insist that he be retained in the position where his talents will be of the widest value.

But public opinion did not change the rules. He carried on a heavy schedule of operating throughout the summer, and on August 17, the day before he sailed for Rome and the International Physiological Congress, he performed his last operation. The rush of departure robbed the occasion of its finality and not until he returned did he realize that he was no longer head of the hospital, that his connections with Harvard and the Peter Bent Brigham were officially ended.

When Cushing arrived in Europe, Arnold Klebs was awaiting him, and his extensive knowledge of Italian history, literature, and art added much to the trip as they journeyed toward Rome accompanied by Henry Viets and John Fulton. The plenary session in the Campidoglio on the Capitoline was opened with a speech of welcome by Mussolini, and Cushing, seated beside Pavlov, was highly amused when Pavlov remarked audibly as Il Duce gave the Fascist salute: "A conditioned reflex." Cushing's own paper, given on the last day of the Congress, summarized his evidence for the existence of special centers in the human hypothalamus for the regulation of visceral processes. As soon as it was finished, Klebs and his party left Rome by the Flaminian Way, whose tempestuous history seemed exceedingly remote on that quiet September afternoon. The old walled towns on the route fascinated H.C., and they stopped in several for a hurried glimpse of their particular treasures in art or architecture. In Venice they visited the library of San Marco in order to examine its rare copy of Vesalius' six anatomical tables published prior to the *Fabrica*. In Munich they again sought Vesalius and had the exciting experience of examining the original wood blocks used for the *Fabrica* which had recently been discovered in the basement of the University library.[4]

After several days' rest at Les Terrasses, Cushing flew to Paris and then, with Henry Viets, to London. He had only a day before the *Berengaria* sailed but he managed to visit the Sherringtons, the Geoffrey Keynes, Hugh Cairns, William Wright, the Vesalian scholar, and several other friends.

His return to the Brigham was something of a shock to him. Only when he found Elliott Cutler fully established in the offices he had occupied for so many years and discovered that he had no further part in the hospital activities did he fully realize what retirement meant. Not to enter the operating room, not to have an eager group of assistants and patients awaiting him was hard to get used to. Somehow he had expected to be a kind of senior adviser to both Cutler and the junior staff, but this was not to be. Dr. Cushing concealed his hurt and disappointment from all except those who knew him best and settled himself in the Surgical Laboratory, where a place had been made temporarily for him to continue his work.

On the boat coming back from Europe, Cushing had renewed acquaintance with R. Scott Stevenson, a well-known London surgeon whom he had met in France. When he discovered that Scott Stevenson was to be in Boston, he invited him to spend a week end at his house. After taking him to the Boston Public Library, where Stevenson wanted to see the Sargent murals, Cushing then wanted to show him his favorite painter, so they drove to the Isabella Stewart Gardner Museum on the Fenway to see "one of the most beautiful

---

[4] These wood blocks were used to print a handsome edition (price $105) sponsored by the New York Academy of Medicine in 1935. The book was published by Mr. Willy Wiegand of the Bremer Presse and the blocks remained in Munich where they were destroyed in the bombing attacks of World War II.

Vermeers in the world." En route Cushing quizzed Scott Stevenson about Vermeer: "Don't you know that he died young and in debt, and that there are only thirty-seven authentic Vermeers known—a dozen of them in America—and that his friend, van Leeuwenhoek, the inventor of the microscope, was his executor?" They studied the picture—"The Concert"—for a long time and Stevenson later commented: "I could certainly understand the appeal of Vermeer to Cushing: the perfection of craftsmanship, the essentially architectural construction of the painting, the serene air of fastidiousness, the superb skill in detail, the refined delicacy and perfect harmony." After they left the museum, Cushing showed him around the wards at the Brigham and even a stranger sensed his nostalgia that they were no longer his.

During the autumn, Cushing followed the Presidential campaign with considerable interest. Although still an Ohio Republican, violently opposed to the so-called "New Deal," he had come to appreciate many of Mr. Roosevelt's virtues and he wrote a warmhearted letter congratulating him on his overwhelming victory over Mr. Hoover. At the same time he greatly admired Mr. Hoover and wrote to John Fulton that Mr. Hoover would be a splendid candidate for an honorary degree at Yale. Dr. Fulton replied: "Your suggestion about Mr. Hoover's degree is first-rate. I shall forward it to the Honorary Degrees Committee and I am still optimistic enough to hope for your personal support in February. You don't know how exciting it is to back candidates before the Corporation. It has the Derby backed off the board!"

The reference to personal support followed an earlier prodding: "I cannot bear the idea of your toasting your toes all winter in Brookline. A decision will be just as difficult in June as in January, but I am not going to write you any further about it because you know where my heart lies. I shall be popping up to Boston very soon to see you. You mustn't fear bargaining with University Boards, because that is the one thing that keeps us all young; it's rather fun, you know."

Despite this and other urging to come to a decision, Cushing continued to procrastinate. He resumed work with Dr. Eisenhardt on a book begun many years previously on the meningiomas, since the clinical material was all in the Brigham records that would soon be unavailable to him if he decided to go to New Haven. He also worked on five lectures, one of them the Harvey Lecture in New York—a particular honor, as he was giving it the second time. Since in the first he had reported his initial work on the pituitary, he chose as a title, "Dyspituitarism Twenty Years Later," and summarized the progress made in the twenty intervening years, culminating with the most recent disclosure in the field—pituitary basophilism.

In December word came that Dr. Welch had had a slight illness. In February he entered the Hopkins for a kidney operation. Cushing stopped to see him twice during the spring on his way to meetings, the second time, in May, he found Welch, despite three operations, sitting up reading a book, cheerful, and full of interesting talk. Although he was not again to leave the hospital, he so far recovered as to live on for nearly a year. It was William T. Councilman, Cushing's loyal friend for even longer than he had known Welch, who slipped away during this month. The appreciation Cushing wrote, one of his best, revealed how deep had been his admiration and affection for this forthright teacher and colleague. He concluded it with a moving description of Councilman's fight, during the later years of his retirement, to preserve the trailing arbutus of which Cushing himself was so fond.

During the twentieth anniversary celebrations of the Brigham, also in May, the Boston Surgical Society conferred on Cushing the Bigelow Medal. His devoted colleague, David Cheever, made a particularly gracious presentation speech which closed with: "But this medal is a symbol—not of a trade, but of a splendid profession; its exquisite workmanship typifies the consummate perfection of your handicraft, and the metal of which it is composed, which does not tarnish or corrode with age, symbolizes the changelessness of scientific truth, for which you have striven. And we dare to believe that among your honors it will not rank least, because it will always remind you of our admiration and affection."

There was another tribute during the reunion when an oil painting, executed by Mrs. Calvin G. Page of Boston, was presented by Gilbert Horrax to the Hospital on behalf of Cushing's students. At the same time, Dr. Francis Blake of New Haven presented a painting of Dr. Christian on behalf of his students. On the heels of these honors came the announcement that Cushing had been elected to foreign membership in the Royal Society of London, the first surgeon among the thirty-four American scientists who had been elected to this distinguished society over a period of one hundred and fifty years.

Always behind these various activities lay the undecided matter of his future. In March he had written Dr. Fulton: "The newspapers here say I am going, or have gone, to New Haven to live in one of the new colleges to inspire the undergraduate. For my own part, I have about come to the conclusion (1) that my surgical days are over; (2) that in these troublous and uncertain times it's inadvisable, both for me and for the University, to take on any new obligations; and that consequently (3) the latter had better postpone action at their April meeting, at least until June, so that everyone can find out where they are at." [5] Two weeks later: "Though I often have yearnings to get back into surgery, I am beginning to feel that it would be foolish for me to do so, even if I limited myself wholly to cases of pituitary disorder. And the Sterling Professor of the Pituitary Body would hardly go, I am afraid."

Finally it was John Fulton, in a tactful and understanding letter, affectionate but firm, who forced him to take definite action. Cushing consequently wrote Mr. Angell that he might announce the appointment at Commencement, and Mr. Angell reported on June 23: "Even your modesty would have been flattered by the tempestuous applause when I announced to the great gathering of our alumni Wednesday the fact that you

---

[5] The collapse of the Boston banking firm which had handled his local business affairs for years added to his uncertainty, for he was not sure what arrangements he would have to make to reassure the financial security of his family.

were coming back to your first love and that the new Sterling Chair was at your disposal."

Early in October, Cushing had the satisfaction of attending the 150th anniversary of the founding of the Medical School and of hearing the forceful speech of James Bryant Conant, Harvard's new president, which gave him new hope for the future of the school in whose interests he had himself striven untiringly for twenty years.

On October 12—the day given over to honoring the discovery of a new world—Harvey Cushing left Boston. He took formal leave of President Conant and made a final visit to the hospital, escaping unnoticed through a side door. On the drive to New Haven the tensions and strain of the years seemed to slip away, and with the same eagerness that had drawn him back to Yale again and again he looked forward to his new life.

PROFESSOR OF NEUROLOGY
AT YALE

Chapter XXVI

THE YALE TO WHICH HARVEY CUSH-
ing returned in 1933 was a far cry from the college he had
known as an undergraduate, and yet he had kept so closely in
touch with its growth that he did not feel nostalgia for the old
days as strongly as did some alumni returning after long years
away. The chimes in the Branford Tower at twilight and at
curfew were as sentimentally regarded by present sons of Yale
as the old Fence and other landmarks of treasured memory.
The beautiful new Sterling Library had supplanted the old
Chittenden Annex with its much-admired Tiffany window.
These and other manifestations of growth and development
had come gradually. He was familiar with them and applauded
them. And there still remained enough of the old and tradi-
tional to make him feel at home. There were still Senior Societies and Tap Day and harmonizing songsters, although they
now gathered at the "tables down at Mory's" instead of on the
Fence. And there was a warmth and wholeheartedness about
the welcome he received on all sides that he had never felt
at Harvard.

While the house the Cushings had rented at 691 Whitney
Avenue (a large frame house not unlike 305 Walnut Street)
was being settled, he sailed for Europe, where he was to inaugurate a new lectureship at the invitation of the Medical
Research Society of University College, London, and also to
receive an honorary degree from the University of Paris. The

faithful Klebs met him in London and accompanied him to Paris when his lecture was over. One among those who welcomed him was Professor Henri Hartmann—recalling to mind a welcome over thirty years earlier when he was a stranger in Paris. In addition to the degree ceremony, he attended the state funeral at Notre Dame of the great French bacteriologist, Émile Roux, and gave an impromptu speech at the Salpêtrière in the old lecture room of another great French scientist, Charcot, the neurologist. He found these activities strenuous and when he reached New York on his return trip on November 18, he looked worn and weary, but he recovered enough strength to join in the welcome to Professor Arturo Castiglioni, the eminent Italian medical historian, who had come to New Haven to speak before the Yale Medical Society. Dr. Castiglioni was followed by Henry Sigerist, who had been invited by the Beaumont Club to talk on William Beaumont, it being the hundredth anniversary of the publication of his classic book on the gastric juice.

These functions over, Dr. Cushing succumbed to the gastric ulcer that had been causing him pain for nearly a year and entered the New Haven Hospital. Much of his indecision about the future had stemmed from the fact that he had been feeling miserable, but it was not until September that he had admitted the gastric pain and had submitted to an examination and X-rays. He had tried to keep it in check with rest and diet, but the trip abroad and the invitations that were showered upon him when he returned were his undoing. The gastric pain was accompanied by increased pain in his feet, and he slept poorly and had little appetite. But although at times acutely depressed and bored by his Sippy diet and hospital confinement, he managed to be cheerful on occasion. To Mrs. LeRoy Crummer, who with her husband was a book collector, he wrote on December 14: "As before, I haven't allowed them to separate me from my trousers which are in the second bureau drawer—at least they told me they were. There is nothing so humiliating, not to say terrifying, for a man as to be separated from his pants."

To Mrs. Ruth Mitchell, a patient who had come to him in
1922 after seventeen years of suffering with Raynaud's disease,
he wrote early in the new year:

Dear Mrs. Mitchell: How nice of you to have sent me this
Christmas letter which has found me still laid up in bed here in
New Haven, incidentally losing the end of one of my toes. It
quite serves me right for not having done better by you and your
fingers and toes. Dr. Fulton will be so happy to have your message
and to know that you still remember him. He drops in to see me
every day. . . .

It's perfectly beastly that you should be having these bad fingers
on your right hand. . . . I wish that I could show as much courage
and fortitude about my present malady as you for so many years
have shown toward yours. In fact, you always did more to help
other people by your cheerfulness than any of us ever succeeded
in doing to help you.

And to Barbara at Westover he wrote in the light vein he always assumed for her benefit:

Dearest Babe: What do you mean by lying in bed on a Thursday
morning looking out a window on the world. I think it is a form
of plagiarism. I have been lying in bed here looking out of the
window viewing the works of creation so far as I could see them
from a small window for some two or three months; but I little
wot that you were going to be a copy-cat.

. . . I am glad you noticed my stylish pyjamas. Just now I am
in silk, kind of greenish blue; but up to now pretty much all day
I have been, as you might say, in the pink, having things done to
me.

I wish that you might have been here today to have seen the
flow of people who came in, beginning with Lucia about an hour
ago and ending with John who has just gone flippity-flop down
the hall. I don't know just what it is, but I think he must have
springs in his tendo Achillis which makes it impossible for him to
let the soles of his shoes come down quietly after his heels have
once struck the ground. Then there came a skinny man named
Day and a medical student named Ehrlich, and then Francis Blake,
my doctor; and then Mother, and then Auntie Mame.

It was early in March before he was able to take up his work again in his hospital office [1] and he turned once more to the meningioma monograph. In May he laid it aside to write an appreciation of Dr. Welch, who had died on April 30. He called it "The Doctors Welch of Norfolk" and its warmth was token of his deep fondness for the man so many had loved.

There is a touch of sadness and melancholy about Autumn which would seem the more natural time of year for an old man to die. But so far as anyone could ever tell, sadness and melancholy were moods of which he was incapable and it was as though he whose youthful spirit and reactions so belied his years had deliberately waited for Spring. . . . It was wholly consistent and typical of him that he should choose to rest where to the future passer-by he would be just another of the many Doctors Welch of Norfolk. . . .

During May, Cushing was also engaged in preparing a major address for the centenary celebration in June of the College of Medicine at Syracuse, founded at Geneva, New York, in 1834. He chose as a theme, "The Pioneer Medical Schools of Central New York," and the necessary delving into their history was a task much to his liking. He received an honorary LL.D. at the close of the ceremonies and returned to New Haven just in time to be present when Yale bestowed the same degree on Mr. Roosevelt, President Conant of Harvard, and Yale's popular professor of English, William Lyon Phelps. Cushing wrote a classmate: "The Alumni luncheon, too, was excellent, and Conant and Mr. Roosevelt both made a great hit. They certainly do stage these things well here, in the tradition of Anson Stokes well carried on by the present Secretary, Carl Lohmann."

His work on the meningioma volume, pursued spasmodically during the summer, received welcome impetus when Louise Eisenhardt arrived in September to help him, bringing with her all of the specimens of his brain tumors. This unique

---

[1] Cushing continued his interest in experimental work during his years at Yale and directed several investigations suggested by his studies on pituitary basophilism. He brought Kenneth W. Thompson from the Brigham to be his research assistant.

collection had been the subject of debate for over a year. Since the pathological specimens were of little use without the clinical histories, Cushing had expected to give the collection to Harvard to be housed in the Warren Museum of the Medical School across the street from the Brigham, but securing funds for its maintenance had presented difficulties. While Harvard was dallying with the problem, Dr. William Van Wagenen, the president of the Harvey Cushing Society, suggested that the collection be made the basis of a brain tumor registry to which neurosurgeons might send obscure specimens for diagnosis. Since Harvard had displayed little real enthusiasm for the project from the beginning, Cushing eventually decided to obtain authorization from Mr. Conant to move the collection to New Haven where such a registry [2] could be established. This accomplished, he then had to have the clinical histories photographed, and Frederic Ludwig of the University Library staff began the extensive process.

In September, Cushing gave an address at the opening of a new Neurological Institute in Montreal—an institute conceived along lines similar to the national institute of neurology for which he had striven so enthusiastically in 1919. "We may well expect," he said, "that under the widely trained and many-sided director [Wilder Penfield] of this new institute, neurology will receive a new impetus, making of this place still another mecca for workers in the great subject in which we all feel so vitally interested. We may rest assured that here not only will the story of neurology's great past be cherished but that a new and significant chapter will be added to it." He was delighted with the inscription in the foyer (which Dr. W. W. Francis, who had been Librarian of the Osler Library since its arrival at McGill, had found in the

[2] The Brain Tumor Registry, under the directorship of Dr. Eisenhardt, was financed at first from the Bolton Fund with generous grants from the Childs Fund (a fund established by Dr. Cushing's classmate, Starling W. Childs, and his sister) until it was endowed at the time of Dr. Cushing's death by Mr. Howard M. Hanna of Cleveland. A number of graduate physicians come each year to work under Dr. Eisenhardt in the Registry, which is now in the Department of Physiology.

works of the great Greek physician, Galen): "I have seen a badly wounded brain heal." But he was startled to find his own name on the foyer wall along with Sherrington, Cajal, Pavlov, and many others.

This visit to Montreal was to have far-reaching results, because while there he of course visited the Osler Library and seeing the books, which he knew so well, arranged in the friendly room in the midst of the Medical School, gave him, during a disturbed ride home on the sleeper, an idea for his own collection. After discussing the matter with Mrs. Cushing and pondering on it for several days, he wrote Arnold Klebs that, although he had always intended to have his books dispersed at auction after his death so that others might have the fun of collecting them, he was now thinking of leaving them to Yale as the basis of a medical-historical collection. "I waked up in the middle of the night with the thought—why not a Klebs-Fulton-Cushing Collection so that the three could go down to bibliographic posterity hand in hand? Just imagine some young fellow long hence stumbling on our diaries and papers and correspondence about books. I envy him to think what fun he would have, for I think in a certain way our three collections have a more personal and intimate provenance than has W. O.'s library."

Klebs was somewhat startled at this suggested disposition of his library, but after considering its many angles he gave wholehearted approval to the idea: "I am heart and soul with your plan if you can insure to it, as well as is in one's power, the continuity of personal interest and influence. If you can give ten more years to it, perhaps with a little help from me and a great deal from John, something lasting might be started." Dr. Fulton claims to have first heard of the idea from Switzerland, but he, too, was enthusiastic and all three began to limit their collecting to specific fields so as to avoid duplication and achieve greater unity and coverage when the libraries were brought together.

The problem of a suitable building next concerned Cushing and he turned his attention to a consideration of the most desirable type of building and the means of achieving it. He had

long had a good friend in Mr. Andrew Keogh, the Librarian
of the University Library, and he promptly consulted him.
Mr. Keogh thought space would be available in the University
Library, but it was nearly a mile from the Medical School, and
Cushing throughout his entire career had held tenaciously
to the idea that since medical students and interns had so little
leisure at their disposal, any library for their use should be
immediately at hand. He therefore insisted that the books
should be housed near the Hospital. Dean Winternitz and
President Angell gave him ready support, and the Corporation
shortly appropriated money for architectural plans. The "part-
nership" he had once contemplated with Grosvenor Atterbury
was at last a reality when Mr. Atterbury was engaged to draw
the plans for "the special library."

During the autumn of 1934, Cushing was able to enter more
actively into the life of the University and the community.
He had become a member of The Club—an organization similar
to The Club in Boston which enjoyed the fast-disappearing
art of conversation—and he began to attend their meetings.
The programs of the Beaumont Medical Club had always interested him and he also thoroughly enjoyed dropping in at
the Elizabethan Club [3] because it gave him a chance to meet
undergraduates. He also made a point of dining on Thursday
nights at Trumbull College, of which he had been an Associate
Fellow since 1932. Trumbull was presided over by Dr. and
Mrs. Stanhope Bayne-Jones, who became close friends of the
Cushings and who made his visits there particularly enjoyable.
But here again he was interested especially in the students, for
through them he seemed to live again the happy days of his
own college years.

With the impetus provided by the new plans for his library,
Cushing began to collect in earnest and also to put his books
in order. He lovingly mended backs and tears, inserted his

---

[3] The Elizabethan Club is a literary organization founded by Alexander
Smith Cochran of the Class of 1896. Cochran had become a collector of
Elizabethan drama and especially Shakespearian quartos and he endowed
the Club that professors and students might meet informally with the
stimulus of some of the classics in English literature at hand.

bookplates, and gathered together correspondence and memorabilia for binding. His correspondence with Dr. Welch filled four volumes, that with Arnold Klebs also four—because hardly a week went by that letters didn't pass between them, full of bookish gossip and information.

In the midst of this pleasant existence there came a letter calling him back to professional responsibilities. It was an invitation from Miss Frances Perkins, Secretary of Labor, to serve on a Medical Advisory Committee to the Committee on Economic Security [4] appointed by President Roosevelt in June of 1934. The function of the Advisory Committee was "to study practicable measures for bringing about the better distribution of medical care in the lower income groups of the population and more satisfactory compensation of physicians and others who render medical services to individuals in these groups." Cushing in accepting the invitation wrote: "I am glad the Committee has thought of establishing such an advisory group, particularly since most of the agitation regarding the high cost of medical care has been voiced by public health officials and members of foundations most of whom do not have a medical degree, much less any actual first-hand experience with what the practice of medicine and the relation of doctor to patient mean."

As with all responsibilities of this nature, Cushing took the assignment seriously and sought advice from his colleagues on the Medical School faculty and from others he knew to be well informed on the matter of health insurance. From William J. Mayo he received this reply:

I do not know that the burdens in the medical profession are any greater than in any other line of work, but I quite agree with you that to put an office holder, probably a politician, between the doctor and the patient will not do either of them any good. Personally, I do not know of any poor person who is not able to

---

4 Its members were Frances Perkins, Secretary of Labor; Homer S. Cummings, Attorney General; Henry Morgenthau, Jr., Secretary of the Treasury; Henry Wallace, Secretary of Agriculture; Harry L. Hopkins, Federal Relief Administrator, and Edwin E. Witte, the Administrative Director.

get good medical attention, without regard to money. And especially do I believe that this is a poor time, when the Aimee McPhersons are running the heavens, the Upton Sinclairs the earth, and the Townsends taking care of the aged, for the medical profession to permit itself to be drawn into the whirlwind of uninformed opinion.

Cushing's particular contribution to the work of the committee was that of balance-wheel. On the one hand he counseled those favoring drastic health insurance measures to proceed slowly, and on the other he urged Drs. Olin West and Morris Fishbein of the American Medical Association to take the initiative, since some kind of sickness insurance was inevitable, in offering their own solution to the problem. To Fishbein he wrote: "You have it in your hands more than anyone else to make things run smoothly and to get the profession adjusted to the possibility of some sort of sickness legislation. I am sure that if we bury the hatchet about the C.C.M.C. report [Committee on the Costs of Medical Care of the Milbank Fund] and make a fresh start, we may be able to get somewhere and preserve the things which most of us regard as precious to our age-long profession."

The Committee, after several months of correspondence and deliberation, recommended in May 1935 that additional Federal funds be appropriated for more adequate public health service and for extension of public medical service, but in regard to the program for social insurance against illness they voted: "We . . . recommend that any Federal or State legislative action be deferred until these various experiences under different conditions in diverse localities can be suitably analysed and made available for the ultimate drawing up of a satisfactory plan adaptable to the needs of our people and acceptable both to them and to the medical profession."

Out of Cushing's thinking on this problem came a suggestion which he forwarded directly to Mr. Roosevelt. He asked why, since there was on foot a movement for establishing national sickness insurance, "would it not be a good move just at this time to take into consideration the establishment—if not of a governmental department—at least of a super-bureau of public health to coordinate a number of welfare agencies? Such a department would naturally include such scattered interests as infant welfare and the Children's Bureau, old age insurance, possibly the matter of the veterans' hospitals and health compensation, vital statistics, the administration of the Food and Drugs Act, and the existent public health and marine hospital service."

He went on to say: "I know that such a fusion would be difficult owing partly to inter-departmental jealousies . . . but I am sure that opposition could be overcome and it certainly would mean a great saving of energy, prevent much duplication of work, and lead to a proper concentration of authority on subjects that have to do with public health." Cushing felt that if such a department or bureau could be formed, the matter of sickness insurance might better be postponed until there was a department that could permanently and properly administer it. President Roosevelt's reply indicated agreement with Cushing on the soundness of the idea, but he felt that the time was not ripe for such a move.

There was also mention of health insurance in a less formal exchange, Cushing writing on January 6, 1935:

Dear Franklin: Herewith a few messages:

(1) Thanks much for the Christmas box of preserved fruit—all too rapidly disappearing.

(2) The children had a grand time at the White House parties. Barbara says you accused me of being "high hat" and worse than that. But I wasn't feeling so in the least—I had to address some scientists *a la Henry* Wallace on their duties to the Government, etc.

(3) Your message to Congress was A++. I hope my repeated cheers over the radio did not interrupt you. I'm glad *you* did not stress immediate sickness insurance—though friend Witte seems to be doing so. We need more time, and more local experiments with the various plans proposed if the backing of the profession is to be secured. This will be necessary to the success of any plan, though public officials backed by the Milbank Fund don't seem quite to realize this.

(4) Herbert Putnam and Senator Fuess have some new ideas about what might be done with the Surgeon General's Library: viz to install it on one floor of the new Annex to the Congressional Library. It might be the best solution of the problem.

(5) I enclose something I came across last night which I thought might interest you.[5] Cicero's maxim I take it is yours also; that the *well being* of the people is the most important thing. *Salus* appears to mean that as well as Security and I suppose they go together.

More power to your elbow and love to you all. H.C.

To this President Roosevelt replied:

Dear Harvey: I am delighted to know of that new suggestion in regard to the Medical Library. We might even add another story to the new annex, and architect it to look like a pill-box.

What a grand quotation that is from Mackail! You are right about that word "salus." We have no exact equivalent, though "well-being" is the nearest.

I hope the Supreme Court will remember that when they decide

---

[5] The quotation, from J. W. Mackail's *Classical Studies*, is interesting in the light of subsequent events: "No more than other communities was Rome free from the selfishness of privileged and the discontent of un-privileged classes, from wrecking demagogues and obstinate reaction-aries. But no other city or nation has so splendid and continuous a record of citizens who subordinated everything: wealth, power, office, the inter-est of their own class, life itself, and what was dearer still, the life of their children, to the service of the Republic, to the national ideal. Patri-otism was with them less a passion than a law. It is put with the incom-parable Roman brevity in the maxim laid down by Cicero as the central rule to be observed by all those who for their term of office were in-vested with the imperium, the delegated sovereignty of the Roman people, *Salus populi suprema lex esto*. In that maxim they rose to the conception of a law beyond law; and they carried it out in practice. Their fundamental principle of the sovereignty of the people did not make them hesitate in creating, and using when need arose, the device of dictatorship, supreme power, military and civil, over the whole magis-tracy and the whole commonwealth conferred on a single citizen for a fixed period and for a prescribed purpose. It is the most striking testi-mony to the patriotism both of the Roman people and of individual citizens, that no abuse was ever made of this absolute power; that the dictator always laid down his office as soon as he had finished the special task assigned to him."

the Gold case. Also I hope they will remember one of the earliest
recorded law cases where the question of the terms of the contract were being considered from the point of view of "well-
being." You can read all about it in a funny old play called "The
Merchant of Venice."

Early in 1935 Dr. Cushing had a letter from Edward Weeks
of the Atlantic Monthly Press, whose persistent efforts to
persuade him to publish portions of his war diary were finally
bearing fruit. This was followed by a letter from Ellery Sedg-
wick, Editor of the *Atlantic Monthly*. Encouraged by their
enthusiasm and by the letters which were pouring in following publication, during the preceding autumn, of four excerpts
from the diaries in the *Atlantic*, Cushing decided to go ahead
with the project. The instalment entitled "The Battle of Boston Common" brought him letters which indicated that the
issue was by no means dead, even after twenty years. He also
drew fire from another quarter—from his friend Henry D.
Dakin for reference to him in connection with his widely
known bactericidal solution for the irrigation of wounds.

Dear Cushing, How *could* you have done such a thing! "The
Incomparable Dakin." My wife titters every time she looks at me
—my acquaintances point at me behind my back and guffaw. Dale
who has been staying here says that your phrase ranks with "The
Admirable Crichton," "The Venerable Bede" and "The Unspeak-
able Turk." In despair I sought solitude on horseback when a
wretched banker mounted on a fast Irish hunter galloped up to
me and began "Did you read this month's Atlantic?"—I saw a cruel
grin on his face & bolted, almost breaking my neck as well as my
horse's.
I am thinking of seeking refuge in our cess-pool.
Do, for God's sake, send me a sworn, witnessed affidavit that the
word you intended to use was "incompetent" & that a printer's
error was responsible for the outrage.
In spite of it all, my wife and I send you and Mrs. C. our love.

Cushing attacked the task of editing his journal much as he
went about the Osler biography, sparing no pains to ensure
that his facts were correct. He wrote letters such as this to

Mrs. Reginald Fitz: "Dear Phoebe: Do you possibly recall two very nice people who were, I suppose, associated with the Red Cross in Boulogne and whose job was to get in contact with the relatives of patients on the D.I.L. who came over from England? In my journal I called them Captain and Mrs. Langridge, but whether I spelled the name correctly, I am not quite sure." Or this one to his good friend Richard P. Strong: "Dear Dick: I am in train to get out some more sections of my war diary and am having a bad time with names of people that I never knew how to spell. At the moment, it concerns the two possible candidates we had for louse experts: namely, Bacot (?) of the Lister Institute and as an alternative if we failed to get Bacot, Bruer (?) from the U.S.A. Do let me know if I have spelled these names correctly."

In the meantime he continued a lively correspondence with Edward Weeks, who wrote in July: "The Boston newspapers tell me you are going to Russia. I welcome the idea as the source of new journals and thus the makings of a new book. But not, pray Heaven, before August 1st, by which time, if the wind continues in the right quarter, we shall have completed the assembling of your *magnum opus*." To this Cushing returned: "I decided to go to Russia after reading the blurb [which advertised the book] in Little & Brown's Summer and Autumn catalogue. But I don't know how the news got in the Boston newspapers. . . . Moral: 'Whenever you see something in the newspapers [or in book catalogues] that you had supposed was true, begin to doubt it at once. (W. Osler)' "

When the book was entirely set up in galley proof, Dr. Cushing suddenly suggested a format similar to that of the *Atlantic*, which brought a vigorous protest from Weeks: "I must go on record as being firmly, sternly and impetuously against any idea of a double column type page. . . . That's a Welsh rarebit idea. If it occurs to you again, take some soda." As a matter of record, the book was entirely reset in a style more to Dr. Cushing's liking, although not in a double column page. When it was published, the reviews were most favorable, as well as the reactions of friends and unknown readers. Weeks reported: "Incidentally, there were a hundred re-orders [from

booksellers] for the *Surgeon's Journal* on this very day. What
are you going to do with all that money—bury it in the cellar?"
Dr. Cushing replied that if any royalties were forthcoming,
Weeks had better deposit them in his bank in Boston quickly
because his book bills the preceding month had shocked him.

One reference to the book in the public press annoyed Cushing, and he sputtered to Weeks:

That awful thing that appeared in a smarty journal called *Time*,
picking out the items of my clinical history and asking the world
what was the diagnosis has resulted in my getting many letters
from people to say that Grandpa had exactly the same symptoms
and what could be done about it. . . .

He also complained to Arnold Klebs, who consoled him but
chid him at the same time:

I know this *Time* article must annoy you in some ways for it is
so d——d personal, but truly since they took it from the book that
you yourself allowed to go out, there is no indiscretion and certainly a great deal of warm interest in yourself and gratitude for
your achievements to say nothing of a very respectful admiration.
"That medically significant author's own activities" was written
by a man I should like to know and I agree in his complaint that
you did not give more of them, for what in the world is a better
lesson for suffering man and those that tend him than to hear one
who feels and knows tell us just what he went through in one of
those trials . . . ?

The work of getting out the *Surgeon's Journal* had occupied a large portion of Cushing's time for a year, but he interrupted it on many occasions to turn his attention to other
things. In April of 1935 he persuaded Richard Light, who had
returned a few months earlier from a flight around the world,
to fly him to Washington so that he might attend a meeting
of the National Academy of Sciences in whose affairs he had
always been keenly interested. Dr. Light's own plane was
away for repairs and he was reluctant to fly the only plane
available at the New Haven airport, but Dr. Cushing was not
to be denied. He felt unable to make the journey on the train

and he was particularly anxious to stop on the way at Philadelphia to see Thomas McCrae, who was seriously ill.

The trip proved all that Light had feared, with a heavy rainstorm on the way down and more rain on the return trip, which had been delayed until after dark because Dr. Cushing had insisted on conducting him on a tour of the Folger Library. But Light, being an experienced pilot, was able to land his precious cargo safely despite the failure of battery and lighting system, and finally the engine itself over the New Haven airport. Dr. Cushing was not alarmed—rather he seemed amused at the predicament he had brought them into, but thereafter (with one exception) he was content to have a second-hand report of the National Academy proceedings. Dr. Walter R. Miles, professor of psychology, a fellow member, was always particularly thoughtful to drop in and bring him news of these and other meetings in which he knew Dr. Cushing would be interested.

In May the Harvey Cushing Society met in New Haven and was entertained at a buffet supper by Dr. and Mrs. Cushing. During the two-day meeting Dr. Cushing presented an account of pituitary basophilism and Dr. Eisenhardt introduced the members to the newly established Brain Tumor Registry. A week later Cushing received the gold medal of the National Institute of Social Sciences in recognition of his "distinguished contributions to modern medicine and . . . to science and literature."

The three hundredth anniversary of the settling of Connecticut coincided with the 150th anniversary of the birth of William Beaumont, and during the spring Governor Wilbur Cross, as a part of the tercentenary celebrations, dedicated a state highway through Lebanon (Beaumont's birthplace) as the Beaumont Memorial Highway. Russell Chittenden, now nearing eighty, presided at the ceremony in the church on the Lebanon Green, and Cushing delivered the principal address, entitled "William Beaumont's Rendezvous with Fame."

Autumn brought a recurrence of his gastric symptoms, with an attendant increase in the pain in his feet. At the end of November Dr. James White was called from Boston to consider an interruption of the sympathetic nerve supply to his legs. Drs. Horrax and Homans also came down to consult with Dr. Ashley Oughterson, who was the surgeon in charge, as to whether his left foot or the toes should be amputated. Early in December, Dr. Oughterson and Dr. Samuel Harvey operated on Cushing's gangrenous left middle toe, with Dr. Cushing supporting himself on his elbows to watch while they tried with difficulty to sever the tiny nerve roots. This operation helped, but it did not save his toe which was amputated on January 8. Despite the poor circulation in his entire leg, the wound healed nicely and his other toes were soon improved. For the second operation Dr. Oughterson made certain that Dr. Cushing had a general anesthetic!

The birth of a second daughter to Betsey and James Roosevelt shortly after Cushing returned home in February was an excuse for an amusing exchange with Mr. Roosevelt who had talked with him for ten minutes from the White House on New Year's Day to wish him cheer.

Dear Franklin: One of my "fat cat" [Mr. Roosevelt had previously used this designation for certain Wall Street Republicans] friends in Boston having seen the announcement of your new grandchild in the same paper which announced the Supreme Court's T.V.A. decision suggests that the child should be called Tennessee. I thought you might be interested. Much water-power to your elbow, Always aff'y, H.C.

P.S. You might tell son Franklin that the next time he takes Barbara to a night club, whether or not he allows photographs of the fact to be taken, all will be over between us.

To which the President replied:

Dear Harvey: I think Tennessee would be a splendid name for our new grandchild, provided her fond parents give her "Authority" for her middle name. That is only fair to her future husband! Notwithstanding, I prefer Kate—and so do you.

When will you ever become old enough to realize that the new generation goes to a Night Club instead of Sunday School and that being photographed there is the modern parallel of the pretty colored card you and I used to get for good behavior and perfect attendance?

I am so glad to hear that you are really feeling so fit again. I do hope that you will come to Washington sometime this spring. Be sure to stay at the White House this time.

Home after his two-month sojourn in the hospital, Cushing began the compilation of a bibliography of the works of Galvani, the colorful Italian physiologist whose work on animal electricity had led Volta to discover the electric battery. He also wrote a tribute to his Yale classmate, Lafayette Mendel, whose work on nutrition and vitamins had brought fame to himself and great prestige to Yale.

During these years of comparative inactivity, Dr. Cushing continued to keep in touch with scientists from other countries and he saw or entertained many who came to New Haven. It was now mostly a matter of people coming to him, for he did not feel able to go very far from home base. He was disappointed not to be present at his son Henry's marriage in June of 1936 to Marjorie Estabrook of Marion, Massachusetts. Nor was he able to attend Harvard's tercentenary in September, but he relayed to Klebs how the heavens had opened in the midst of the impressive ceremonies and had given Mr. Angell a chance to get off his now-famous jest—that this must be Harvard's method of soaking the rich.

Cushing was keenly interested in the centenary of the Army Medical Library in November. In August he had pointed out to Mr. Roosevelt that it would be an ideal time to announce the allocation of funds for the new building so urgently needed. Mr. Roosevelt replied: "I wish I were the dictator you assume me to be!" and went on to explain that the matter of housing for the Surgeon General's Library would require an act of Congress, and he hoped that the next Congress would authorize it, but this would not be in time for the centenary celebrations.

H.C. did not reopen the subject the next time he saw President Roosevelt, for the occasion was in the midst of the 1936 election campaign when he came to New Haven to give a speech on October 22. Mr. Roosevelt arrived for luncheon over an hour late with a large retinue, and although Mrs. Cushing

had calmly played solitaire in the drawing room, Dr. Cushing
had become somewhat disturbed, as had the crowd on the
Green impatiently awaiting his appearance. It was clearly not
a proper time for conversation about personal interests.

During 1936 two books appeared which for Cushing had
special interest—*We Northmen* by his friend Lucien Price, and
Trail Blazers of Science by the physician-writer, Martin Gumpert. The latter was significant in that a contemporary pictured
Cushing as typical of the scientist of the future. "In order to
avoid any hypothetical survey of human greatness and scientific genius, we will close with the description of a life-work
that fixes the standard of inspired research—past, present and
future—as the *organic unity of daring and knowledge*." There
followed a vivid presentation of Cushing's contribution to
medicine—a personal tribute to Cushing but a tribute as well
to the unselfish ideal toward which all physicians strive, each
in his own capacity.

Price's book was dedicated to Cushing with a quotation from
Balzac's *Pierrette:*

To
Dr. Harvey Cushing

. . . There now took place between the doctor and the disease
one of those struggles which physicians alone comprehend,—the reward of which, in case of success, is never found in the venal pay
nor in the patients themselves, but in the gentle satisfactions of
conscience, in the invisible ideal palm gathered by true artists from
the contentment which fills their soul after accomplishing a noble
work. The physician strains toward good as the artist toward
beauty, each impelled by that grand sentiment which we call virtue.

The book contained a stirring account of Mr. Price's meeting
with the great Finnish composer, Jean Sibelius, as well as
chapters on Wagner and Bach, and prompted Dr. Cushing to
write Edward Weeks, who had had a hand in its publishing:

Dear Ted: . . . I have just finished reading Lucien Price's book
last night with a great thrill. I haven't seen any reviews of it yet and
hope he gets some good ones. It certainly deserves them. Being
entirely unmusical myself, even though I went to hear the Whif-
fen-Poofs sing last night, I can only sentimentally understand his

great enthusiasm for music and realize that something valuable is missing in my make-up. Nevertheless I am sure I would have enjoyed his talks with Sibelius and it's all so vivid that I almost feel as though I had been there myself.

With the coming of the new year, Cushing faced his second retirement, for he would be sixty-eight in April and the retiring age was sixty-seven. Again he viewed the prospect with no eagerness and was not satisfied with any of the titles suggested for his approaching "Emeritus" state. Finally, in view of his hopes for his library, the designation of Director of Studies in the History of Medicine was decided upon as being acceptable to all.

Meanwhile, he "pegged along," as he called it, at the meningioma monograph. "But it's slow business," he wrote Klebs, "for I find composition increasingly difficult, my sexagenarian loss of orientation, which grows worse rather than better, proving a great handicap, for I can never find my place in the MS. and can't remember overnight what I have written." However, he felt well enough in April to attend a dinner meeting of the Yale University Library Associates in New York arranged by Frank Altschul (President of the Associates), and then to go to Washington to the meetings of the National Academy, where he saw many Hopkins friends. He reported that everybody looked surprised, having supposed he was long since dead and buried, and he sent Klebs an amusing account of the sessions, which, he said, were dominated by astrophysicists who wrote complicate formulae on blackboards that he could not understand.

But this trip was a rare occasion—he now spent most of his days writing or working on his books. The frequent letters that passed between him and Klebs discussed not only their purchases, but the progress of plans for the library. Late in April Klebs suggested that they use as an emblem the clover leaf or "the more acid one of *oxalis* . . . the green of oxalis is a lovely green and the inversely heart-shaped leaves 'obcordate' are quite appropriate." Later he wrote: "Your idea of making choice collecting as the center of efforts is perhaps after all the most promising. The notice in the Report of the President of

Yale for 1936/7 about the Director of Studies in the History of Medicine, just received, also the approval of Grosvenor Atterbury's plans, are pleasant reading. . . . The day perhaps will come when we can learn something for today from the lessons of the yesterdays. With John in the offing, you have at Yale a sort of insurance for continuity.[6] I only wish I could be of more help, but I am afraid my 'positive uselessness' is increasing to an alarming degree."

Shortly after receiving this letter, Dr. Cushing reported that their plans were attracting other donors—or so he hoped:

Your welcome dossier arrived yesterday—a day that I wish you had been here to share, for John and I had a most enjoyable afternoon and evening with E. C. Streeter and George Smith of our local faculty who is a bibliophile after your own heart. I don't remember whether you met him when you were here, but he collects fish and has a superb ichthyological library with all the early books on the subject. He is much interested in our trifoliate project and I have no doubt plans to turn his things in with ours when the library plans are consummated. . . . Incidentally, Ned Streeter got quite enthused and I think will, with a little cajoling, let us have his books on weights and measures in which he has been specializing these past several years.

After this first meeting, Dr. Smith made a habit of dropping in frequently and, having so many common interests, he and Cushing became warm friends. Since he was confined, Dr. Cushing particularly appreciated the visits of those who sought him out. During the spring he enjoyed a spirited conversation with Sinclair Lewis, whom his good friend, Chauncey B. Tinker, Professor of English, had brought to tea, and he was delighted to welcome the Geoffrey Jeffersons of Manchester, who had come over for the Philadelphia meeting of the Harvey Cushing Society which he could not attend. And he was always glad to see Carl P. Rollins, Printer to Yale University, not only because he admired his talents as a designer of beautiful books, but because Rollins viewed printing much as he did medicine—they both had the same

---

[6] Dr. Cushing named Dr. Fulton his literary executor with final authority over the disposition of his library.

love of craftsmanship, the same practical approach to their arts, the one aspiring to be above all a good printer, the other a good doctor.

In June, Cushing "retired with the Angells," as he called it. His speech at the alumni luncheon afforded a welcome opportunity to pay affectionate tribute to "Sunny Jim" Angell, who had been responsible for much of the recent growth and development of the University. "Those of you who yearn for 'the good old days,' and, in a changing world, regret that you can't send your sons to an unchanged Yale, would feel quite otherwise could you have shared with me in the great privilege of coming back to enjoy this extraordinary new Yale that has emerged during the wise and courageous administration now drawing to a close." It was on this buoyant note that Cushing entered upon his retirement.

THE EVENING YEARS

Chapter XXVII

SEVERED NOW FROM EVEN THE
slight responsibilities that had been his as Professor of Neurology, Cushing could at last fulfill the promise made to Mrs. Cushing in 1909: "We will spend our evening years on the back porch, ruminating on the past, knitting side by side." They were particularly happy years, for he was surrounded by friends and books and could choose those activities which gave him the most pleasure. In the autumn of 1937 he had been elected president of the Elizabethan Club and he made a habit of dropping in almost every afternoon at the house on College Street. There was often a group of students around him, for with his wide knowledge of the library's books and their interesting provenance, he easily attracted an audience. He enjoyed arranging meetings and often planned dinners beforehand, as he had done at the Hopkins and at Harvard, for the distinguished scholars and writers who came to address the Club.

These stimulating sessions were described to John Fulton, then on sabbatical leave and hunting Tarsius monkeys in the Pacific Islands. He also reported on the progress of the committee to choose a successor for Mr. Keogh, University Librarian, of which he was a member. "We are now on the trail of a man named Knollenberg, a New York lawyer of scholarly instincts who at odd times is writing a history of the Revolution. The members of his firm, all of whom are Yale men, don't want to see him as the Sterling librarian because he is their tax expert. Just what this means I am not sure though I assume his task is to instruct people into ways of reducing their taxes by manipulating their returns. Some of us might be able to use him should he come down here." Later that month, Bernhard Knollenberg was appointed Librarian and was to hold that post until he was called to fill an important position in Washington during World War II.

Tea hour at the Cushings attracted many from all parts of the university, for Dr. Cushing's lively interest in everything that was going on was a source of inspiration to old friends and new. In the summer tea was served out of doors, as had been their custom in Boston, croquet having replaced tennis as the attraction. Dr. Cushing was no less devastating at this game than he had been at tennis, but he rarely lacked opponents among those accustomed to dropping in—Dr. Clements C. Fry, a fellow collector particularly interested in Weir Mitchell; Mr. Donald Wing of the University Library and Mrs. Wing; Mr. and Mrs. Burton Paradise; Miss Mary Nettleton and her fiancé, Gordon Haight; the Bayne-Joneses; Mr. James T. Babb, a young man interested in books who was to succeed Mr. Knollenberg as University Librarian; and many others. Deane Keller, of the Yale School of Fine Arts, with whom Dr. Cushing shared an interest in art and baseball, tried to sketch him on various occasions but, as had so many others, found it most difficult to catch on paper the warmth that was his particular charm. He made several charcoal drawings, and although he was never at all satisfied with any of them, others have thought he succeeded better than his predecessors.

In February of 1938 the meningioma monograph at last went to press. Dr. Cushing reported to John Fulton, who was still away: "I have no local news for you except that we are sitting here waiting for proof; and Charles C (without a period) Thomas says it will be a book of 750 pages with an illustration on every page at least. We knew there were a great many so we clustered them, giving them a single number, sometimes as many as six or eight to a cluster, hoping he wouldn't notice it."

Early in March, Cushing went to Philadelphia to attend a

dinner for his old friend, Max Brödel, given by Lawrence
Saunders, President of the W. B. Saunders Company. "It was
a delightful affair," he wrote Klebs, "with a great turn-out of
some two hundred people to pay tribute to the man whose
name, I suppose, will outlive most of his Hopkins contemporaries owing to the uniqueness of his contribution to medicine." It was the first time in years that Cushing had seen so
many of his Hopkins friends together, but he greatly missed
Thomas Futcher, who had died suddenly during ward rounds
one morning in February.

Although he had grave doubts as to the wisdom of it, Dr.
Cushing decided during the spring to go to England in July
to receive the D.Sc. which Oxford was to confer upon him. He
was accompanied by his nephew, Dr. Edward H. (Pat) Cushing, and Klebs, although he also had been in uncertain health,
was in London to greet him. In the *Lancet* for July 23, under
the heading of "Dr. Cushing at Oxford," there was the following notice:

On Saturday last the honorary degree of doctor of science was
conferred by the University of Oxford on Dr. Harvey Cushing,
professor emeritus of neurology at Harvard [*sic*]. The event was
more than academic, for in receiving this new degree, Dr. Cushing
also received expressions of respect and affection that few men
could command. It was also more than English, for colleagues and
old pupils from many parts of Europe had gathered to do him
honour.

There was then a long list of those who attended a luncheon in
his honor, and besides friends such as Sir Almroth Wright, Sir
Richard Livingstone, Sir D'Arcy Power, Sir Cuthbert Wallace, Mr. R. T. Gunther, and Professor George Gask, there
were Dr. George Riddoch, Mr. Geoffrey Jefferson, and Professor Raffaele Bastianelli, who had come from Rome for the
occasion, as had Dr. Thierry de Martel and Dr. Clovis Vincent
from Paris. As always, there was also a group of his pupils—
Georges Schaltenbrand, Paul Martin, Jean Morelle, Ignaz
Oljenick, Norman Dott, George Armitage, W. R. Henderson,
A. R. D. Pattison, Hugh Cairns, and J. Paterson Ross. Klebs
called it "a great gathering around a beloved master such as the

world has rarely produced." Before leaving Oxford, H.C. held a clinic at the Radcliffe Infirmary on pituitary basophilism.

Cushing now had degrees from many of the great universities of Europe—Cambridge, Lwów, Dublin, Glasgow, Edinburgh, Strasbourg, Brussels, Budapest, Berne, Amsterdam, Paris, Leeds, and Oxford. In America he had been honored by Washington University, Western Reserve, Yale, Jefferson Medical College, Dartmouth, Harvard, Rochester, and Syracuse. Honorary membership in one form or another had been conferred on him by the most distinguished scientific and medical bodies on both sides of the Atlantic. England had made him a Companion of the Bath, France an *Officier* of the Légion d'Honneur, and Peru had given him the order of El Sol del Perú. It was a list to savor in the evening years, but although each had brought him deep gratification, he did not linger on them.

In September Reinhold Gehner, the talented book designer of the George Banta Publishing Company which had printed the meningioma volume for Mr. Thomas, brought the first copy to New Haven. It represented some twenty-five years of work and it has been said that "It is the embodiment of all the things he [Cushing] has stood for during his career as a clinician: his painstaking case records and photographs, his unusual artistic ability evident in his own numerous operative sketches, and his extraordinary knowledge of the day-to-day life of his patients." With this volume (which has come to be regarded as his greatest clinical monograph) he had now completed studies of the more important types of brain tumor—those impinging on the pituitary body, tumors of the nervus acusticus, the gliomas (with Percival Bailey), tumors of the blood vessels (also with Bailey), and the meningiomas. A reviewer wrote: "If the art falls into disrepute because of present practices, it will be from neglect of the main lesson which he [Cushing] attempted to teach."

For over a year, Dr. Cushing had been concerned over the growing tenseness in Europe caused by Hitler's activities. He became addicted to the radio, and he frequently mentioned to Klebs the appealing letters he was constantly receiving from friends in Europe who were having to flee for their lives. After a visit in March from L. L. Woodruff, Chairman of the Zoology Department, he wrote Klebs:

This botany [Sir John Hill's *British Herbal*] is an amazing book, and it led us to look at some other botanies, and then he asked if I had a copy of Valerius Cordus, of whom I knew nothing but he said he thought he was the most important of all German botanists. So I made a note of it and in a few days I had an offer of a copy of the *Annotationes* of 1561 which by chance had been bound for Maximilian II, King of Bohemia and much else. I wonder what he would have had to say could he have been in Prague yesterday and have witnessed Hitler's triumphant entry at the head of his highly mechanized troops.

I wonder, too, about other things: How would Switzerland react should he decide to lop off the German-speaking cantons on the grounds that they were being imposed upon by the Republic and really belonged, like all other good Germans, in the Reich? I had always supposed that Bohemians and Czechs had a very high national spirit of their own, and I wonder if they won't make very uncomfortable subjects for the Reich to handle.

The Harvey Cushing Society had planned their meeting in 1939 to coincide with Cushing's seventieth birthday. On April 5 he wrote Klebs that "Cairns and Geoffrey Jefferson who were planning to come over for my birthday party are being kept at home by the present political uncertainties whereas Putti, who had also planned to come, is in bed with the yaller janders." As it happened, Klebs was already on the high seas on *his* way to the birthday party, unknown to Dr. Cushing, who was completely astonished and more than delighted to see him. The dinner on the evening of April 8, climaxing the usual two days of papers and clinics, was a gala and happy affair, with Dr. Eisenhardt, President of the Society, presiding over the large gathering of pupils and old friends. Mr. Arnold Muirhead, who had been a "latch-keyer" at the "Open Arms" in Oxford, brought messages from the Osler Club in London, and his old friend W. W. Francis was one of the speakers. Dr. Francis reminisced about the "latch-keyer" days in Baltimore when he was living with Osler: "I wonder if two adjacent houses, with a couple of boards knocked out of the intervening backyard

fence . . . can ever, before or since, have sheltered such a pair
of congenial geniuses, so useful, hard-working, stimulating,
informative, Vesaliolatrous, and withal so exuberant, cheery,
witty and playful. . . ."

Olof Sjöqvist of Stockholm, a Rockefeller Fellow at Yale,
presented a birthday volume of papers from Dr. Cushing's
friends in Sweden, and a few of the cables received from friends
and colleagues throughout the United States and Europe were
read.[1] Even Cushing's faithful operating orderly, Adolph
Watzka, who had adjusted his surgical headlight and mopped
his brow during operations for many years, was present.[2] A
bibliography of Cushing's writings—twelve books and 330
papers (as well as 328 additional papers from his laboratory)—
which had been prepared without his knowledge was presented by Dr. Eisenhardt. Dr. Cushing's happily chosen words,
addressed to "My fellow co-workers, guests and friends; neurologists, neurosurgeons, ophthalmologists, printers, publishers,
and others unclassified and unexpected including an interloper,
Dr. Arnold Klebs, also Dr. William Francis and Adolph," concluded seriously with a verse from the Talmud:

"The day is short and work is great. The reward is also great
and the Master praises. It is not incumbent on thee to complete
the work but thou must not therefore cease from it."

When life had again returned to normal, Cushing resumed
work on his biobibliography of Vesalius. During the preceding
autumn he had decided to do something about his long interest
in Vesalius and his works, but when he announced his intention
to Klebs, the latter thought he was assuming a task more pre-
tentious than he realized: "And now you *ganz allein* tackle the

---

[1] The *Yale Journal of Biology and Medicine* (under the editorship of one
of his colleagues, Dr. George H. Smith, Professor of Immunology)
devoted its May issue to commemorating his anniversary.

[2] In order to distinguish Adolph from interns at the Brigham, Dr. Cushing had told him to wear special trousers of blue and white stripes. One
day Frederic Schreiber and Adolph were walking down the hospital
corridor when Dr. Homans came along and teased Adolph about his
pants. Adolph turned to Schreiber and said with great scorn, "Where
der's no respechs, der's no nothings."

Vesal bibliography. God bless your innocence!" Despite
Klebs' apprehensions, Dr. Cushing went on with the project,
and a picture of him at work comes, strangely enough, from
a letter from Klebs: "Your good letter of July 13 without any
steamer indication got here on the 22d at the same time as
John's July 14 'Clipper' letter and Sir Henry's [Viets] 'Aqui-
tania' letter of July 14, all of which must be terribly disappoint-
ing to dear old John [there was ever a race to get letters back
and forth by the fastest means]. At any rate he gives me a
much better description of your present activities than you do
yourself and for this I am very grateful. Sitting behind an im-
mense, oilcloth covered table with documents spread all over
and fortifications of reference books à la Vauban, for sixteen
hours a day, would merit the brush of a Vermeer."

While Dr. Cushing was thus engaged, anyone who called
and was suspected of having a knowledge of Latin might very
likely be set to translating a difficult passage. This happened to
one of his former colleagues from Boston, Dr. Frederick T.
Lewis, whose visit coincided with one from Herbert M. Evans
of California, with whom Cushing shared an interest in rare
books and, since Hunterian days, in the pituitary.[3]

Shortly after the visit of these friends, Dr. Cushing had word
that he had received a most unusual honor—election to honorary fellowship in the Royal College of Physicians of London. Until he had a reply to his letter of acceptance and appreciation, he did not realize that he was the only surgeon who
had ever been so recognized. "I shall have to watch my step
carefully," he wrote H. M. Barlow, the Secretary, "lest I do
something in my remaining years to cause the College to regret
its action." During the year he was also granted honorary fel-

[3] Dr. Evans had long been working on the growth hormone of the anterior pituitary—an impure extract of which Dr. Cushing had tried in the
summer of 1929 on John and the others whose growth he hoped to stimulate. When Evans' paper announcing his success in obtaining a pure
extract was published, Dr. Cushing wrote: "It [the paper] is admirably
presented and most convincing, and I think it is the best thing you have
ever done. It shows how worthwhile is slow maturity of thought on
such a complex subject and is worth dozens of papers on isolated facts."

lowship in the Société Suisse de Neurologie, the Société d'Endocrinologie of Paris, and in the Royal Society of Medicine of Edinburgh.

While the Yale Corporation was sitting in June of 1939, Cushing wrote to Klebs in a state of some excitement: "I am expecting to hear from them any minute to the effect that they have allocated a half million dollars to us, that Atterbury will immediately go ahead to modify his plans for the Y-shaped building in the middle of the present Medical School group and to enlarge it to hold a possible 400,000 books instead of the 200,000 his plans originally called for, and that they propose to start building immediately." He later added, after the good news had come: "I think I ought to say that it was our friend Lefty Lewis who apparently pushed the library program through the Corporation of which he is the youngest and most enthusiastic member. He frequently asks about you."

Klebs, too, was delighted, and satisfied with the ultimate decision not to have a separate building: "I am not at all sorry that the grand plans that you had about the Library cannot materialize. The simpler they are, the better they will please me. . . . We have now to put all our trust in John and I think we can do it with a good conscience. He has wonderful vitality and I am so glad to hear that he works in close cooperation and sympathy with Knollenberg who also seems to me a very promising fellow. Of course we old fellows have to take a back seat but I think we are very lucky to have such fine young men working in line with our ideals."

The declaration of war depressed Cushing deeply, and although he had the engrossing preoccupation of Vesalius and the revising of the Library plans, he could not keep his mind off his many friends and pupils in Europe. He was further upset to hear of the deaths, just two months apart, of Charles H. and William J. Mayo, to whom he had long been devoted, and he immediately tried to express his feelings in an appreciation.

On September 11 he wrote Klebs with something of his old light touch:

I have been sadly remiss as a correspondent of late. Altogether too much time has been passed glued to the radio—a habit easily acquired. But I have now sworn off, and the world can go to the bow-wows for all my listening in can prevent. I will hear news about it when it is all over.

Just twenty-five years ago W.O. and I were planning to participate in the Brussels celebration [of the birth of Vesalius] planned for December 1914. This summer, which has gone on the wings of the wind, I have, as you well know, given over once more to Vesalius whose books are sprawled all over the dining room table, expanded with extra leaves to fill the room. I begin to think he is a dangerous man to deal with, for renewing my acquaintance with him seems to have now precipitated World War No. 2.

But a letter from Mrs. Cushing to an old friend, Captain Frank Pleadwell, late in October told in retrospect the true state of affairs: "What good times we used to have when we both lived in Boston and the bibliophiles got together. Harvey was happy in New Haven too. His association with the Library and the Elizabethan Club gave him such pleasure. His book on Vesalius written last summer in a terrific burst of energy, he left almost finished and Billy Francis has consented to write the last part. He did so want to finish it but he never could concentrate after the war started."

During the evening of October 3, Dr. Cushing had an attack of pain around his heart—much sharper than the warnings he had had occasionally during the summer. By noon of the 4th he was admitted to the hospital. Signs of heart block developed during the evening and he was placed in an oxygen tent. He smiled when his nephew Edward H. Cushing arrived the next day from Cleveland, and again on the 6th when the news was brought to him that the building of the Library, threatened by the war, would proceed regardless. Early the next day he died.

On October 9, in the Center Church on the New Haven green there gathered from far-scattered places many friends of Harvey Cushing to pay their final tribute. The majestic strains of Sibelius' *Finlandia* swelled from the open doorway of the church. Outside, automobiles moved swiftly along Temple Street—far more swiftly than the horse-drawn vehicles which had pursued their leisurely way along the same street that autumn over a half century before when, as an eager boy, he had come from Cleveland to enter Yale College as a freshman. But the yellow leaves dropping quietly in the clear sunshine of the perfect autumn afternoon were from the same elms that had shaded him in his youth and on the many occasions of his return to the scene of those happy days.

As the simple service proceeded, more than one must have let his mind wander back through the years to think how far the Ohio lad had traveled since first he came to New England, the home of his forebears. The journey ended where it had begun—in the Western Reserve—when his ashes were taken to the hilltop where his mother and his father, his sister and his brothers had preceded him, to the hilltop where Dr. Kirke had planted crocuses to keep memory green with each returning spring.

"BE YOU BUT BRAVE AND DILIGENT"

Chapter XXVIII

Hᴉs ᴅʀᴇᴀᴍ ꜰᴏʀ ʜɪs ʙᴏᴏᴋs ᴡᴀs realized, and the Historical Library will be his most enduring monument. The Rotunda from which one enters the Library was the gift and tribute of his classmates in '91. And carved in stone over the fireplace are words of eloquent beauty in which his friend, the Reverend George Stewart, captured the essence of his hope for the future of his books—the essence, as well, of his own gallant search for truth:

> Here, silent, speak the great of other years, the story of their steep ascent from the unknown to the known, erring perchance in their best endeavor, succeeding often, where to their fellows they seemed most to fail;
>
> Here, the distilled wisdom of the years, the slow deposit of knowledge gained and writ by weak, yet valorous men, who shirked not the difficult emprize;
>
> Here is offered you the record of their days and deeds, their struggle to attain that light which God sheds on the mind of man, and which we know as Truth.
>
> Unshared must be their genius; it was their own; but you, be you but brave and diligent, may freely take and know the rich companionship of others' ordered thought.

His death was not the end. Harvey Cushing, like a truly great teacher, had merely turned over his work to his pupils. You will find them in clinics and operating rooms the world over. And in his library you will encounter scholars at work among the rich materials whose collection had been his lifelong pleasure, and students and interns reading quietly or, worn out by a bedside vigil, asleep with a book in their laps. The afternoon sun, slanting through the clerestory windows near the arched ceiling, lights up the face of Vesalius in his portrait over the fireplace on its way to the shelves where his great book, *De humani corporis fabrica*, stands in its many editions. "Though lives die, the life is not dead; and the memory of lives such as these will be reverently and forever shared not by a profession alone, not by a nation alone, but by the universal brotherhood of man."

IN WRITING THIS BIOGRAPHY I HAVE BEEN grateful that the Cushing family were constitutionally opposed to throwing anything away. Dr. Henry Kirke Cushing saved many of the letters Dr. Erastus wrote him in medical school; Betsey Maria Williams kept those her father wrote to her whenever he was away from home. They both preserved all the weekly letters Harvey wrote to them from 1887 on. The files also contain deeds, cuttings, programs, photographs, and all manner of other memorabilia that make the way of the biographer easier. Mrs. Harvey Cushing likewise saved Dr. Cushing's letters; and there are fourteen file drawers of letters to and from other correspondents between 1891 and 1939. The bound manuscript materials include the following:

Memorabilia of Erastus Cushing and Mary Ann Platt

Memorabilia of Betsey M. Williams (Cushing) and her Forebears

Memorabilia of Henry Kirke Cushing
(*These three volumes were put together by Dr. Cushing during the last four years of his life*)

The Western Reserve and Its Medical Traditions

Yale College—2 scrapbooks

Harvard Medical School—15 course notebooks

Baltimore—1 scrapbook

Diaries:

Harvard Medical School 1893-94
Columbian Exposition 1893
Havana 1894
England 1894
Bermuda 1895
Canada 1896
Le Puy 1900
European Notes 1900-01—3 vols.
Oxford 1904—2 vols.
Budapest 1909—2 vols.
Clinical Society Tour 1912—3 vols.
Harvard Unit in Paris 1915—4 vols. (all handwritten)
Base Hospital No. 5, 1915-17—9 vols.
Rome and the Physiological Congress 1932

Correspondence and memorabilia of

William S. Halsted—1 vol.
William H. Welch—4 vols.
S. Weir Mitchell—1 vol.
Leonard Wood—1 vol.
James Ford Rhodes—1 vol.
Arnold C. Klebs—4 vols.
Sir William Osler—1 vol.

Correspondence on University and Hospital Appointments

Pamphlets on Full-time for Clinicians

Correspondence and Papers on Full-time

Letters about the Osler Biography (1925-29)—2 vols.

The Annual Reports of the Peter Bent Brigham Hospital 1914-33 have been most helpful. Dr. Cushing's published works, both clinical and nonclinical, have been an excellent source oftentimes of historical background. In addition, I have consulted the following:

[Bagg, L. H.] *Four Years at Yale.* By a graduate of '69. New Haven, Charles C. Chatfield & Co., 1871. xiv, 713 pp.

Beecher, H. K. "The First Anesthesia Records (Codman, Cushing)." *Surgery, Gynecology and Obstetrics,* 1940, *71:* 689-693.

Bernheim, B. M. *The Story of the Johns Hopkins; Four Great Doctors and the Medical School They Created.* New York, McGraw-Hill Book Co., 1948. xi, 235 pp.

———. *A Surgeon's Domain.* New York, W. W. Norton and Co., 1947. 253 pp.

Cheever, David. "The Turn of the Century—and after." *New England Journal of Medicine,* 1940, *222:* 1-11.

Flexner, Simon and Flexner, J. T. *William Henry Welch and the Heroic Age of American Medicine.* New York, The Viking Press, 1941. x, 539 pp.

Fulton, J. F. *Harvey Cushing: A Biography.* Springfield, Ill., Charles C Thomas, 1946. xiv, 754 pp., 64 plates.

Garrison, F. H. *John Shaw Billings. A Memoir.* New York, G. P. Putnam's Sons, 1915. v, 432 pp.

Gumpert, Martin. *Trail-Blazers of Science: Life Stories of Some Half-Forgotten Pioneers of Medical Research.* Tr. from the German by Edwin L. Schuman. New York, Funk & Wagnalls Co., 1936. viii, 303 pp.

Jefferson, Geoffrey. "Harvey Cushing." *Manchester University Medical School Gazette,* 1943, *22:* 37-45.

Livingston, W. K. "Harvey Cushing. April 8, 1869–October 7, 1939." *Western Journal of Surgery, Obstetrics and Gynecology,* 1939, 47, 716-718.

MacCallum, W. G. *William Stewart Halsted, Surgeon.* Baltimore, The Johns Hopkins Press, 1930. xvii, 240 pp.

Paget, Stephen. *Sir Victor Horsley. A Study of his Life and Work.* London, Constable and Company, 1919. xi, 358 pp.

Price, Lucien. "Olympians in Homespun." *The Atlantic Monthly*, 1926, *137:* 433-447.

Rand, C. W. "Doctor Cushing as I Knew Him." *Bulletin of the Los Angeles Neurological Society*, 1940, *5:* 1-8.

Stalker, Hugh. "The Warrens of New England and Their Friends." *New England Journal of Medicine*, 1940, *222:* 517-529.

Stevenson, R. S. Review of *Harvey Cushing: A Biography* by John F. Fulton. *Medical Bookman and Historian*, 1947, *1:* 41-44.

ACKNOWLEDGMENTS

I wish to express my appreciation to the following:

Charles C Thomas for permission to quote from John F. Fulton's *Harvey Cushing. A Biography;* Cushing and Eisenhardt's *Meningiomas; A Bibliography of the Writings of Harvey Cushing;* and from *Harvey Cushing's Seventieth Birthday Party, April 8, 1939.*

The Oxford University Press for permission to quote from Harvey Cushing's *The Life of Sir William Osler.*

Little, Brown and Company and The Atlantic Monthly Press for permission to quote from Cushing's *From a Surgeon's Journal 1915-1918*, and from Lucien Price's *We Northmen.*

The *Manchester University Medical School Gazette* for permission to quote from Geoffrey Jefferson's "Harvey Cushing."

The *Bulletin of the Los Angeles Neurological Society* for permission to quote from Carl Rand's "Dr. Cushing as I Knew Him."

The *Medical Bookman and Historian* for permission to quote from R. Scott Stevenson's review of *Harvey Cushing. A Biography.*

The Rowfant Club of Cleveland for permission to reproduce four illustrations from *A Visit to Le Puy-en-Velay* and to quote from *Henry Kirke Cushing. A Memorial.*

And, finally, to all who have generously allowed me to quote from their letters and writings, published and unpublished.

INDEX

Abernethy, John, 199
Acland, Sir Henry, 129
Acromegaly, 159, 172, 249
Addison, Thomas, 96
Adiposity, asexual, 159, 160
Adson, A. W., 209n
Aesculapius, 239
Agassiz, Louis, 179
Altschul, Frank, 310.
American Ambulance, Paris, 186 *et seq.*; organization, 186; Harvard Unit arrives, 187
American Association for the Advancement of Science, 276
American College of Surgeons, 228
American Expeditionary Forces, 199
American Journal of Science, 19
American Medical Association, 155, 161, 171, 261, 267, 300
American Neurological Association, 140, 155, 182, 230
American Physiological Society, 141, 160, 177
American Red Cross, 192
Amerman, G. L., 54, 56
Amsterdam. University, 316
Anderson, N. M., 15-17
Anesthesia, discovery of, 44, 95; early use of at M.G.H., 48; local, 86; *see also* Ether charts
Angell, J. R., 213, 272, 298, 308, 312; letter from HC, 283; letter to HC, 283, 290

Archibald, Edward, 209n
Arderne, John, 269
Armitage, George, 280, 315
Arthur Dean Bevan Lecture, 276
Asepsis, 44, 95
Asher, Leon, 110, 268, 280
Asher, Mrs. Leon, 268
Atterbury, Grosvenor, 34, 36, 51, 87, 163; visit to Le Puy, 98-9; plans for medical library, 298, 311

Babb, J. T., 314
Babinski, J. F. F., Sign of, 285
Bach, Johann Sebastian, 309
Bacon, Robert, 186
Bagdazar, Dimitri, 280
Bagley, Charles, Jr., 209n
Bailey, Percival, 182, 206, 214, 230-1, 240, 241, 274, 280, 316
Baldwin, Mrs. A. D., 32, 63
Baldwin, H. P., 221
Baldwin, H. T., 55
Balfour Lecture, 278
Ballance, Sir Charles, 183, 229n
Baltimore, dining habits, 73; Druid Hill Park, 73; fire, 142, 149; market, 73
Balzac, Honoré de, 309
Banks Memorial Lecture, 163
Banta Publishing Company, 316
Banti, Guido, 108
Banti's disease, 88, 108
Barker, L. F., 119, 147
Barlow, H. M., 319